THE
·GRACE·
AND THE
·SEVERITY·
OF THE
·IDEAL·

THE ·GRACE· AND THE ·SEVERITY· OF THE ·IDEAL·

John Dewey and the Transcendent

VICTOR KESTENBAUM

THE UNIVERSITY OF CHICAGO PRESS
CHICAGO AND LONDON

VICTOR KESTENBAUM is associate professor of philosophy and education at Boston University. He is author of *The Phenomenological Sense of John Dewey: Habit and Meaning* (1977) and editor of *The Humanity of the Ill: Phenomenological Perspectives* (1982).

The University of Chicago Press, Chicago 60637
The University of Chicago Press, Ltd., London
© 2002 by The University of Chicago
All rights reserved. Published 2002
Printed in the United States of America

11 10 09 08 07 06 05 04 03 02   1 2 3 4 5

ISBN: 0-226-43215-7 (cloth)
ISBN: 0-226-43216-5 (paper)

Chapter 4 originally appeared as Victor Kestenbaum, "Humanism and Vigilance," *Man and World* 20 (1987): 149–69; © Martinus Nijhoff Publishers, Dordrecht, reprinted with kind permission from Kluwer Academic Publishers. Chapter 6 originally appeared as Victor Kestenbaum, "The Undeclared Self," in *Dewey Reconfigured: Essays on Deweyan Pragmatism*, ed. Casey Haskins and David I. Seiple (Albany: State University of New York Press, 1999), 19–38; © 1999, State University of New York, all rights reserved. Chapter 7 originally appeared as "'Meaning on the Model of Truth': Dewey and Gadamer on Habit and *Vorurteil*," *The Journal of Speculative Philosophy* 6, no. 1 (1992): 25–66; copyright 1992 by The Pennsylvania State University, reproduced by permission of the publisher.

Library of Congress Cataloging-in-Publication Data

Kestenbaum, Victor.
    The grace and the severity of the ideal : John Dewey and the transcendent / Victor Kestenbaum.
    p. cm.
    Includes bibliographical references and index.
    ISBN 0-226-43215-7 (cloth : alk. paper)—ISBN 0-226-43216-5 (pbk. : alk. paper)
    1. Dewey, John, 1859–1952.   2. Idealism.   I. Title.
B945.D44 .K46   2002
191—dc21

2001008481

∞ The paper used in this publication meets the minimum requirements of the American National Standard for Information Sciences—Permanence of Paper for Printed Library Materials, ANSI Z39.48-1992.

·CONTENTS·

1. Under Ideal Conditions   1
2. The Pragmatic Struggle for the Good   28
3. "In the Midst of Effort"   54
4. Humanism and Vigilance   78
5. The Rationality of Conduct: Dewey and Oakeshott   99
6. The Undeclared Self   122
7. "Meaning on the Model of Truth":
   Dewey and Gadamer on Habit and *Vorurteil*   139
8. Faith and the Unseen   175
9. Dewey, Wallace Stevens, and the "Difficult Inch"   200

   Notes   227
   Index   253

· CHAPTER 1 ·

Under Ideal Conditions

The central aim of this work is to propose that at least one version of pragmatism, John Dewey's, has an important place for the ideal, intangible, and transcendent. I wish to discredit the view that pragmatism generally, and Dewey's in particular, is simply a philosophical apology for what Tocqueville called the American "taste for the tangible and the real." Dewey's pragmatism, I propose, is not a philosophical or cultural substitution of tangible goals for intangible ideals. His pragmatism is an attempt to respect the authority of the "tangible and the real" at the same time that it does justice to meanings which transcend the verified and the evident and which, in their most perfect expressions, are intimations of the ideal. Dewey's pragmatism does not simply, or only, "naturalize" ideals by bringing them "down to earth." His pragmatism is far more complicated than the instrumentalist and naturalistic interpretations which render ideals as "tools" to be used in the natural world. Ideals for Dewey are situated at the intersection of the tangible and the intangible, the natural and the transcendent.[1] Ideals were the best evidence he had that in the realm of meaning, but not of fact, something simultaneously can be and not be.

My intent is not to argue that instrumentalist and naturalist interpretations of Dewey's pragmatism have no basis in his texts or in his own formulations of philosophical purpose. I do argue for the view that some of the most interesting and important aspects of Dewey's philosophy are those which are at best only obliquely related to his instrumentalism and naturalism. Sometimes at crucial points in an article or chapter, and other times in less telling moments, Dewey's pragmatism transgresses the expectations of a well-behaved instrumentalist-naturalist philosophy. The essays in this book give Dewey's transgressions a sustained and appreciative hearing.

Much of my argument depends upon the development of what I call the "primacy of meaning thesis" in Dewey, his contention that "meaning is wider in scope as well as more precious in value than is truth"[2] This thesis is not unique to the early, middle, or late Dewey. It is there in "The Postulate of Immediate Empiricism," and it is there in *Art as Experience*. Meaning exceeds its verifying instances and is not to be equated with them.[3] Further, meaning transcends—because experience transcends—the inquirable, the reflective, and the practical. We are, as Glenn Gray puts it, "attached to the world in a thousand ways."[4] What is the proper place of *ideal* meanings in a world where meaning is "wider in scope as well as more precious in value than is truth"? In other words, when one speaks of the "pragmatic meaning" of an act, a value, or a fact, how do ideal meanings function in that pragmatic meaning? How are ideal meanings sustained, thought, and fulfilled in practical experience? In aesthetic experience? In poetic experience? In educational experience? In short, what is man's relationship to the transcendent and intangible meaning which may, on occasion, provide an intimation of the ideal?

This primacy of meaning thesis is distinguishable from Dewey's theory of prereflective, habitual meaning but ultimately each notion reinforces and deepens the other. In a previous work, I attempted to show, in the context of Merleau-Ponty's phenomenology of the habitual body, the centrality of habit in *Art as Experience*.[5] I did not then see in what sense habits were the transcendentals of experience for Dewey, what that might mean for his entire philosophy, and what trouble it would cause him.[6] The trouble derives from the fact that as Dewey asked more and more from the concept of habit, he was forced to accept more and more of the invisibilities of habitual meaning and the transcendental contribution it makes to experience. It certainly helps to avoid any hint of trouble if his middle and late periods can be regarded as continuous refinements of a naturalistic theory of habit, but it does not appear to me that the process happened quite that smoothly, if at all. For example, *Human Nature and Conduct* is Dewey's most concentrated and extended consideration of habit and comes closest to constituting what one might call his "theory of habit." Yet just three years later in *Experience and Nature*, habit plays a distinctly less prominent role. It is not that an equivalent concept has taken its place or that it has been abandoned. It is in the background, subdued.

Dewey did not, because he could not, sustain a wholly naturalistic interpretation of habit. He asked so much from the concept of habit in *Human Nature and Conduct* that his naturalism could not accommodate it all. In that work, habitual meaning is for the most part "trued up" to experience: to the social, to language, to context. But if meaning is "wider in scope as well as more precious in value than is truth," then meaning which has become funded in habit may find ranges of expression and fulfillment which transcend the requirements of truth or the need for inquiry. How does meaning unsteered by truth, but not indifferent to truth, function in deliberation? Neal Coughlan is correct to note that "much of what was new in *Experience and Nature* was there to *ground* human activity, so to speak, in the immediately felt qualities of things and in consummatory, as distinguished from instrumental, values."[7] One of the most demanding and rewarding hermeneutic challenges in reading Dewey, however, is to understand how much of the human contribution to the instrumental and the consummatory is "offstage," in the background, under the surface, in habit.

Dewey often, but not always, grasped how radically the concept of habit unsettled what should be counted routine in experience and what was radiant. It begins to look as if habit is a strange ally for a pragmatist seeking to understand "ordinary experience." There is something ordinary about habit, but it had become increasingly evident to Dewey that there also is something extraordinary about habit. William James influenced Husserl significantly, but it was Dewey, not James, who saw that habit is not merely conservative but also is intentional: it creates and sustains meaning on a prereflective, preobjective level of experience. On this level, the solicitations of habit and world establish an accord which is both immanent and transcendent. My presence to the world, my opening to the world, is grounded in habitual meaning, which my reflective acts can only partially encompass or direct. Habit has been at work before I have predicated my ends-in-view; it is the source of what comes into view and is the limiting condition of what is viewable, that is, of what transcends my view. Pragmatic intelligence, grounded in transcendental habit, is situated in a transcendent world horizon. For such an intelligence, the ideal makes demands which are immanent and transcendent.

The essays in this book tend to be incompatible with, but not indifferent to, the standard view of Dewey's idealism. This view holds that having passed through his "idealist period" from 1882 to 1903, Dewey gradually but decisively turns away from idealism. The usual corollary to this view is that traces of Dewey's idealism can be found in his later philosophy and that indeed, in the case of the *Psychology*, in Herbert W. Schneider's words, it "foreshadows much of Dewey's later philosophy."[8] "Foreshadows" does not adequately formulate the place of the *Psychology* and other early writings in Dewey's later development. My interpretation of Dewey proposes that there is good reason to believe that Dewey did not "break with" or reject idealism. He recast it. The difference is crucial, and not simply for gaining a better understanding of Dewey and American pragmatism. Dewey's understanding of the intangibility of ideal meanings focuses some of the most difficult, interesting, and enduring issues in the empirical and theoretical study of culture, politics, religion, and education. A careful study of the transcendent and the ideal in Dewey shows that the search for the good life cannot be conducted without a "taste for the tangible and the real." It also shows that significant progress in the pursuit of the good life, and a large element of its realization, requires what Dewey in *Human Nature and Conduct* calls "the need of a continuous unification of spirit and habit."[9] This is not an unusual idea in Dewey's later, "mature" philosophy. It is merely one of the more vivid formulations of his desire to see how the spiritual and ideal are possible for the habit-grounded and habit-transcending human being. Viewed from this perspective, his early idealism does more than foreshadow his later pragmatism. It sets some of the philosophical requirements for an acceptable pragmatism, of what is involved in striving to see something under ideal conditions and acting in accord with such seeing. Even more fundamentally, his early idealism attends to the not seen, the invisible, the intimated, the undeclared. When he said in 1891 that "morality works by faith, not by sight," he set a path for his pragmatism which he could not steadily follow but one he would not abandon.[10]

Dewey did not have a steady and clear vision of how such ideal, transcendent visibilities and invisibilities could be incorporated into a habit-based practical life. This may account for the range of interpretations we find concerning his idealism, interpretations arguing that he completely rejected idealism, essentially embraced it, or accepted and transformed some of it. I shall not attempt to provide a detailed account of this range of interpretations at this point but shall instead simply note a few of them.

Among his contemporaries, Edgar S. Brightman's view is fairly typical of what might be called the "repudiators," those who take Dewey to have rejected idealism and thereby to have lost his way. Brightman says that "John Dewey repudiates idealism and traditional religion but gives himself to the service of humanity and educational advance." Brightman then groups Dewey with those philosophers who "think that ideals are alien to the real world in which they arise."[11] There are those, small in number, who note Dewey's affinity with idealism but simply wish to consider this a victory for idealism rather than an occasion to look deeper into Dewey. In this group, the remarks of R. F. Alfred Hoernle are interesting. In an article titled "The Revival of Idealism in the United States," he cites some passages from *Experience and Nature* and then says:

What Dewey here calls his own empirical method is, in spirit and principle, if not in the actual details of its execution, identical with the idealistic method, especially when one adds, from Dewey's *Preface* the references to "faith in experience when intelligently used as a means of disclosing the realities of nature," and to the character of human experience as "a growing progressive self-disclosure of nature itself." If in these utterances we substitute for "nature" simply "Reality," or even the "Absolute," they might have been written by any true-blue Idealist.[12]

Hoernle's first premise is simple: the idealist way "is to take experience as 'ultimate,' i.e., as itself the context or whole within which all differences are found."[13] His few quotations from Dewey are clearly meant to show that Dewey takes experience to be ultimate. The argument is, at best, elliptical. Nonetheless, there is at least a recognition that Dewey's pragmatism involves ultimates and that it may be a loftier thing than responses of organisms to their environments.

For some, Dewey's pragmatism is so lofty that it loses touch with material reality. Maurice Cornforth remarks that "Dewey's philosophy, which he parades as 'naturalism,' in opposition to idealism, is actually nothing but a subtle and disguised form of subjective idealism."[14] With respect to Dewey's idealism, the distance from compliment to condemnation is indeed very short.

H. S. Thayer contends that "Dewey's use of much of the language of idealism was as unidealistic in intent and diverged as much from traditional idealism as his use of the word 'experience' departs from traditional empiricism."[15] Thomas M. Alexander's account of Dewey's "idealist period" is exceptionally discerning, but he adopts the consensus view that "in 1903, Dewey officially broke with idealism and joined the new pragmatic movement with his *Studies in Logical Theory*."[16] It is hard to judge the depth or length of this break, however, because Alexander notes various ways in which the idealism of *Psychology* is "retained" in Dewey's later philosophy, allowing one to find an "analogy" here (the role of rhythm), or "parallel" there (feelings as objective modes of revelation).[17] Indeed, throughout much of his work, Alexander acknowledges that idealism leaves numerous traces, but these are, in his view, absorbed by and subordinated to experimentalism, empiricism, naturalism. Dewey's philosophy of experience puts idea and meaning in their proper instrumental, solve-a-problem place. In aesthetic experience, meaning is less labored and is more expressive of the possibilities of ordinary experience; in other words, it is consummatory. On Alexander's account, the line from the instrumental to the consummatory is continuous; there are no breaks. Ordinary experience may be transcended, but it is still, in his view, the "ground" of the intense moments of aesthetic experience because "they are *its* possibilities."[18] The "ground," I think, presents more of a challenge for Dewey than Alexander's analysis allows or can allow. In aesthetic, moral, and religious experience, our confidence in, and reliance upon, the ordinary is disrupted by the drama of habits undergoing reconstruction, maybe reinvention, and perhaps even transcendence.

While Alexander's approach to Dewey's idealism aligns him pretty well with the "rejection" school of interpreters, there is more than a hint of what can be called "reconciliation" in his treatment of Dewey. This is the view that Dewey did not really reject idealism and that its presence in the later works is not a "leftover" or residue. On this view, it was Dewey's intention to reconcile ideals and experience. Russell B. Goodman presents this case in his chapter on Dewey in *American Philosophy and the Romantic Tradition:* Two main themes dominate Dewey's work: reconciliation and reconstruction. Under the former comes his interest in something akin to James's project of uniting empiricism and spiritualism: Dewey thinks of it as reconciling "ideals" and experience." Of particular interest to Goodman is "the sense in which Dewey remains an idealist and also the respects in which he, like James, incorporates a strong element of realism into his idealism."[19] This is interesting, as is his claim that "although Dewey rejected 'traditional supernaturalism' because it placed ideals apart from human experience and control, he accepted the natural and humanized supernaturalism of the Romantics." Dewey's 1890 commencement address, "Poetry and Philosophy," occasions Goodman's remark that poetry for Dewey cannot be separate from life nor can it be separate from truth. It cannot be "transcendental." Goodman takes Dewey's belief in the "spiritual possibilities of the natural" to be an indication of his sympathy with the Romantics. In response to the sentiment summarized in Dewey's affirmation that poetry is "the genuine revelation of the ordinary day-by-day life of man," Goodman says: "Dewey here embraces the key Romantic idea of a spiritualized commonplace, achieved by or in poetry." Thus, the extraordinary is there in the ordinary: hidden, latent, unperceived, and, too often, unappreciated. There is no transcendence here, no "overweening Beyond and Away," as Dewey calls it in his 1903 essay on Emerson. According to Goodman, Dewey "shows ideal objects to be a part of nature, that is, how the secular and sacred (as well as many other oppositions) can be reconciled." Again, extraordinary possibilities are possibilities of ordinary experience. They are continuous with, resident in, the commonplace.[20]

The notion of "reconcile" is well suited to describe many of Dewey's troubles with the ideal. The term is usually used in the sense of settling, harmonizing, making consistent. But it also has a different usage: submitting to. The former usage points toward equitable convergence; the latter usage points toward the authority, or at least the power, to elicit compliance. Dewey was keenly interested in reconciling, in the sense of harmonizing, what Max Otto called "tangible things and intangible ideals."[21] But the authority of an ideal which could be realized only imperfectly, if at all, was not without appeal to Dewey. The ideal was the "what for," the moving force that had the power to, as Dewey liked to say, stir us. When Dewey balked at transcendent ideals it was almost always because they were presented as fixed or absolute or both. But ideal meanings or essential meanings, he maintained, could function in experience in ways which were not fixed or absolute, that is, in ways which encourage their fuller realization. The primacy of meaning for Dewey did not require a quest for primordial meaning, first meaning, absolute meaning.

Dewey's reconciliations are, then, complex and elusive. They are not always what they appear to be. A comparison with William James is helpful here. In the last paragraph of *Psychology* (the abridgement of *Principles of Psychology*), James says:

> When, then, we talk of "psychology as a natural science," we must not assume that that means a sort of psychology that stands at last on solid ground. It means just the reverse; it means a psychology particularly fragile, and into which the waters of metaphysical criticism leak at every joint, a psychology all of whose elementary assumptions and data must be reconsidered in wider connections and translated into other terms.[22]

If Dewey's naturalism and instrumentalism stand "on solid ground," I doubt that it is because of the reasons typically offered by his proponents. Likewise, if his naturalism and instrumentalism are fragile, I doubt that it is because of the reasons offered by his critics. The "waters of metaphysical criticism" did not leak into his philosophy; rather, it is the transcendent which leaks in at the many joints where the tangible and the intangible meet in Dewey. The aim of my work is not to offer a wholesale rejection of the more or less prevailing stance in Dewey scholarship, that the ideal has a natural basis and that when the natural seeks ideal fulfillment, the latter must be reconciled to the former. The chapters of the present work suggest another, quite different interpretive stance. The "elementary assumptions" regarding Dewey's naturalism "must be reconsidered in wider connnections and translated into other terms." I set out to discover what aspects of Dewey can be translated into terms which seem unlikely candidates as sources of illumination for his pragmatism: the transcendent, the unrealizable, the ideal, the intangible, the spiritual, and the imagination when it is unreconciled to actuality.

Some of the connections and terms through which I approach Dewey are derived from the work of philosophers: Michael Oakeshott, Hans-Georg Gadamer, and John Findlay. Some come from Wallace Stevens. A few emerge from analysis of works from Dewey's "idealist period." Finally, some find their way into our conversation by implication and inference, suggestion and intimation. An example of the latter is chapter 4, "Humanism and Vigilance." "Vigilance" is not a common term in Dewey, yet it helps to extract from, and infuse into, his pragmatism a resonance which is missed without its solicitations. It does not take hermeneutical finesse but simple common sense to respect the fact that much of Dewey cannot survive such a translation project. A certain portion of Dewey's thought can be forced into such terms and connections but only at the cost of distortion. Much, however, not merely survives the translation but actually becomes more intelligible, interesting, and important when seen in terms which do not initially appear coincident with the "elementary assumptions" of pragmatism.

Collected here are what might be called pragmatic occasions of transcendent and intangible ideals. Thus, not all the chapters are "about" Dewey, although almost all are deeply inspired by him. Some attend more closely to the "letter" of Dewey; others are more concerned with the "spirit" of Dewey. Given the nature of my argument, it should not be surprising that quite often what I take to be the spirit of Dewey lacks a letterlike equivalent in the text. This is far from conceding that there is nothing, or little, "in" the texts to "support" my interpretations. The matter of what is there, in a text, and of what is supportable, defensible, and valid in an interpretation, are of course hermeneutical issues of a complex nature.

The studies in this volume are not exercises in hermeneutical cleverness, hermeneutical daring, or purposeful hermeneutical misreading. In his book *Hermeneutics: Interpretation Theory in Schleiermacher, Dilthey, Heidegger, and Gadamer*, Palmer says: "To focus purely on the positivity of what a text explicitly says is to do an injustice to the hermeneutical task. It is necessary to go behind the text to find what the text did not, and perhaps could not, say."[23] This passage is found in the section titled "On Being Able to Hear What the Text Did Not Say." I am in accord with much of what Palmer says in this section, summarized in the above quotation. However, such a viewpoint invites abuse. To misinterpret what the text *did* say cannot be defended by recourse to what the text did not say. Hermeneutical accountability requires acknowledgment that the objects of interest to me in Dewey's texts often are not clear, not well defined, not as tangible as an argument posed, defended, won, or revised. I have found enough, though, to convince me that a great deal of Dewey scholarship has focused on the "positivity of what a text explicitly says" to the detriment of what "what the text did not, and perhaps could not, say." I do not believe, however, that it is necessary, or wise, or maybe even possible, "to go behind the text" in order to attend to what "the text did not and perhaps could not, say."

Let us attend to what the text did say, but differently. The difference I have in mind is suggested by the distinction Heinrich Wölfflin draws between the linear and the painterly:

> Everything depends on how far a preponderating significance is assigned to or withdrawn from the edges, whether they *must* be read as lines or not. In one case, the line means a track moving evenly round the form, to which the spectator can confidently entrust himself; in the other, the picture is dominated by lights and shadows, not exactly indeterminate, yet without stress on the boundaries.[24]

Like most enduringly rewarding philosophers, Dewey's style and his philosophical vision is a mixture of the linear and the painterly. Dewey does not lack lines of reasoning starting from the beginning of a book to its last pages. He does not lack lines of reasoning and argumentation starting from his earliest writings to his very last works. The masses bounded by these lines may be thought of as his positions, his standpoints: pragmatism, naturalism, experimentalism, instrumentalism. The "edges" around these positions have been drawn, I believe, too sharply, too confidently. Even when these lines have been softened so as to cast doubt on whether they "*must* be read as lines," the effect has been simply to call attention to the ways in which pragmatism has parallels with other philosophical positions. So one can talk about pragmatism *and* Wittgenstein, pragmatism *and* Heidegger, pragmatism *and* Habermas, pragmatism *and* law, pragmatism *and* literary theory. When Dewey plays a prominent role in such trespasses of boundaries, as he increasingly does, very rarely do his trespassers question whether his positions "*must* be read as lines." I should like to place less stress on the lines and boundaries of Dewey's thinking and more on its play of lights and shadows.

Dewey does not make this easy. In his autobiographical essay "From Absolutism to Experimentalism,"[25] he gives considerable comfort to those who do their best philosophical work with what James Collins calls the "from-to perspectives." Collins has in mind historical from-to orderings: from Plato to Kant, or from Kant to Heidegger. I think, though, that his analysis of from-to developments in the history of philosophy sheds considerable light on the nature of from-to development in the history of a philosopher:

> Historians of modern philosophy who are attentive to the interpretive present come to regard every from-to perspective as being *porous in principle*. It brings to meaningful unity some themes and arguments in a grouping of philosophers. But the grouping is never intended to be so fixed and isolated that it blocks the development of still other historical relationships, still other modes of synopsis for understanding the company of modern philosophers.[26]

Does this mean, or do I mean, that Dewey did not understand his own from-to development? Not necessarily. It does mean that Dewey is not eager to be "fixed and isolated":

> The philosopher, if I may apply that word to myself, that I became as I moved away from German idealism, is too much the self that I still am and is still too much in process of change to lend itself to record. I envy, up to a certain point, those who can write their intellectual biography in a unified pattern, woven out of a few distinctly discernible strands of interest and influence. By contrast, I seem to be unstable, chameleon-like, yielding one after another to many diverse and even incompatible influences; struggling to assimilate something from each and yet striving to carry it forward in a way that is logically consistent with what has been learned from its predecessors.[27]

This passage has been cited fairly often in studies of Dewey, usually as evidence that he was always growing, changing, experimenting. I take it rather differently: as a hint that there is much in his philosophy which is not "distinctly discernible" and that attention to its lights and shadows will not go unrewarded.

Two recent publications offer different—and compelling—approaches to the from-to perspective. Neither, however, succeeds in capturing the more painterly effects in Dewey. In *Dewey's Empirical Theory of Knowledge and Reality*, John R. Shook undertakes a "genetic account of Dewey's philosophical development."[28] He offers an exceedingly detailed account of such topics as absolute idealism, Wundtian voluntarism, the centrality of experience (particularly the centrality of purposive, active experience), and so on. The aim of Shook's book, at least a central aim, is to show the complex relationship between idealism and Dewey's "later" philosophy. It would be unjust to characterize his book as a linear account of Dewey.

Indeed, it seeks to combat certain standard accounts of Dewey's development. Yet what emerges from the finely detailed analysis of Dewey is a picture not unlike the Dewey of those accounts. Thus, Shook claims that by 1891 "Dewey held that the only reality is that of ordinary experience." And further: "Meanings always project forward toward future possible experiences; a thing's meaning is just those activities in which the thing may play a role as a means." And finally: "Experience is all we have, and only it, not some transcendentally ideal existence, contains the resources of intelligence to reduce fragmentation and uncertainty."[29] In what follows, I try to show a few of the ways that "some transcendentally ideal existence" motivated Dewey's philosophical vision.

Louis Menand informs the reader that his book *The Metaphysical Club* "is not a work of philosophical argument" but rather "a work of historical interpretation."[30] One takes this not as a defense against philosophical scrutiny and criticism, but simply as a clarification of scholarly intent. So, in the preface, we gain our first sight of how Holmes, James, Peirce, and Dewey are to be historically interpreted. What did they have in common? "They all believed," says Menand, "that ideas are not 'out there' waiting to be discovered, but are tools—like forks and knives and microchips—that people devise to cope with the world in which they find themselves." In case one should miss the central point of these thinkers, Menand offers an even more compact declaration of their position: "The belief that ideas should never become ideologies—either justifying the status quo, or dictating some transcendent imperative for renouncing it—was the essence of what they taught."[31] The "story," as he calls it, which Menand wishes to tell, his from-to, is about the value of tools and the lack of value of transcendence. I propose a different interpretation of Dewey, one which acknowledges the power of Randolph S. Bourne's criticism of Dewey—"that there is no provision for thought or experience getting beyond itself"—but not its accuracy.[32] Menand also does not appear to see any "beyond" in Dewey, no basis upon which to respond to Bourne's brilliant, chilling, inaccurate criticism of Dewey's philosophy: "You never transcend anything."[33]

Two brief examples of linear approaches to Dewey will help to distinguish, and perhaps clarify, my more painterly attitude. In an essay titled "What's the Use of Calling Emerson a Pragmatist?" Stanley Cavell says: "The following sentence from Dewey's *Experience and Education* is, I assume, characteristic of what makes him Dewey: 'Scientific method is the only authentic means at our command for getting at the significance of our everyday experiences of the world in which we live.'"[34] Cavell does not believe such an outlook on experience can be of much help in understanding something like Emerson's "Experience," which, Cavell notes, "may be understood as written to mourn the death of his young son."[35] Cavell's indirections direct us to this: science, and thus Dewey as proponent and champion of science, cannot do justice to the work of mourning. Its kind of objectivity, that is, intersubjectivity, is precisely what "neither Emerson nor Wittgenstein can assume to be in effect; the human subject has first to be discovered, as something strange to itself."[36] Dewey the experimentalist does not see in what ways the "human subject has first to be discovered," that is, in what ways experiments of language and sensibility can occasionally reveal the strangeness of the self to itself.

One way to respond to Cavell's cautionary tale regarding Dewey is to propose that Dewey's account of the consummatory in his aesthetic theory takes care of Cavell's Emersonian and Wittgensteinian pressure on Dewey. The strategy is simple and certainly not lacking power. Art, not science, is Dewey's ultimate, his end-in-view which consummates possibilities of meaning rather than merely preparing them for the next problem or situation. The aesthetic line of attack would reprimand Cavell for neglecting Dewey's declaration that "'science' is properly a handmaiden that conducts natural events to this happy issue."[37] The "happy issue" to which Dewey refers are meanings which are "immediately possessed" and which are "the complete culmination of nature." Not only has Dewey, so the argument would go, put limits on the instrumental meanings, he has placed them there in order to acknowledge that pragmatic meaning is not merely on the way. In art, meaning arrives; it reveals, thrills, astounds, and terrifies with no further destination.

This defense of Dewey is convincing as far as it goes, but it begins and ends too soon. What is unsettled, opaque, luminous, silent, rapturous, peaceful, for example, does not wait for the promise of aesthetic consummations to be at work and at play in ordinary experience. It slides in and out of our experience with far less tangible provocations than Monet's water lilies, Fred Astaire's dancing, a setting sun, Beethoven's late quartets, a roiling ocean, a John Updike or Henry James short story. Our experience is opened and sealed in ways which cannot always be told or retold, made and remade as aesthetic consummations. Meaning occasionally requires a patience, an alertness to the accidents and hazards which may befall it, and which perhaps Deweyan aesthetic experience cannot meet on its own, fragmentary, spotted terms. "Having an Experience" is both the title of a chapter in *Art as Experience* and the declaration of a standard for experience. But the qualitative world attended to by Dewey is not so quick to resolve itself into unifications, wholes, and harmonies. In other words,

Dewey's attention to the qualitative in experience, call it phenomenological or not, had opened horizons of meaning which his own preferred categories could not control.

Rather than account Cavell's view of Dewey wrong or unfair or insensitive, we can say it takes the line of least resistance. Likewise, we can say that the defenders of Dewey who advance the centrality of the aesthetic in his philosophy also take the line of least resistance. I propose that both lines leave too much of Dewey unattended, unserved. One can, however, attend to places in Dewey where the edges dissolve, where pragmatic equivalents of Platonic *aporeia* occur. At such places in Dewey's philosophy, things fly into motion. Emerson might admire and Wittgenstein might condemn these apparently unnavigated conceptual flights, but their existence invites attention. They cause us to be less certain than Cavell and most Dewey interpreters of what is "characteristic" of Dewey. For example:

> In the assertion (implied here) that the great vice of philosophy is an arbitrary "intellectualism," there is no slight cast upon intelligence and reason. By "intellectualism" as an indictment is meant the theory that all experiencing is a mode of knowing, and that all subject-matter, all nature, is, in principle, to be reduced and transformed till it is defined in terms identical with the characteristics presented by refined objects of science as such.[38]

Dewey turns away from epistemological reductions and transformations of experience and, on the way out, takes science with him. When he readmits science, it is in a more chastened, instrumental form, but it frequently still threatens to reduce and transform what is qualitatively irreducible and nontransformable. The qualitatively rich, stubborn, elusive, massive, halting, flowing, expectant, nostalgic meanings of ordinary experience are not so easily reconciled with the qualitatively reduced and instrumentally ordered meanings of scientific knowing. As Husserl saw, a science of the lifeworld is no easy thing.

I offer two other instances of Cavell feeling along the edges of Dewey and pragmatism generally. He says: "In Dewey's writing, the speech of others, whose ideas Dewey wishes to correct, or rather to replace, especially the speech of children, hardly appears—as though the world into which he is drawn to intervene suffers from a well-defined lack or benightedness." Cavell is not finished with pragmatism: "Pragmatism seems designed to refuse to take skepticism seriously, as it refuses—in Dewey's, if not always in James' case—to take metaphysical distinctions seriously."[39] Such claims are easy to refute, though no less perplexing and frustrating to friends of

Dewey and pragmatism. But there are texts in Dewey which take Cavell and pragmatism's defenders to a more shadowy landscape. In the chapter titled "Custom and Habit" in *Human Nature and Conduct*, Dewey says:

> We come back to the fact that individuals begin their career as infants. For the plasticity of the young presents a temptation to those having greater experience and hence greater power which they rarely resist. It seems putty to be molded according to current designs. That plasticity also means power to change prevailing custom is ignored. Docility is looked upon not as ability to learn whatever the world has to teach, but as subjection to those instructions of others which reflect *their* current habits [Dewey's emphasis]. To be truly docile is to be eager to learn all the lessons of active, inquiring, expanding experience. The inert, stupid quality of current customs perverts learning into a willingness to follow where others point the way, into conformity, constriction, surrender of scepticism and experiment. When we think of the docility of the young we first think of the stocks of information adults wish to impose and the ways of acting they want to reproduce. Then we think of the insolent coercions, the insinuating briberies, the pedagogic solemnities by which the freshness of youth can be faded and its vivid curiosities dulled. Education becomes the art of taking advantage of the helplessness of the young; the forming of habits becomes a guarantee for the maintenance of hedges of custom.[40]

Note the remarkable precision and compactness of Dewey's emphatic "their." His recognition of how tempting, indeed, unavoidably natural, it is for the adult to "correct" and "replace" the speech of the child could not be clearer. It is equally clear that Dewey is determinedly set against such impositions and subjections. What, though, is a teacher to do? Not correct and replace what is false, bad, self-defeating, or self-deceiving?

It is not difficult to pull Dewey out of this apparent nosedive toward terrain marked egoism, subjectivism, and relativism. Dewey risks and then resists these dangers because he senses, but does not quite have an account of, the slightly mysterious nature of praiseworthy growth. When it occurs, for the first grader or the parent of the first grader, how is the individual, unique soul to be respected in the calm and turbulence of a habit-made world? Habit, the middle term between "their" and "me," draws the person inward and outward. Dewey takes skepticism very seriously because a "surrender of scepticism and experiment" eliminates one of the major inducements to Emersonian self-transcendence, what Dewey more quietly refers to as growth.

And it is here, at or near transcendence, that Cavell rests his case against calling Emerson a pragmatist:

> I have, accordingly, wished to place Emerson's writing in a tradition of perfectionist writing that extends in the West from Plato to Nietzsche, Ibsen, Kierkegaard, Wilde, Shaw, Heidegger, and Wittgenstein. Both Dewey and Emerson are necessary for what each of them thinks of as democracy. To repress Emerson's difference is to deny that America is as transcendentalist as it is pragmatist, that it is in struggle with itself, at a level not articulated by what we understand as the political. But what Dewey calls for, other disciplines can do as well, maybe better, than philosophy. What Emerson calls for is something we do not want to hear, something about the necessity of patience or suffering in allowing ourselves to change. What discipline will call for this if philosophy does not?[41]

The central aim of the studies in the present work is to call into question the assumption (and, one senses, the conclusion) underlying Cavell's, but not only Cavell's, thinking about pragmatism: pragmatism has no place for transcendence. In its desire to keep ideal ends from straying too far from concrete means, to see how things are verified and worked out in experience, in short, in its desire to be practical, pragmatism foreshortens the power of what is in principle, as well as in fact, unrealizable. On this view, the high price of metaphysical impatience is the limited and self-limiting taste for the "tangible and the real." No pragmatic consummation can soar so high, or range so distantly, that the shores of the ordinary and everyday are not in sight.

If Cavell compresses the reach of Dewey's pragmatism from above by placing a ceiling on that to which it can be imagined to aspire, one must recognize as well that pragmatism also can be chained from below. A recent example of this perspective on Dewey is found in the treatment of ideals in Michael Eldridge's *Transforming Experience: John Dewey's Cultural Instrumentalism*. Early in this work, Eldridge argues: "To say that [Dewey] was an idealist in a realist's body would make the dualist's mistake against which he was constantly alert. Rather, he participated fully in the society as it was, grasping the possibilities for improvement that were inherent in the existing reality."[42] Eldridge expresses no disappointment in a possibility which is "inherent in the existing reality." Most often, neither does Dewey. But sometimes Dewey moves in the direction of a possibility which stands off from the current situation, a possibility which suggests terms not "inherent" in the situation but which may be found to be relevant and revelatory. We say, "one would not have known" or "one would not have imagined." In order for the natural, the given, the problematic to seek and find ideal fulfillment, it must occasionally transcend the terms on which its identity and self-identification has been established. The growth of persons and of situations involves arcs of meaning which fall above and below the site lines of the present standpoint. What is needed but absent is not always determinable on the basis of what is present.

Eldridge's position regarding ideals is apparent in the section title "Deweyan Ideals as Generalized Ends-in-View."[43] Ideals can be seen and viewed. Actual, specific situations solicit from consciousness actual, specific goals, that is, ends specified as ends-in-view and acted upon as realizable goods, goods for this situation. This, for Eldridge, is Dewey. But Dewey frequently confounds such unrelieved instrumentalist interpretation. In the chapters which follow I direct attention to instances and occasions when "ends-in-view" reflect their debt to the transcendent and horizonal. Occasionally, and always tellingly, Dewey recognizes that there are ends which cannot be viewed, ends given to consciousness as intimations of ideal meaning rather than courses of action. At such times his pragmatism is at its most daring and confusing. The many and various goods we can discern "in" a situation, that is, what Dewey repeatedly and without much clarification says we have in moments of "appreciation," may not all find application in that situation. Transcendent ideals, unfixed and nonabsolute, can exert an inspiring and elevating influence on determinations of what is "useful" in a situation. We appreciate more than we apply.

The possibility that the eyes of the pragmatist can be raised above the level of "what works" to solve a problem is not merely undermined by sentiments such as the following, it is rendered unnecessary:

> There is no "best" beyond the "discovered good" of the situation. One can determine what is better or worse than what existed at any point relative to the felt need; valuation is possible. But one need not find the best action over all, regardless of the specific problematic situation one is trying to resolve. Such a search was pointless from Dewey's instrumentalist perspective. One must be content with the better course of action that has been discovered through deliberation. The better is all the good there is.[44]

As I shall discuss in greater detail in chapter 2, "The Pragmatic Struggle for the Good," there is too much contentment here, too little ambition. One can indeed determine better and worse relative to "felt need," but what prompts, motivates, activates the "felt need"? To propose the problematic situation is circular, as is the proposal that "the fullest justification for both a method and an ideal is found in their usefulness, not in their correspondence to reality."[45] Determinations of better and worse are made in Dewey relative to desire, not simply "felt need." This desire to do justice to the phenomenon is attentive to the situation and to ideal meanings, which have outgrown the restrictions of time and location. Whether, and for what reasons, and for what purposes, we must be "content" with a "better" course of action has little practical force apart from an intimation of what, under ideal conditions, we might aspire to in this situation. The horizon of the better is the good, and unless the better has no horizon or context, it is an unfortunate misrepresentation of Dewey to say on his behalf that "the better is all the good there is." John William Miller puts it well: "Men do not set limited goals for themselves. In fact, and in principle, there is no such sort of goal. All particular enterprises occur in the context of something other than their own limits and because of that context."[46] This transcendent context profoundly complicates notions like usefulness, merging (of actual and ideal), instrumentality, tool, end-in-view, practice, as well as problem and solution.

It may appear as if I am simply urging a larger and deeper place for Kant's regulative ideals in Dewey's philosophy. That is not my intent. The suggestion does, though, helpfully focus one of the chief objectives of the studies in this volume. What transcends the visible and tangible, including, but not limited to, orienting and regulative ideal meanings, was not for Dewey an annoyance which impeded the smooth functioning of instrumental rationality. Neither was the intangible an incidental prop or prompt for the consummatory destination of instrumental rationality, namely, aesthetic experiences. Throughout his career, the transcendental contribution of habit to experience, or, more precisely, the habit-grounded transcendental constitution of experience, attracted and repelled Dewey. Habit set meaning loose for Dewey in ways with which his science and instrumentalism could not always keep pace. In certain respects, Dewey's pragmatism was an attempt to put ordinary, determinate validations of meanings in their extraordinary, intangible, and transcendent place. I assemble in this work a number of occasions in which what I term the "primacy of meaning thesis" allows, invites, and ultimately requires Dewey's pragmatism to respond to the transcendent.

If transcendence, intangibility, and unattainable ideal meanings in Dewey's philosophy are as atmospheric as I claim them to be, they will not be easily visible. Iris Murdoch captures the essence of my approach to these ideas in Dewey in her response to a hypothetical question: "If someone says, 'Do you then believe that the Idea of the Good exists?' I reply, 'No, not as people used to think that God existed.'" Murdoch then continues: "All one can do is to appeal to certain areas of experience, pointing out certain features, and using suitable metaphors and inventing suitable concepts where necessary to make these features visible. No more, and no less, than this is done by the most empirically minded of linguistic philosophers."[47] In the present work, I try to attend to the transcendent, the ideal, the intangible, even the Good, in a roughly similar way. Dewey invites such attention but often frustrates it. For example, his theory of qualitative immediacy is a familiar subject of Dewey studies and, with some justification, can be thought of as a central component of his approach to the intangible. I do not think, however, that the qualitative is nearly as composable and composed as most commentators on Dewey, pragmatism, and American philosophy seem to believe. The qualitative in Dewey cannot explain more than his theory of meaning can explain, since the qualitative is an account of how meaning functions in experience in certain ways, in certain circumstances. The intangible is buried in Dewey's theory of meaning and habit, with a small, though not exclusive, entry point through the familiar territory of the qualitative.

The place of ideals and ideality in Dewey is even more familiar than the intangible. It often is thought of as one of the crowning achievements of his philosophy that ideals are not merely thought, but used. The notion of unattainable ideal meaning is not a common feature of Dewey studies, other than in its role as a bad thing Dewey wished to avoid. Here again, though, buried in his theory of meaning and habit are ideal meanings which are only horizonally available to mind and action. The point is that there are at least starting places in Dewey in connection with intangibility and ideal meaning which permit me to point out "certain features."

A starting place is nearly impossible to find with respect to transcendence. When Dewey discusses transcendence or a cognate, it usually is to criticize it and then to reject it. Given the pervasiveness of his criticism, it is not surprising, or indefensible, for Goinlock to refer to "Dewey's scorn for remote and transcendent ends."[48] Whatever difference transcendence makes to experience, it must occur within experience. Dewey thus appears to steadfastly steer his pragmatism away from whatever cannot be experienced in the ordinary or in its consummations in aesthetic experience. Thus, to gain a starting point with transcendence, it is advisable to review a few formulations of it, which will help to make its presence in Dewey more visible.[49] I do not contend that there are exact equivalents in Dewey of the conceptions which follow. Rather, these ideas about transcendence settle into his thought with surprising ease, animating it and complicating it.

Murdoch's own reflection on transcendence is a stimulating place to begin:

> How do we know the very great are not the perfect? We see differences, we sense directions, and we know that the Good is still somewhere beyond. The self, the place where we live, is a place of illusion. Goodness is connected with the attempt to see the unself, to see and to respond to the real world in the light of a virtuous consciousness. This is the non-metaphysical meaning of the idea of transcendence to which philosophers have so constantly resorted in their explanations of goodness. "Good is a transcendent reality" means that virtue is the attempt to pierce the veil of selfish consciousness and join the world as it really is. It is an empirical fact about human nature that this attempt cannot be entirely successful.[50]

There are enough recognizably "pragmatic" instincts here to satisfy most determined pragmatists. The self pushes not simply ahead but "beyond," seeing that the Good for here and now invites further elaboration, further seeking, further specification. The aim of such seeking is self-seeking and self-knowing, but its attention is not only to the self. The Good solicits virtuous attention to the "real world," to the problems of men and women, children, institutions, families, societies, cultures. The virtuous self deftly or clumsily makes an object of itself and thereby appropriates and transcends itself. One ought not to say that pragmatism is the well-intentioned but limp desire to do the best we can when we know that "this attempt cannot be successful." Say, rather, that pragmatism abjures the absolute because the present realization—small or large—of an ideal meaning has not, in William James's phrase, brought us to "the bottom of being."

There is much to be learned from Stuart Hampshire's remarks on imagination and transcendence in *Innocence and Experience*. Referring to activities that may or may not engage us deeply—"working in the garden, skiing down a slope, climbing a mountain, designing an experiment in a laboratory, suddenly seeing a connection in philosophy, drinking and talking with friends, watching children and grandchildren play, buying a first house, returning to a childhood home"—he says:

> In the peculiar workings of their individual imaginations during these activities, men and women may arrive at a sense of transcendence, a kind of epiphany, in which they seem to themselves to have escaped for a time from the usual limits of possible experience, and to have alighted on a privileged moment that takes them outside their ordinary and

confined routines. In moments of transcendence we feel free from the lapse of time.[51]

It is important to note that while transcendence very well may spring from the ordinary, from gardening, drinking, talking, watching, buying, it involves an escape from the "usual limits of possible experience." To exceed or surpass what we take to be actual, usual experience is not unusual, but what, practically, is involved in an escape from the "usual limits of possible experience"? Perhaps only that some inventions or exertions of mind and meaning escape envisionment of how they could be fulfilled in experience. On such occasions, the routines and typifications of ordinary experience are insufficient to regulate and hence to determine what such escaped meanings "really mean." How such "outside" meanings would appear in, or to, a possible but real experience, is something we cannot know a priori. If the quest for certainty is misplaced in ordinary experience, is it less so for the out-of-the-ordinary?

Peter L. Berger gives a charming example of the border or frontier between the ordinary and the transcendent. He describes an experience in a hotel lobby in Honolulu. As he is waiting with a friend for others to join them for dinner, a "group of elderly Japanese ladies dressed in kimonos" come through a door and into the lobby. "Then the door open[s] again, releasing another group of similarly clad elderly Japanese ladies. And again. And again." This goes on for a long time and moves Berger to remark to his friend: "'Look, I think we are seeing here a hole in the universe. This is it: There is a hole. And out of it will come an unending number of elderly Japanese ladies in kimonos. They will keep coming. This will never stop.'" It finally does stop and the entire hotel lobby is filled with our Japanese ladies. Berger concludes the episode with a number and a reassurance: "In the end, there were about a hundred ladies in the lobby, and of course there had to be a perfectly ordinary explanation." But Berger is not convinced by his own "of course." Even after acknowledging that the experience was trivial, hardly good for a dinner story, and not in any way frightening, he says: "And yet, for a few minutes, the reality of ordinary life was put in question."[52] One wonders, How does Dewey respond to such an experience? First, it is not quite "an experience" in the sense in which he would intend that phrase. Further, inquiry is not absolutely required, not unless what is "put in question" is appreciated solely as a problem to be solved. And while the qualitative richness of the situation is manifest, it is not manifest how what qualitatively appears (puzzlement, fun, strangeness) opens out to what is nonapparent yet present in experience.

Berger sets his example in a larger philosophical context, one which does not seem to overlap very much in Dewey:

> My point is that ordinary reality can be punctured quite easily and once this has happened, anything is possible. This insight is certainly not the result of an act of belief. It is typically not an act of any kind; not something I did, but something that happened to me. All the same, these ruptures of reality disclose or at least intimate a *transcendent* reality lying beyond. The insight is not faith. But it opens up the possibility.[53]

Berger of course is not arguing that One Hundred Elderly Japanese Ladies is the basis of faith in God. What his example does provide is an empirically determinable event which allows response in the terms and language of transcendence. The meaning set loose by the ordinary exceeds what the ordinary can grasp, understand, fathom. How is such a volatile, bewildering "ordinary" to be managed by Dewey's empiricism?

Perhaps, though, the transcendent need not be viewed as so wholly other to the ordinary. Maurice Natanson proposes such a possibility:

> I am interested in the symbolic as a bearer of transcendence. Obviously, the word "symbol" can be used in contexts which are quite different, from symbols in the sense of special notation to systems of highly complex scientific meanings, and to mythic and culture-encompassing world views. The symbolic, as far as I am concerned here, is that which announces, presents (or "appresents") meaning whose elements are in the mundane world but whose qualitative unity and coherence are strange to common sense. The transcendent, in this approach, is not opposed to the mundane but penetrates it in such a way that the naive attitude of daily life is forced to the edge of its limits.[54]

This phenomenology of transcendence has important relevance to Dewey's phenomenology of experience. It complicates the notions of continuity and reconciliation which are typically used by Dewey supporters to keep the everyday and the transcendent in contact with each other. Truth sets limits for itself beyond which it cannot go and still present itself as truth. Meaning is pleased to venture further from the ordinary, further from ordinary explanations and ordinary verifications. Such transcending arcs of meaning do not detour around the mundane, nor do they simply collide with it. They pass through it and penetrate it. A transcendence-penetrated mundanity is not only possible in Dewey's philosophy, it is, I propose, a requirement and outcome of what I term his "primacy of meaning thesis."

It might be objected that the everyday forced to "the edge of its limits" does not transgress limits, is not "beyond" reach of the arts and sciences of intelligently controlled practices. Natanson provides stimulus for a closer consideration of the "beyond" in Dewey's pragmatism:

> It would seem that, if not by definition, then almost by its very nature, transcendence is "beyond" mundane experience; yet it is appresented within the reality of the symbolic self. The "beyond" needs qualification, for transcendence is a pointing, an intentional arrow, which itself lies within experience but which intends an object (the transcendent) which does not. In appresentation, however, the transcendent is brought within the experiential reality of the individual, but the individual not as a mundane being but as a symbolic self.[55]

A surprising amount of Dewey is captured in the phenomenological language of intentional arrows of meaning, which originate in experience but intend objects which do not exist within experience. There are good, practical reasons to wish for meaning's fulfillment to occur within experience besides the logical constraint that there is no other place for it to occur. Dewey was mindful of this. But he also sent aloft intentional arrows which promised more than they could predictably deliver to experience. The mundane self in Dewey's pragmatism—not "a symbolic self"—is ennobled by the capacity for, and possibility of, self-transcendence. In its transcendent moments, meaning, and thus reason, lives beyond its means, beyond its history and habits.

Poetry offers other ways of approaching transcendence. My first example is a work about transcendence in poetry, the other, a few lines from a poem by Charles Tomlinson. The title of Thomas Weiskel's book does not promise a set of concepts easily linked to Dewey: *The Romantic Sublime: Studies in the Structure and Psychology of Transcendence*. Nonetheless, his account of the sublime "as a symbol of the mind's relation to a transcendent order" is an account of habit's hold on the world viewed from the perspective of transcendence.[56] Reflecting on Weiskel's characterization of "three phases or economic states" of the sublime brings Dewey to mind quicker and more convincingly than Emerson, Wittgenstein, or Heidegger.

According to Weiskel, the sublime experience begins with the mind and object in "smooth correspondence":

> In the first phase, the mind is in a determinate relation to the object, and this relation is habitual, more or less unconscious (preconscious in the Freudian sense), and harmonious. This is the state of normal perception or comprehension, the syntagmatic linearity of reading or taking a walk or remembering or whatnot. No discrepancy or dissonance interrupts

representation, the smooth correspondence of inner and outer. Boredom signals an incipient disequilibrium which is not yet strong enough to break into consciousness and bring to a halt the automatic linear rhythm of sensation and reflection.[57]

The habit-made world goes about its business without discord, discrepancy, trouble, or problem. Such mundanity doesn't seem to offer much promise of the sublime. But for Dewey's pragmatism, of course, it does.

The determinations of habit are disrupted and then the second phase begins:

> In the second phase, the habitual relation of mind and object suddenly breaks down. Surprise or astonishment is the affective correlative, and there is an immediate intuition of a disconcerting disproportion between inner and outer. Either mind or object is suddenly in excess—and then both are, since their relation has become radically indeterminate. We are reading along and suddenly occurs a text which exceeds comprehension, which seems to contain a residue of signifier which finds no reflected signified in our minds. Or a natural phenomenon catches us unprepared and unable to grasp its scale.[58]

The "indeterminate" relation of mind and object can become, can be made to become, more determinate by finding means, specifying ends, and reconstructing both. There is not, however, a desire interior or natural to habitual meaning, which restricts its exercise to moments of practical repair or aesthetic consummation. The tear or rent in the ordinary attunement of self and object elicits, as D. H. Lawrence calls it, a new "effort of attention." We can attend to the breakdown of habit as a problem, a puzzle, a mystery, a wonder, a challenge, a comedy, a tragedy. Sublimity, though, has not yet announced itself.

The third phase of the sublime moment is what Weiskel calls the "reactive" phase. How is one to attend to the breakdown?

> In the third, or reactive, phase of the sublime moment, the mind recovers the balance of outer and inner by constituting a fresh relation between itself and the object such that the very indeterminacy which erupted in phase two is taken as symbolizing the mind's relation to a transcendent order. The new relation has a "meta" character, which distinguishes it from the homologous relation of habitual perception. (In the case of poetic imagery, however, it is notoriously difficult to draw a clear line between the image as perception and as sign standing for the nonsensible or the unimaginable—a fact that accounts for a history of quarrels over what is or is not sublime.) Should there be a reversion to

habitual perception, the sublime moment subsides or collapses into something else. For it is precisely the semiotic character of the sublime moment which preserves the sublimation necessary to the sublime.[59]

This is interesting but not quite satisfying. Straining to get as much as he can from Kant, but not wishing to accept Kant's idealist interpretation of the sublime, Weiskel leaves us wondering precisely why indeterminacy should symbolize the "mind's relation to a transcendent order." Not all the breakdowns or collapses of ordinary meaning warrant the distinction, dignity, or inflation of being termed transcendent. Why is the "order of meaning" which follows habit's unsettlement transcendent? Because it overwhelms the meaning on hand and in habit? Because the tangibilities of practical reason face, and are faced with, the intangible and invisible?

From Charles Tomlinson's poem "Ode to Arnold Schoenberg: On a Performance of His Concerto for Violin," we have the following:

> Meshed in meaning
> by what is natural
> we are discontented
> for what is more,
> until the thread
> of an instrument pursue
> a more than common meaning.[60]

While it leaves too much out to be fully adequate, the idea that we are "meshed in meaning" is an acceptably compact description of central features of Dewey's pragmatism. We are not meshed in society, history, or language but rather in the meanings—tangible and intangible—which they institute and sustain. Further, we are meshed in meaning "by what is natural." The ranges of "natural" here exceed the specifications, themselves inexact, of philosophical naturalism, including Dewey's naturalism. It is not difficult to see, however, that our discontent does not arise from the state of being "meshed in meaning" but from being "meshed in"—as in "hemmed in"—by meaning which is restricted to the natural. We are discontented "for what is more."

To uncover the nature of "what is more" was rarely the explicit aim of Dewey's philosophical work. Yet the "more" is the background of every area of philosophy in which he wrote: epistemology, metaphysics, ethics, education, politics, and art. Usually, the more is reclaimed by the natural. Dewey's "mores" are determinable mores, they are more *than* something in the present state of affairs, for example, some specifiable matter which is more stable, more effective, more just, more aesthetically satisfying. His pragmatism, in other words, is committed to working with the world that is *there*. Whatever surpasses the here and now has a path of transcendence — its more — which is determined by the limits of the actual and natural and not by the meanings proposed by the subject: "Instruction in what to do next can never come from an infinite goal, which for us is bound to be empty. It can be derived only from study of the deficiencies, irregularities and possibilities of the actual situation."[61] This type of more might be called the "natural more," and on most interpretations of Dewey, it is the only kind of more he needed or wanted.

Dewey was drawn by another "more," one less determinable, less certain in its appearance, less tangible. Reason's desire — its practical and idealizing desire — is not content with what is there, and it can take only limited instruction from what is there. The ideal, says Dewey, "marks something wanted, rather than something existing. It is wanted because existence as it *now* is does not furnish it. It carries with itself, then, a sense of contrast to the achieved, to the existent. It outruns the seen and touched."[62]

What is noteworthy even without much analysis is how easily Dewey projects a horizon of meaning which "outruns" the seeable and touchable, the empirically verifiable. That such a horizon of meaning should respond, via plans and deliberations, to the needs of this situation, this *now*, is a good thing. But the good intimated in the horizon is not reducible to its good in this *now*. It surpasses its local application and may become, as a habit of mind, a way of appreciating what is possible in such situations. Through habit, we are meshed in the ordinary meanings of the actual and the practices of the actual. Through the projection of a horizon of meaning — ideal meaning — not closed or secured by the verifications of the seen and touched, our sights can be raised. In a violin sonata, a thank-you note, a photograph, a conversation, we are opened to transcendence, opened to "a more than common meaning."

Dewey's pragmatism is, on my account, an attempt to understand how such ideal-aspiring and, often, transcendent discontents (not to be confused with problems) might be incorporated and cultivated in experience. I do not contend that Dewey's pragmatism can accommodate all such idealities, intangibilities, and transcendencies. What I do propose is that when he refers to "a sense of contrast to the achieved, to the existent," he does not simply mean a contrast to what we know, or believe, the actual to be really "like." The pragmatic occasions of intangible idealities and transcendencies are not merely flashes of unlikelihood, ordinary departures from the ordinary. Dewey's pragmatism is an oscillation between moments when the ideal and transcendent are absorbed by the actual and immanent, and moments when they resist such absorption. On these occasions, the ideal "outruns" the actual, leaving our practices and habits, and pragmatism itself, in a less certain state.

The occasions when this happens in Dewey's pragmatism do not form a direct and clear path, say from "Knowledge as Idealization" (1887) to *Experience and Nature* (1925).[63] Thus, my attention to pragmatic occasions of the transcendent ideal is meant to acknowledge the fact that one cannot find a program or position explaining it in Dewey, refined over the course of his career. Nonetheless, there are times, occasions, when habit, meaning, and the ideal dissolve some of the contours of Dewey's pragmatism. In "Knowledge as Idealization," he says: "A mind which does not come to sensations with an ineradicable pre-judgment that the sensations are interpretable, that is, possible bearers of an ideal quality, does not have the starting point for any interpretation, and its sensation could not ever get a beginning on the road of meaning."[64] This outlook does not settle perfectly into the middle or late Dewey, but neither is it wholly foreign or strange to these later periods of his philosophy. Certainly, in the next forty years Dewey made revisions to such an outlook. These revisions invite analysis in the context of an assertion in the final chapter of *Experience and Nature*: "By an indirect path we are brought to a consideration of the most far-reaching question of all criticism: the relation between existence and value, or as the problem is often put, between the real and ideal."[65] The pragmatic occasions studied in the present work recommend the view that Dewey's desire to promote "ordinary experience," "concrete human experience," and "common experience,"[66] could not be fulfilled without a conception of a transcendent ideal, "a more than common meaning."

This meaning is not likely to be ready-to-hand, ready-made, tangible. Dewey agrees with Arendt: the reality and continuity of "the whole factual world of human affairs" depends upon others and their remembrance, and "on the transformation of the intangible into the tangibility of things."[67] Arendt does not stop here, and neither does Dewey, though she thought pragmatism did. Thinking, for Arendt, returns us to the invisible and intangible. For Dewey, thinking *and* acting, sensing *and* trying, afford intimations of the transcendent and intangible. The difference between Arendt and Dewey is simple. Dewey attempted to understand practice and action from the inside and sometimes found more than he could reconcile with his instrumentalism and experimentalism. Arendt says: "I think I understood something of action precisely because I looked at it from the outside, more or less."[68] I do not believe Arendt understands less about action than Dewey *because* she is outside it. But neither does Dewey understand less about what is outside of action and its visibilities simply because he seems to stand so firmly inside of it. We should thus be prepared to be surprised by Dewey.

The studies in the present work attempt to illuminate some of the surprises in Dewey, some of the ways in which intangible, ideal meanings are to be found along stretches of what he calls the "road of meaning." Dewey's "road of meaning" moves from the finite to the infinite, from the visible to the invisible, from the material to the spiritual, from the concrete to the transcendent—and then back. Dewey is not just an empiricist; he is an *excellent* empiricist. He understands that transcendently distant places sometimes offer the promise of "a more than common meaning." To move along the "road of meaning" is, for him, more than a problem solved, intelligence applied, experience had and aesthetically consummated. It is to be alert for all the "possible bearers of an ideal quality." If, as he says in *Human Nature and Conduct*, there is "need of a continuous unification of spirit and habit," then Dewey would not refuse to look into "the hiding places (which are the dwelling places) of spirit."[69] These "hiding places" may not be perfectly visible, and the bearers of a "more" they conceal may not be immediately productive or useful. They may not present themselves to consciousness as ends-in-view. Or facts. Or practices. And, if Dewey is right, they are unlikely to present themselves as the more which is everlasting, the evermore, the eternal. The transcendent ideal transcends its own manifestations. In its presence, in its light "that never was on land or sea,"[70] we still have not reached, as James says, "the bottom of being."

The transcendent for Dewey is no metaphysical sedative; neither is it a metaphysical justification to keep things moving and growing. What the transcendent ideal *is*—specifically, what he called "the grace and the severity of the ideal"[71]—was the most consistent background and stimulus for Dewey's philosophical work. We begin with the grace and severity of the moral struggle, with action that gives us the opportunity to claim the ideal, to live in accordance with it.

· CHAPTER 2 ·

The Pragmatic Struggle for the Good

Dewey's moral idealism is admirably summarized in the following "early" remark from *Outlines of a Critical Theory of Ethics*: "To surrender the actual experienced good for a possible ideal good is the struggle."[1] The remark occurs in the first paragraph of the chapter "The Moral Struggle or the Realizing of Ideals." The rest of Dewey's chapter amplifies this epigrammatic utterance, and with no exaggeration it can be said that the rest of Dewey's career amplifies the chapter. Here I look at some of the continuities between the early and middle idealisms of Dewey through an analysis of "Goodness as a Struggle" (the first section of "The Moral Struggle or the Realizing of Ideals") and one chapter of *Human Nature and Conduct*, "Desire and Intelligence."

I quote a great deal from Dewey in this analysis for two reasons.[2] The first, most obvious reason is that I want to provide a basis, if not evidence, for my interpretations. The second reason is that the power and cogency of some of Dewey's early writings have not been sufficiently noticed or properly appreciated. Even when his thought is most programmatic on behalf of idealism, it often has a suppleness and analytic precision which contradicts the view that his early work was simply a dispensable warm-up for what was to follow later.[3] If one sets aside the fact that what is being read is the "early" Dewey and instead reads the text as an attempt to grapple with certain philosophical issues, a surprising thing happens. The work emerges as interesting and important regardless of its chronological place in the Dewey corpus.

We begin not with Dewey, but with Wittgenstein, Wittgenstein pitched by Stanley Cavell:

Dewey's picture of thinking as moving in action from a problematic situation to its solution, as by the removal of an obstacle, more or less difficult to recognize as such, by the least costly means, is, of course, one picture of intelligence. Intelligence is to overcome inner or outer stupidity, prejudice, ignorance, ideological fixation. Intelligence has its beauties. Wittgenstein's picture of thinking is rather one of moving from being lost to oneself to finding one's way, a circumstance of spiritual disorder, a defeat not to be solved but to be undone. It has its necessities.[4]

The "beauties" which Cavell contemplates for Dewey's thinking are not insignificant. It certainly is clear, though, that their character, if not their worth, is quite different from the "necessities" which Cavell attributes to Wittgenstein's picture of thinking. Problematic situations are at stake for Dewey. Finding the way out of "spiritual disorder" is at stake for Wittgenstein. In this chapter, I do not respond directly to Cavell's striking underestimation of Dewey. I simply consider how Dewey puts the very self at stake in the moral struggle: actual and incipient "spiritual disorder" was the context and motivation for the struggle.

Dewey sees goodness as a struggle because it involves not one, but two kinds of transcendence. The first is captured in the common saying that there is more to something—a person, an event, a remark—than meets the eye or senses. A quality, aspect, consequence, or association is not readily apparent or apparent at all; it transcends what is given now and here to the senses. The second kind of transcendence might be formulated thus: "There is more here than meets the idea," that is, the idea and ideal I presently have regarding honesty, fairness, evil, happiness. The idea and ideal I have of something may not be irrelevant to the present situation, but it is more a repetition or resonance of a previous success or good rather than a compelling sense that this, here and now, is good. Let us begin our examination of the moral struggle and moral transcendence with their history.

Neither kind of transcendence is easily launched, since both are rooted, grounded, in the past:

> The past satisfaction speaks for itself; it has been verified in experience, it has conveyed its worth to our very senses. We have tried and tasted it, and know that it is good. If morality lay in the repetition of similar satisfactions, it would not be a struggle. We should know experimentally beforehand that the chosen end would bring us satisfaction, and should be at rest in that knowledge.[5]

What has been "tried and tasted," what has become second nature and part of our character, "speaks for itself." Dewey's point, however, is that the "past satisfaction" recorded in our habits does not speak for, or regulate, the requirements of *this* situation, *this* time. It is important to note the phenomenological hints he supplies in order to drive home the depth and intimacy of what has become habitual, second nature. Worth is not simply registered in our minds or thoughts; it has been conveyed to our senses. Indeed, not simply to our "senses" but to our "very senses." We look at the world, are in the world, through our habits. Worth conveyed to the senses goes down to habit. This of course is essentially Dewey's stance in *Art as Experience*: "There is no limit to the capacity of immediate sensuous experience to absorb into itself meanings and values that in and of themselves—that is in the abstract—would be designated 'ideal' and 'spiritual.'"[6] Ideal meanings held aloft and secured by habit are those which have been "tried," tried by experience and in experience. They have been held accountable. And they have become so much a part of our character, so internalized, that they are not simply tried and tested, they are "tried and tasted." Idealities have entered our minds and our bodies.

Given the ease, the naturalness of our prior moral accomplishments or satisfactions, what moves us to transcend them? Dewey's answer is quite remarkable: "Some satisfaction has been enjoyed in a previous activity, but that very satisfaction has so enlarged and complicated the situation, that its mere repetition would not afford moral or active satisfaction, but only what Kant terms 'pathological satisfaction.'" On the basis of what he had worked out in the 1887 *Psychology* regarding imagination, Dewey is now able to attribute to habit both a conservative and creative function. Habitual meaning draws the moral demand into its compass and thereby narrows it, focuses it. But habit is expansive, even inventive, and thus it has "enlarged and complicated the situation." It is not so much that past meaning, past experience, is inadequate because it is too small to fit the current situation. The problem is that it is too large. The resources brought to bear on the matter at hand complicate it and do not simply replicate it. The assurances, the confidences of the conserved past are important to Dewey because they make liberating demands on us now. Repetition is not liberation and thus Dewey says: "If morality lay in the repetition of similar satisfactions, it would not be a struggle. We should know experimentally beforehand that the chosen end would bring us satisfaction, and should be at rest in that knowledge."[7] The good of "past satisfactions" is so enormous that repetition is a constant temptation and struggle becomes almost a sign of failure or breakdown. If something has worked before, say a principle or a virtue, why doubt it now? Why struggle if one can "be at rest"?

The answer is that self-cultivation demands it. We can do better, be better. If character is to be improved, the moral self must strive: "When morality lies in striving for satisfactions which have not verified themselves to our sense, it always requires an effort. We have to surrender the enjoyed good, and stake ourselves upon that of which we cannot say: We *know* it is good. To surrender the actual experienced good for a possible ideal good is the struggle."[8] These ideas are not rough sketches which the later Dewey develops and, in developing, outgrows or, more dramatically, rejects. These ideas constitute a rather large part of the meaning of his mature pragmatism. They reward close consideration.

To be at rest, and to seek to stay at rest, is only natural. Equilibrium between organism and environment is not, in Cavell's terms, either a small beauty or a small necessity. It is important. Rest, though, may not be possible. When a problem disrupts our rest, we call upon prior experience to respond to the disruption. On the basis of previous experience, we can "know experimentally" what end to choose. But such experimental knowing is a sense-bound knowing, a knowing which must have its past arrayed before the senses, verified by the senses. Having been "tried and tasted," having become habitual, it slumbers until a problem causes a breakdown. Then, stirred by trouble, habit and experience are reconstructed and reorganized.

This picture of Dewey is inadequate. It leaves out the central elements of striving, surrendering, and staking. It leaves out the struggle. First, there is the striving, the desiring. These states admit of degrees. The desire to be and to do good ranges from the wholly absent to the fully developed. Max Otto says that ideals are "campaigns to win desired satisfactions from existence."[9] The state of individual and collective campaigns varies in sincerity, intelligence, imagination, and of course, effort. For this reason, it does not help to understand the phenomenology of the moral struggle to claim that one must first be the kind of person for whom struggle is possible. The struggle may be weak, virtually undetectable, just a wisp of a second thought or doubt. Precisely because the struggle is motivated by something so intangible as an ideal, it is easily quickened or retarded by small influences: a mood, a memory, a rebuke, an encouragement. The moral struggle involves striving for something which transcends presentability to the senses, and in this respect Otto's comparison of ideals and campaigns is inadequate. A campaign seeks a result, a determinate result. An ideal good is not determinate or determined. It has not been verified "to our sense," that is, verified through trying and tasting. It is supersensible.

Because the projected good is uncertain, unknown, intangible, the movement to it from the presently "enjoyed good" involves nothing less than a "surrender" of the latter. The determinations and declarations of good in the past are not without value. Their worth lasts and their lastingness is achieved through habit. But a habit can grow—can become, say, more differentiated, textured, responsive—and in its growing it must release or surrender its present hold on the world. This of course does not mean that all of one's habits and their goods are surrendered, but simply that with respect to *this* struggle, in *these* conditions, certain habits and their goods are more relevant than others, and these must be surrendered. The struggle begins, then, on the immanent side of the habitual and opens to what must be surrendered, left behind, transcended. We "stake ourselves" on what transcends our ability to fulfill itself perceptually or epistemologically. The ideal we project is not seen with the senses, nor is it that about which we can say "We *know* it is good." Moved by desire for the good, we "stake ourselves" on a transcendence of the eye and mind.

Note the similarity of Dewey's account of the struggle to Iris Murdoch's rather well known description of a mother's struggle to give "careful and just *attention*" to her daughter-in-law (for whom she initially "feels hostility"):

> M *looks* at D, she attends to D, she focuses her attention. M is engaged in an internal struggle. She may for instance be tempted to enjoy caricatures of D in her imagination. (There is curiously little place in the other picture [what Murdoch calls the "existentialist-behaviourist" view] for the idea of *struggle*.) And M's activity here, so far from being something very odd and hazy, is something which, in a way, we find exceedingly familiar. Innumerable novels contain accounts of what such struggles are like.[10]

It might appear as if Murdoch contradicts Dewey, since he places so much emphasis on what cannot be visualized, while she is emphatically concerned with looking, attending, seeing. But the contradiction does not exist. The mother's attending is "something progressive, something infinitely perfectible."[11] What leads the attending on, what sustains the struggle? Murdoch's answer is the Good, and it transcends vision:

> The Good itself is not visible. Plato pictured the good man as eventually able to look at the sun. I have never been sure what to make of this part of the myth. While it seems proper to represent the Good as a centre or focus of attention, yet it cannot quite be thought of as a "visible" one in that it cannot be experienced or represented or defined.[12]

We attend to the Good not by seeking to look at it—or for it—as if it were a tangible object or event or state. Rather, we seek to give tangible expression to intangible ideals which reside beyond the tangible. Seen from Murdoch's perspective, it does not seem to me misguided to suggest that Dewey's early and mature pragmatism is essentially a series of proposals on how to give tangible, visible expression to authorizing, transcending, intangible ideals. Such expression is not complacent or self-absorbed or solipsistic or relativistic or historicist.

Its character becomes clear in the last sentence of Dewey's paragraph: "To surrender the actual experienced good for a possible ideal good is the struggle." The sentence contains almost too much, attempts too much, and this despite appearing to attempt so little. "Actual experienced good" is contrasted with "possible ideal good," and the constant is "good." The "actual" must be surrendered for a "possible," and the "experienced" must be surrendered for an "ideal." This surrender removes one, for a while, from actual, ordinary, concrete experience. It is not a historically determinate, reassuringly actual "ideal good" which calls one forward, but rather a "possible ideal good." Having surrendered the tangible good, one so tangible that it can be tasted, we "stake ourselves" upon an intangibility. To be precise, it is not one, but two, intangibilities which pull us forward: the intangibility of the possible and the intangibility of the ideal. Dewey's pragmatism, viewed not simply as a philosophical theory but as an encompassing view of the human condition, is a generalization of the idea that our lives are lived in the realms and intersections of the tangible and the intangible.[13]

Dewey thus gets immediately to what he calls the "heart of the moral struggle," the opposition of desire and duty. In (what has come to be) his expected dualism-avoiding fashion, Dewey starts his analysis by saying, "Of course, taken strictly, there can be no opposition here."[14] To have even minimum "appeal to the mind," a duty must awaken some desire. It is apparent, though, that the distinction he goes on to make is stronger and more ontologically divisive than a mere functional distinction: "But we may distinguish between a desire which is based on past satisfaction actually experienced, and desire based simply upon the idea that the end is *desirable*—that it ought to be desired."[15] Dewey's "and" is really "or": we can define ourselves on the basis of past satisfactions and goods, or we can move ourselves forward into less well charted territory "based simply upon the idea that the end is *desirable*—that it ought to be desired." The general habitual past is not rejected, forgotten, rescinded. But habit's power cannot be less than its freedom, and its freedom requires that habit attune itself to the present, to take on new meaning at this time and in this place. If habit could not transcend itself, Kant's worries about habit would be fully justified. But habit can transcend itself. Surrender is the perfect concept to capture the phenomenology of this transcendence. It captures just how difficult it is for habit to momentarily ask less of itself so as to eventually ask more. But the striving, the desire, for a "possible ideal good" has the power, sometimes, to surmount the difficulty. And this desire is inspired by such intangibility, being "based simply upon the idea that the end is *desirable*—that it ought to be desired." "Simply" testifies on behalf of transcendence, the possible, the ideal, the good.

This is not new, it is there in the first paragraph of "The Moral Struggle or the Realizing of Ideals," and the second paragraph asks us to attend more carefully to what is not holistically bound together in the first paragraph—the self. Precisely because the "past satisfaction" and "actual experienced good" are "surrendered," we are not of one mind. We are not whole. We struggle and we strive. We are divided selves, divided in what we have been and what we can be, divided in what we have known and what we do not know; we are even divided in what we can see and what cannot be brought before our senses. In an important sense, we also divide experience. We ask experience to function as evidence for our hypotheses, our adventures with experimental meanings, and we also range beyond experience as evidence pushes into what is not evident, into what Dewey in the next paragraph calls faith. In striving for a "possible ideal good," we ask of ourselves and experience more than they can provide at the moment.

Dewey is not finished with "simply": "It may seem strange to speak of a desire based simply upon the recognition that an end *should* be desired, but the possibility of awakening such a desire and the degree of its strength are the test of a moral character."[16] Desiring is quite tangible, possessing phenomenologically specifiable characteristics like urgent, restrained, focused, vague, halting, committed. But desire's intentional object is rather more intangible in the case of the moral struggle. The intentional object is a "possible ideal good," an end that "*should* be desired." The number of intentionally nonexistent objects is almost staggering: possibles, ideals, goods, shoulds, ends. That moral life should balance on such an array of intangibles is well captured by Dewey's repetition of "simply." It was remarkable for Dewey that so much depends on an intangible—an ought or should. Hidden behind the cautious "it may seem strange" is Dewey's wonder and awe. The moral struggle turns on something as immaterial and insubstantial as an ought pledged to a "possible ideal good." On such intangibilities we pledge—and stake—ourselves and our character.

Thus, what Cavell does not see in Dewey is precisely Dewey's chief concern, what Cavell calls "a circumstance of spiritual disorder." The "spiritual disorder" for Dewey is the self at stake in moral struggle. Naturally, the disorder and struggle cannot even have a start unless we are awakened by an end that ought to be desired. Desire and the ought are stirred by a "possible ideal good" and are continued into action. But Dewey realizes that such a stirring of desire, such awakening, is far from automatic, since it must overcome, must transcend, the satisfactions and resources of habit. Equally important, the desire or intent must be fulfilled, brought further into the experience which calls it forth. He asks two questions which are not fully rhetorical; that is, they are questions he asks himself: "How far does this end awaken response in me because I see that it is the end which is fit and due? How far does it awaken this response although it actually thwarts some habitual satisfaction?"[17]

It is not at all clear how we come to "see" which end is "fit and due." The seeing is not merely a recognition that this or another end is the ideal. The seeing involves a forecast, seeing how the ideal fits the demands of this context, this place, this time.[18] Further, one must see what is due the ideal end, the ideal good. What does it concretely require of us? The surrender in such seeing involves self-transcendence and self-definition. Desire inspired by an ideal good may not "fall into line with past satisfactions." Indeed, desire for the good may thwart a "habitual satisfaction." In other words, the habitual accomplishment which appears best suited to respond to the present circumstance may not be best suited to respond. I must ask more of myself because the situation may be asking more of me than I realize.

This leads to the recognition that Dewey did not locate the struggle entirely "in one's head," one's mind, or even one's habits. There is something objective and impersonal involved in the moral struggle. To desire the good is not to desire self-satisfaction but rather the satisfaction of the situation which calls forth the struggle. Transcendence, in other words, looks inward and outward; duty draws me through my habits and beyond some of them to the demands of the situation. To rely solely on inclination, preference, or desire is to substitute self-assertion in place of what is due, what is dutiful. But objective duty separated from a subject's habits is not possible; it would have no content or resources with which to meet its own demands.

In what may appear to be the adoption of a modified Kantian position, Dewey says: "Here is the opposition of duty and desire. It lies in the contrast of a good which has demonstrated itself as such in experience, and a good whose claim to be good rests only on the fact that it is the act which meets the situation. It is the contrast between a good of possession, and one of action."[19] The Kantian auspices thus are indirect. Kant's "highest good" measures itself on the basis of the claims of reason, claims which are expected to have practical consequence. Action transfers the findings of reason to human experience. Dewey's "ideal good" measures itself on the basis of whether it inspires "the act which meets the situation." Action is morally significant for Dewey when it is a striving, and striving helps to determine the findings of reason.[20] The ideals which come to mind, dominated though not exhausted by the varied activities of reason, are prospective. They lift up and forward. We strive forward, not backward.

Moral action for Dewey, then, is not an arena simply, or even primarily, for the use or application of means-ends reasoning: "From this point of view morality is a life of *aspiration*, and of *faith*; there is required constant willingness to give up past goods as the good, and to press on to new ends; not because past achievements are bad, but because, being good, they have created a situation which demands larger and more intricately related achievements."[21] Application is nothing without aspiration and is not possible without faith. Habits are the basis of constancy, but constancy requires vigilance, a sort of metaconstancy. As I discuss further in chapter 4, "Humanism and Vigilance," this is the "constant willingness to give up past goods as the good, and to press on to new ends." Transcendence of past satisfactions, achievements, and goods is not a preference for Dewey, in that he prefers to be modern or presentist rather than old-fashioned.[22] Habit not merely allows but requires aspiration if it is to be morally responsive. If we are to cultivate and perfect ourselves, we must "press on to new ends." Transcendence is built into pragmatism.

It might be argued that Dewey was being surprisingly nonempirical. Whether past achievements should be given up is at least partly an empirical question. We do not know before the fact whether these achievements have "created a situation which demands larger and more intricately related achievements." Perhaps what is "fit and due" is roughly proportional to what is tried, tested, and tasted. If so, then a "constant willingness to give up past goods as the good," even in the name of moral striving for ideal good, can only result in the substitution of possibles, mights, and maybes for what has shown itself in experience and to the senses to be workable because it has worked.

Dewey does not shrink from this challenge; indeed, he enlarges it. The willingness to give up past goods is not based on evidence that they are manifestly inadequate or problematic. The willingness to "press on" is "aspiration and it implies *faith*." What Dewey next says is the sort of thing that presumably could never find a place in his later thought: "Only the old good is of sight, has verified itself to sense. The new ideal, the end which meets the situation, is felt as good only in so far as the character has formed the conviction that to meet obligation is itself good, whether bringing sensible satisfaction or not."[23] I will show later in this chapter that he does say essentially the same thing in his mature moral theory. This certainly, though, is a remarkably nonempirical, nonexperimental, non-naturalist thing to say for a pragmatist. The ideal end which leads us forward is not envisioned by the senses: "only the old good is of sight." The ideal is not an intention, but it does prescribe the intentions which steady it in consciousness and which, through action, fulfill it in experience. That I can fulfill, body forth, this ideal is the basis or source of the obligation to which Dewey refers. In meeting this ideal-inspired obligation, I may not be able to body it forth to the senses. Nonetheless, I strive for a "possible ideal good" and I continue the struggle "whether bringing sensible satisfaction or not." For Dewey, what I can see with the senses is neither the beginning nor the end of the moral struggle.

As Dewey moves toward the conclusion of this section, it is apparent that moral struggle is constituted by the accords and discords of the tangible and the intangible. You can show, demonstrate, make evident, prove that one "ought to act so and so." But, says Dewey, "you cannot *prove* to him that the performance of that duty will be good." There may not be "sensible satisfaction" but only the satisfaction afforded by faith in certain high intangibles, the "moral order" and the "identity of duty and the good." This faith is carried through to activity: "Every time an agent takes as his end (that is, chooses as good) an activity which he has not already tried, he asserts his belief in the goodness of right action as such. This faith is not a mere intellectual thing, but it is practical—the staking of self upon activity as against passive possession."[24]

If we strive to perfect ourselves, we are not content with the "tried and tasted." An ideal end which inspires us and moves us to action occasions a most magnificent act of faith: "belief in the goodness of right action as such." This "as such" is not visible to the senses, not tangible. Call this the Platonic faith of Dewey. In moral action we are ahead of ourselves, living at least in part beyond our habitual means. Dewey's final sentence is simultaneously compact and expansive. No "mere intellectual thing," faith continues its journey and furthers its reach through practical engagement with the world. And so Dewey concludes the section with a definition of the practical, a definition which comes close to defining much of his later pragmatism: "the staking of self upon activity as against passive possession." Neither pragma nor dogma is the motivation for the self-transcendence and striving of moral practice. Rather, we stake ourselves on an intangible ideal and we try to act in accord with it, to keep faith with it and ourselves.

Before turning to a consideration of "Desire and Intelligence" in *Human Nature and Conduct*, I wish to look briefly into Dewey's idea that moral practice is grounded in a certain kind of desire. Desire for him is the striving—the active willing—to find the most fitting tangible expression of an agent's faith in an intangible ideal. One can find a number of excellent insights into the nature of such striving in *Plato: Dramatist of the Life of Reason* by John Herman Randall, Jr. In linking Plato and Dewey (through Randall, a philosopher who understood and admired both), I am not suggesting that Dewey was "really" a Platonist.[25] I simply wish to propose that Dewey's account of the motivation for moral struggle is compatible with a great deal of Randall's exposition of Plato. Randall says that for Plato "the important point is, we will *know* and *see* what life is only if we see it as more than it actually is—only if we see what is imperfect in fact as perfectible in imagination. Human life is not only tolerable, it is only *intelligible*, if we idealize it. We do not understand what it really is unless we see what it *might* be."[26] The "tried and tasted," as well as worth which has been conveyed to the "very senses," encourage us to believe that on their basis we know and see what "actually is." We are not ahead of the actual, but rather even with it, symmetrically abreast of it. It makes sense, is understandable, is intelligible, on the basis of what is present to consciousness. But Platonic restlessness is not easily denied. To understand what something "really is," it must be idealized. Intelligibility requires nothing less than the transcendence of the given and the present. It requires the longest of arcs, one moving from "actually is" to "*might* be," from the tangible to the intangible. The actual provides a certain momentum and direction for the "*might* be," even a certain content, but the "*might* be" is not derived from the actual. In Dewey's language, a "past satisfaction actually experienced" will need to be surrendered in favor of perfecting ourselves, or more precisely, in favor of striving to perfect ourselves.

It is customary in Dewey studies to regard the "*might* be" as a hypothesis, the task of which is to bring order, harmony, and equilibrium to a disrupted organism. The disruption may be practical, intellectual, or moral, but the desire is the same in all three: to end the tension, disruption, and turbulence by envisioning and enacting meanings possibly responsive to the situation's needs. The origin of hypotheses may be obscure and perhaps even transcendent with regard to the gap between the facts of a case and the suggested, hypothesized meanings.[27] Once, however, the hypotheses are at work in experience, their "*might* be," more intangible nature is transformed into something rather more tangible, that is, an instrument. Like most instruments, we never lose sight of these hypothetical meanings. The agent projects them, looks to them, looks with them, and looks after them. In this respect, hypotheses are visionary instruments which enable one to experiment with the situation and to seek a solution, a consequence which meets the requirements of the situation. The desire which moves the whole thing, which animates the entire experience, is the desire to resolve a problem and to restore equilibrium. In other words, habit's hold on the world has failed and it must be restored; such restoration may perhaps require some reconstruction of one's habits,[28] but such reconstruction is not to be feared so long as we fix our eyes on the end we have in view.

Modifying Delmore Schwartz just a bit, one might say the self is always at the wheel.[29] Its desire is to survey the road ahead, take careful account of what is there, and perhaps incidentally, to note what is not there. If a breakdown occurs, the hypothetical if/then will shed the necessary light to get us on our way again. The hypothesis must be governed by the present conditions; it cannot project a meaning which has lost sight of the past since the past is what needs to be reconstructed, that is, the past which is no longer satisfactorily working in the present. A hypothetical "*might* be" unrooted in something actually seen could cause distraction and an accident. Pragmatically speaking, desire must know some bounds and these are set by what is in view, coming into view, or foreseeable. Glorious ideals are fine, as are great aspirations, but both have their practical, perceptible origins as well as practical, perceptible limits. The requirements of practice, properly conceived, are not weakenings of the ideal. They are more like the step-down transformers on utility poles, which reduce the volts coming from the power station to a level we can actually use in our homes.

Thirty-one years separate *Outlines of a Critical Theory of Ethics* and *Human Nature and Conduct*. What has become of ideality, transcendence, striving, staking oneself, surrendering, in short, the struggle? It appears that Dewey has brought things down to earth. In the chapter "The Nature of Aims" he says: "Every such idealized object is suggested by something actually experienced, as the flight of birds suggests the liberation of human beings from the restrictions of slow locomotion on dull earth."[30] Well, this certainly is in unmistakable contrast to his assertion of 1891: "But we may distinguish between a desire which is based on past satisfaction actually experienced, and a desire based simply upon the idea that the end is *desirable*—that it ought to be desired."[31] In 1891, Dewey had given the "actually experienced" not simply a minor role in the moral struggle, but of necessity an expendable role: "To surrender the actual experienced good for a possible ideal good is the struggle."[32] One way of approaching pragmatism, not only as a philosophy but as a cultural orientation, is to judge its success or failure by how far away it moves from this standpoint. And it certainly appears as if Dewey judged the success of his pragmatism by how robustly he could keep the "actually experienced" centered, rather than allowing it to slip off into the margins—which it nevertheless does.

Before looking at "Desire and Intelligence," it is worth noting how unsteadily Dewey steers his course to the "actually experienced." In the next to last paragraph of "The Nature of Aims," he says:

> "Idealism" must indeed come first—the imagination of some better state generated by desire. But unless ideals are to be dreams and idealism a synonym for romanticism and phantasy-building, there must be a most realistic study of actual conditions and of the mode or law of natural events, in order to give the imagined or ideal object definite form and solid substance—to give it, in short, practicality and constitute it a working end.[33]

The first point to note is that this is a less strenuous requirement than what he just two pages before had imposed on the ideal, namely, that it is "suggested by something actually experienced." Here, however, the ideal simply must allow "a most realistic study of actual conditions." It is possible that an ideal may not have been suggested by an actual but can still fulfill the second, less stringent, requirement that it permit a realistic study of actuals. One may be surprised by how an apparently remote, impossible ideal actually has possibilities, is *at least* possible.

The second point to note is that an ideal which is presented to consciousness more by surprise than suggestion emphasizes not only the drama of the ideal but also the intangibility of the ideal. An ideal suggested by an actual is already partially formed and carries with it discernible prospects for tangible expression and embodiment. An ideal which is less directly suggested by an actual, that is, more loosely occasioned and governed by an actual, is diaphanous. It is too insubstantial to be used directly as a means of viewing ends, much less actions. Hence the need for the actual "to give the imagined or ideal object definite form and solid substance." Thus, when Dewey says in 1922 that "'Idealism' must indeed come first—the imagination of some better state generated by desire," one cannot fail to ask, "what sort of desire?" But the force of this ultimate question is diluted and misunderstood if one fails to note that Dewey does not say that "the imagination of some better state" is generated by a problem. No, the better is generated by desire, and what will fulfill desire is an ideal suited to, actively made ready for, this occasion. Action fulfills ideality, action which is itself prepared by deliberation and judgment. The largeness of the ideal, the specificity of the ideal, the relevance of the ideal—all these considerations and more must be managed with the greatest care. Through our practices, we demonstrate our care for ideals. Thus, in 1922 idealism is not on his mind as a transcendental nuisance; instead, he is drawn to, drawn back to, 1891 and the "desire based simply upon the idea that the end is *desirable*—that it ought to be desired." The question might be put this way: how is the intangible to be practically managed?

Dewey's chapter "The Nature of Principles" is important on its own terms and as a preface to "Desire and Intelligence." The purpose of the chapter is relatively straightforward: to see how ready-mades, that is, ready-made principles and ready-made rules, do not do justice to situations occasioning moral response. His way of proceeding is to look at actuals. First, he acknowledges that "human history is long"; that is, past experimentations and satisfactions have yielded a cultural repository of principles with "a well earned prestige." The "height of foolishness" would be to disregard them. Then, he says: "But social situations alter; and it is also foolish not to observe how old principles actually work under new conditions, and not to modify them so that they will be more effectual instruments in judging new cases."[34] How do they "actually work"? For the most part, they are adapted: "Yet the choice is not between throwing away rules previously developed and sticking obstinately by them. The intelligent alternative is to revise, adapt, expand and alter them. The problem is one of continuous, vital readaptation."[35]

In 1891, Dewey's phenomenology of the moral struggle emphasized discontinuity—surrender of the old and enjoyed good and the commitment to a new ideal, one which may not even bring "sensible satisfaction." The past is not in sight, nor is the future. In 1922, Dewey appears to want both past and future more clearly in sight. "Continuous, vital readaptation" is not equivalent to continuity of past and future, but it is clear that the work of hypothesis is to keep the actuals of the "previously developed" in touch with the possibles of the yet-to-be-developed. The sight lines connecting past, present, and future may not be perfectly clear, but at least some are discoverable through the hard work of hypothesis forming and testing.

That Dewey wishes to be very concrete is indicated by his choice of an example, the foot as a unit of measure. Quite simply, there is "no fixed foot 'in itself.'" As he pursues the actual, Dewey is steadily moving away from the "fixed antecedent standard." But the actual possesses stresses and strains which blur the sight lines which Dewey just a few pages earlier had constructed through the work of adaptation. Such a fixed standard should be rejected because it is "another manifestation of the desire to escape the strain of the actual moral situation, its genuine uncertainty of possibilities and consequences."[36] "The strain of the actual moral situation" is proleptic. That is, not until the next chapter, "Desire and Intelligence," does it become clear in what way the actual is not fixed, visibly transparent, or even fully tangible. A great deal is at stake in the strain between the fixed and the unfixed. As in Beethoven's Pastoral symphony, the rumble of thunder is distant but grows closer. In the "actual moral situation," there is "genuine uncertainty of possibilities and consequences." Present uncertainty may run deeper than adaptation of the past can manage. So, while he is not content to settle for the assurances of the past, and while adaptation seems to be the most effective way of keeping the past in mind and in use, a question looms for Dewey. Let us suppose that the agent somehow controls the desire to "escape" strain and uncertainty and is instead prepared for them. What desire of the agent ought to animate the moral situation? This question takes us to "Desire and Intelligence."

This chapter is one of the most difficult and obscure in all of Dewey. It also is one of the most rewarding and profound chapters to be found in his entire corpus. Perhaps it is not really that ironic that certain conflicting, or at least competing, intellectual desires of Dewey move in and out of focus in a chapter concerned with desire and intelligence. The strain in the chapter is evident. It begins with what Dewey calls "an independent analysis of desire," and desire, he immediately claims, is an "outcome" of obstacles and obstructions to activity.[37] The chapter concludes with a consideration of "the genuine import of ideals and idealism." This analysis is effected through an amazing tumble of what might be called transcendence-invoking concepts: "indefinite context," "shadowy background," "encompassing infinity of connections," "intimations," "ineffable and undefinable," "effortless and unfathomable," "enveloping whole." The chapter begins, one might say, with severity and ends in grace.

The chapter begins slightly defensively, sternly. "Certain critics" find his position "intellectualistic, cold-blooded": "They say we must change desire, love, aspiration, admiration, and then action will be transformed. A new affection, a changed appreciation, brings with it a revaluation of life and insists upon its realization."[38] His response to this criticism requires an "independent analysis of desire." Presumably, Dewey is going to show that what we desire in the moral situation is far more complicated than what simply intellectual desires can accomplish. One can almost immediately see—mistakenly, it will turn out—what Dewey wants to do: convert cold-blooded to full-blooded. He wants the first step of this conversion to be on a solid, tangible footing so that it does not look as if he is warming things up too quickly or simply too much. In other words, he doesn't wish to be accused of romanticism as he responds to the charge of intellectualism.

Solidity is found in a distinction. "End-in-view" and "the actual end of desire," the outcome, are to be distinguished. The object of desire is an end-in-view, a state of being which does not presently exist but one we aim to bring into existence. However, because the desire is called out by an obstacle or obstruction, the desire must take account of the particulars along its path of satisfaction. Such accounting may, and probably will, require that the end-in-view be modified as new information, new thought, new demands make their claims. The end-in-view functions, in other words, hypothetically, not categorically or absolutely. The revisability of the end-in-view depends on its being truly viewable, or, stated epigramatically, revisability follows visibility.

It should be noted that Dewey has grounded the object of desire in the actual not once, but twice. First, he grounds it in the end-in-view, which is accessible to revision and augmentation. Ends have meanings and can take on new meanings; both change and grow. Growth, though, which is the result of my freedom, requires that I be responsible for the career of the growth, and such responsibility requires that at the very least I be able to see, to view, the ends and meanings which are under cultivation. The second ground in the actual is the obstacle or obstruction: "When the push and drive of life meets no obstacle, there is nothing which we call desire." Not satisfied that he has adequately placed desire squarely in the actual, Dewey notes that desire "is activity surging forward to break through what dams it up."[39] Not merely something actual from the environment, but something physical is needed to break through the dam. Without a discernible, determinate, visible obstruction to satisfaction, desire is not awakened.

Although it appears to be a small one, there is a stumble in the second ground, and it is surprising and it is serious. In an earlier chapter, "Custom and Habit," Dewey warmly remarks: "How delicate, prompt, sure and varied are the movements of a violin player or an engraver!"[40] Not all persons possessing extraordinary talents, skills, capacities, and habits can be claimed to possess extraordinary desire, but of course many do possess just such desire. And of those who do, it would be at least a bit odd to claim that the desire, the love, the eros, embodied in the exercise of their habits is motivated solely by the desire to meet obstacles and obstructions. The latter may be inherent in the practice, and part of the goodness and beauty of the practice may involve overcoming them, but the desire is fueled by something more worthy than the obstruction. The fact that desire can be obstructed tells us that obstruction is not the end, the goal, the motive force of desire. Something transcending the obstruction is the occasion and the perfection of desire.

The violin player and engraver are instances of the larger point about habit and desire which Dewey had made in an earlier chapter, "Habits and

Will," and which he contradicts in "Desire and Intelligence." In the former, he says:

> All habits are demands for certain kinds of activity; and they constitute the self. In any intelligible sense of the word will, they *are* will. They form our effective desires and they furnish us with our working capacities. They rule our thoughts, determining which shall appear and be strong and which shall pass from light to obscurity.[41]

Habits form our desires and are "demands for certain kinds of activity," demands for activities like violin playing, engraving, going to museums, going to ball parks, having parties, praying, writing books, caring for one's family. Habit-grounded desire has moved us into the world prior to any confrontation with an obstacle or obstruction: "We may think of habits as means, waiting, like tools in a box, to be used by conscious resolve. But they are something more than that. They are active means, means that project themselves, energetic and dominating ways of acting."[42] Certainly, habits may meet with obstacles and may require reconstruction. But habits and desires are at work, active and projecting, before trouble and obstruction call them into being. Dewey is simply inattentive to his own phenomenology, to the intentional powers he has attributed to habit and thus to desire. Prior to the specification of distinct objects of consciousness (and desire), and prior to any realization of discord between habitual self and world, habitual meaning mediates, modulates, and energizes our accord with the world.

By the middle of "Desire and Intelligence," Dewey turns to impulse and also returns to the idea of the obstruction-dependent nature of desire. He does not make either turn in order to continue the analysis of desire with which he began the chapter, nor does he commence a detailed analysis of intelligence, the second half of the chapter title. With respect to intelligence, he simply states that it "converts desire into plans, systematic plans based on assembling facts, reporting events as they happen, keeping tab on them and analyzing them." Having disposed of quiescence, pleasure, and perfection as the termini of desire, Dewey winds up with ideality. He does not announce that he has rejected these other termini and that he now wishes to consider the ideal. Its appearance is almost incidental: impulse is easily fooled and intelligence is needed to clarify and liberate impulse. He then says: "Hence the idealism of man is easily brought to naught. Generous impulses are aroused; there is a vague anticipation, a burning hope, of a marvelous future."[43] He does not, however, reject the ideal as the proper object of desire, but instead he attempts to strengthen this possibility by locating the intersection of the ideal and the actual a little closer to empirically determinate, worldly visibilities. The ideal is too strong a force, though, and Dewey loses control of it fairly quickly.

Before it passes out of his control, Dewey once again calls upon obstruction to keep things grounded: "Obstacles are encountered upon which action dashes itself into ineffectual spray."[44] Undirected by thought and intelligence, generous impulses weaken and wither, or persist as "vague enthusiasms" and "cloudy perceptions." Whatever form their future takes, the result is the same: they gain no purchase in the actual. They fall victim to a "baser desire" that takes advantage of acquired habits and "a shrewd cold intellect that manipulates them." His aim low and narrow, his foresight sharp and clear, the "realistic man" has a reliable technique for dealing with what Dewey wonderfully calls "idealistic outbursts." The realist drafts "idealistic desire" into "materialistic reservoirs." Idealism is easily co-opted by an ungenerous realism.

It is important to note the tone, the attitude, the mood of Dewey as he makes life difficult for the sentimental, romantic idealist. He is impatient with, but not dismissive of, "the glorification of affection and aspiration at the expense of thought." Without respect for the empirically determinable and actual, and without their deepening by thought, desire "does not know its way." Almost in a physical sense, desire does not see where it is going. Thought is required to accompany the ideal, guide the ideal, through the actual conditions which foster or hinder its realization. Without the "hard labor of observation, memory and foresight," ideals will be foreshortened and ends-in-view will be vague and ill-defined: "For the moving force may be a shadowy presentiment constructed by wishful hope rather than by study of conditions; it may be an emotional indulgence rather than a solid plan built upon the rocks of actuality discovered by accurate inquiries."[45]

To oversimplify, Dewey does not wish to leave a perfectly good ideal at the door of experience. It must be invited in, carefully watched, and, most important, assisted in its trajectory through promotions and obstructions. Failure to attend to idealistic desire in this manner—this practical manner—is to condemn it to a marginal existence, "a shadowy presentiment constructed by wishful hope." Thus, Dewey does not reject idealistic aspiration but rather what Max Otto nicely calls "a gardenia idealism developed under glass."[46] Dewey wishes to remove the glass, to set the ideal to work in environments and conditions less pure than the ideal.

At this point in the chapter, Dewey seems to have fulfilled his purpose, which is to connect desire and intelligence, emotion and thought, hope and plan, faith and work. In each coupling the first term is a good, but not good enough. The second term realizes or fulfills the promise of the first. He is not, however, finished. He has not said enough about the ideal. The working ideal, like the working hypothesis, is a congenial notion to Dewey, and thus it is not surprising that the chapter has focused on this work. Nonetheless, the ideal cannot be worked into the actual without something describable as the ideal. How is the ideal present to consciousness and mind? How does an ideal-inspired intentionality stand toward the world? Dewey's answer to this question is one of those striking places in his work where the ideal as stimulus to the instrumental or experimental imagination loses ground to the transcendental imagination. Attitudes or stances toward the world which he has just finished criticizing—"romantic faith," " wishful hope," "shadowy presentiment," "burning hope," "cloudy perceptions"—reappear in a new light, in what can be reasonably called a transcendental light.

Dewey of course does not move toward sense-transcending ideals without considerable caution. His first move in that direction is qualified and hesitant and is almost retracted by a less than compelling distinction. First, the transcendental overture:

> Every end that man holds up, every project he entertains is ideal. It marks something wanted, rather than something existing. It is wanted because existence as it *now* is does not furnish it. It carries with itself, then, a sense of contrast to the achieved, to the existent. It outruns the seen and touched. It is the work of faith and hope even when it is the plan of the most hard-headed "practical" man.[47]

Dewey's naturalism is not too helpful here in clarifying the ontological status of the ideal. Not only does the ideal contrast with the existent, the ideal "outruns the seen and touched." The ideal outruns—transcends—the actually existing. Immanence will not do here, that is, a "more" or "beyond" tethered to the actual. There is no transition here, just as there is no transition in 1891 between the "actual experienced good" and a "possible ideal good." Existence does not furnish, *now*, what is wanted. It is beyond what is given to the senses, beyond what a plan can incorporate and enact. Precisely because of this human capacity to transcend the existent, the capacity of consciousness to intend what is not existent or actual, we can do a certain kind of "work." Through faith and hope—and it is important to emphasize that they involve work for Dewey—we intend an ideal meaning which is not, as he says in 1891, "of sight" and which may not, at least initially, admit of a plan.

Thus, Dewey has no difficulty in grasping something in transcendental terms, in terms not governed by the "seen and touched."[48] Ideality cannot take its lead, or its existence, from what appears or is apparent: it "outruns the seen and touched." This does not mean, however, that ideality can never be world-seeing and world-seen, world-touching and world-touched. The work of faith and hope must be undertaken, then the work of planning, but not just planning. Faith, hope, then trying, effort, striving. It is a meager and pallid planning which is not a striving, not a trying or effort to realize some of the sense-transcending possibilities of ideality. Having turned our eyes upward and outward to what "outruns the seen and touched," we bring to the actual something more tangible, an ideal to be worked with and on. Having sketched what is ideal in one sense, that is, in the transcendental sense, Dewey then says: "But though ideal in this sense it is not *an* ideal. Common sense revolts at calling every project, every design, every contrivance of cunning, ideal, because common sense includes above all in its conception of the ideal the *quality* of the plan proposed."[49]

The move Dewey makes here, from ideal as an adjective to ideal as a noun, does more than simply allow him to introduce quality as a consideration. It allows him to return to the transcendental ideal as a source of illumination for answering the tangible demands of the present. It also is a source of illumination for assessing the resources offered by the past. The transcendental ideal provides "a sense of the contrast to the achieved, to the existent." The plan which responds to present need does more than merely solve a problem. It seeks to do justice to what appears and to what does not appear, to what transcends appearance.

As he moves toward completion of the transcendental turn in "Desire and Intelligence," it should be carefully noted that Dewey is asking the moral agent to do two things at once. One is to see, to view, to form ends-in-view, in short, to work toward tangibility. The second request is to be mindful of what is not seeable or viewable as ends or terminations, mindful, that is, of the intangible ideal. Think of the ideal, Dewey says, not as a "ready-made world" but rather as a contrasting world whose contrast with the everyday world is neither final, exhaustive, nor complete.[50] Indeed, it is not a particularly well-defined world. It is a world, though, which enlarges and transforms, perhaps even transfigures, the everyday. This contrasting world tells us not of the actual existence of, say, splendor or sublimity or nobility, but rather of our capacity to intend such meanings. Not merely their importance to experience, but also their availability in experience exceeds or transcends specific ends, specific points of application. The horizon of ideal possibilities—a beyond which "outruns" what is given to the senses and our habitual achievements—keeps us alert and responsive to what is not realized or adequately brought into being in this instance, in this circumstance. What can be foreseen in our plans and efforts, that is, ends-in-view, draw upon what cannot be distinctly seen; they borrow from what "outruns the seen and touched."

For this reason, when Steven C. Rockefeller says that in Dewey "human ideals are ends-in-view, purposes," he is only partly correct. Indeed, much of the following is only partly correct: "These observations lead Dewey to conclude that ideals do exist in nature. There is no gulf separating the ideal and the real, nature and human values. However, he emphasizes that ideals exist in nature as possibilities rather than as actualities. Ideals are possibilities resident in natural events."[51]

If "in nature" means present as an existent, then ideals in Dewey's first, transcendental sense do not exist in nature. He says that what is ideal is in contrast to the "existent." I take "contrast" to mean distinguished from, different from. There are, of course, degrees of difference, and thus there is the possibility that Dewey meant contrast in a weak sense, that is, not wholly other but somewhat other. In other words, Rockefeller might contend that Dewey simply meant not naturally existing now without any reference to a supersensible ideal. It seems clear, however, that nature as the existent is not the foundation for ideality: "[The ideal] marks something wanted, rather than something existing." Thus, the claim that for Dewey "ideals exist in nature as possibilities rather than as actualities" leaves too much unexplained. And certainly the claim that "ideals are possibilities resident in natural events" fails to explain what sort of natural event "outruns the seen and touched."

Dewey's path is circuitous, and it is well to remind ourselves what we are seeking to uncover: how is the ideal, ideality which is antecedent to *an* ideal, present to mind and consciousness? It is *not* present as "final exhaustive, comprehensive perfection," "the source of all generous discontent with actualities," "compensatory dream," "ready-made world," "refuge," "asylum from effort," "ineffable and unrelated to present action and experience," "complete and exhaustive realization." A lot has been rejected, so when Dewey announces that he is ready to "recover the genuine import of ideals and idealism," we expect a lot.[52] He does not disappoint us.

The conception of the ideal and ideality which Dewey presents in the final four paragraphs of "Desire and Intelligence" can be summarized in the following manner. The ideal is not viewable as a "complete and exhaustive realization" of the "better state" offered through imagination and generated by desire. There is a horizon of ends and consequences, what Dewey calls "an indefinite context," which transcends the end-in-view. This transcendent horizon or context cannot be willed as a specific goal, a definite end-in-view. Nonetheless, this transcendent horizon is the source of the ideal: "The consciousness of this encompassing infinity of connections is ideal."

What, though, sort of "consciousness" is it which opens and connects us to such an encompassing, to such transcendence? Dewey identifies art and religion as sources of "appreciations and intimations" oriented to the transcendent, but he considers only religious consciousness at the close of the chapter. That the religious should conclude a chapter on desire and intelligence in Dewey is itself more than a little surprising; even more remarkable is his wish to install it in "the midst of effort to foresee and regulate future objects." Clearly, these four paragraphs warrant careful examination.

This examination is made simpler by virtue of the fact that Dewey weaves a single theme through the four paragraphs: the transcendentally ideal is not fully visible or definite and it cannot be made fully visible or definite. Thus, he immediately acknowledges what we expect him to acknowledge: "The action of deliberation, as we have seen, consists in selecting some foreseen consequence to serve as a stimulus to present action." This "stimulus" serves to bring ideal possibilities into contact with "present tendencies." What we do not quite expect is the radical curtailment of the visible and definite and its effect on the nature of desire: "But the selected consequence is set in an indefinite context of other consequences just as real as it is, and many of them much more certain in fact. The 'ends' that are foreseen and utilized mark out a little island in an infinite sea."[53]

At first glance, it might not seem as if Dewey has gone very far in the direction of anything transcendental. A context transcends a text in a respectably naturalistic fashion: it is more than the eye can in fact, but not in principle, take in. Even "indefinite" does not seriously loosen the moorings of the possible in the actual, since the actual is still present as the authorization of the possible; it simply is indefinitely present. But in the next sentence, Dewey puts visibilities and utilizations—puts the actual, the determinate, the finite, the visible—into a rather reduced and vulnerable ontological position: "the 'ends' that are foreseen and utilized mark out a little island in an infinite sea." Matters are now a little unclear. Does the "infinite sea" of the unseen authorize the seen and foreseen? The indefinite is not in principle indefinable, but a "little island" does not appear to be, in principle, transformable into an "infinite sea." There is a discontinuity, an asymmetry, which Dewey wishes to put in place in the "little island"/"infinite sea" analogy. It is a physical analogy—land masses and bodies of water—which does not satisfy Dewey. He tries another analogy in the next paragraph.

This analogy lacks subtlety in some respects but may actually gain in power as a result. "The 'end' is the figured pattern at the center of the field through which runs the axis of conduct." Figure and background, center and periphery are the same elements of the field theory of meaning which

Dewey sketched in *Experience and Nature*. But he is now not talking about mind and consciousness in general but desire and the ideal and their presence to mind and consciousness. Thus, through the center or figure "runs the axis of conduct." Dewey then commits himself to an "in principle" claim regarding the ability of intelligence to illuminate, to shed light: "At most intelligence but throws a spotlight on that little part of the whole which marks out the axis of movement. Even if the light is flickering and the illuminated portion stands forth only dimly from the shadowy background, it suffices if we are shown the way to move."[54]

The "spotlight" cannot, *in principle*, illuminate the whole. Whatever visibly "stands forth" is but a tiny fraction of the invisibilities of the "shadowy background." This background is felt, and it "forms the stuff of the ideal." The ideal—dim, shadowy, vague, undefined, undiscriminated—does not exist as a perfected state, mental or otherwise. It is not fully formed in consciousness, by consciousness, or for consciousness. Nonetheless, it "enters into the *present* meaning of activity." Dewey has effected a rather remarkable inversion: shadows cast light. Or, more precisely, shadows are essential to the revelations of reason's more visible spotlights.

Deserving a chapter devoted entirely to itself, I shall simply emphasize here that the theme of light, dark, visible, invisible, is central to Dewey's analysis of the ideal. The ideal is resident in the dark and invisible, the offstage, the shadows. The ideal is indefinite, and the extent to which it is definable depends on the various forming activities of consciousness, mind, and imagination. Dewey consistently affirmed, early and late, that although the ideal cannot be brought to perfect visibility, tangibility, or transparency, it can be *better* defined. Such efforts to better define and better realize the ideal require an enduring, passionate desire—aspiration Dewey called it in 1891—which seeks "the way to move" toward the ideal. Such aspiration defeats itself, however, if it takes the visibility of things seen and touched to be a victory or conquest over the invisible. We do most of the practical work of realizing ideals in the "frontier" between the visible and the invisible, the well illuminated and the dimly lit and shadowy. Thus, in seeking a visible, tangible expression of an invisible, intangible ideal, Dewey's moral struggle is necessarily an act of reason and faith. It is, to use a phrase from George Steiner's *Real Presences*, "a wager on transcendence."[55]

The next to the last paragraph of "Desire and Intelligence" continues the ontological placement of the ideal and provides a few central clues to its phenomenological placement. Having brought to light an end-in-view from the shadows of ideality, Dewey is concerned to remind the reader that this "*definite* aim" is "petty" and "infinitesimal." Having set sail on the "infinite sea" of the ideal, finite aims and ends-in-view do not lose their connection with the infinite. Indeed, Dewey three times notes that the finite or definite aim (and act) has "infinite import," is connected with an "infinity of events," and has "infinite reach." The most important formulation of the boundlessness of the ideal's reach permits Dewey to make a necessary transition to the manner in which consciousness entertains infinity: "The consciousness of this encompassing infinity of connections is ideal." In the light of the ideal, a particular, an instance, is seen in the broadest, largest, most encompassing manner possible. In Randall's formulation, we see—see better—what something actually is when we see what it might be, when we see how it can grow in new meaning. When such an infinitizing drive toward the ideal "comes home to us," says Dewey, "the meaning of a present act is seen to be vast, immeasurable, unthinkable."[56] The language is less dramatic than in 1891, but little else has changed with respect to the essential nature of the moral struggle: moved by the ideal, we live beyond our means and are opened to the "vast, immeasurable, unthinkable."

Having oriented the ideal toward the infinite, Dewey still must place it phenomenologically. How does consciousness address the infinite, meaning which is "vast, immeasurable, unthinkable"? He says: "This ideal is not a goal to be attained. It is a significance to be felt, appreciated. Though consciousness of it cannot become intellectualized (identified in objects of a distinct character) yet emotional appreciation of it is won only by those willing to think."[57] Dewey perhaps gives us too little by asking too much of one term, "appreciation." The ideal is not a "ready-made world" which offers itself as an attainable goal. The ideal is a significance, a meaning, which must be felt or appreciated. "Appreciation" is one of those concepts in Dewey which appears again and again, and in almost each instance one is inclined to believe that he has explained it in some *other* place since it rarely is itself explicated. Its meaning becomes clear indirectly, by virtue of how it explains something. But what does appreciation explain here?

Steiner says of the "wager on transcendence" that it

> predicates the presence of a realness, of a "substantiation" (the theological reach of this word is obvious) within language and form. It supposes a passage, beyond the fictive or the purely pragmatic, from meaning to meaningfulness. The conjecture is that "God" *is*, not because our grammar is outworn, but that grammar lives and generates worlds because there is the wager on God.[58]

It is a powerful and strange passage "from meaning to meaningfulness," but it is this passage which allows the person to be what Steiner calls an "executant of felt meaning," one who "invests his own being in the process of interpretation."[59] The ideal for Dewey, as a significance or meaning to be felt, is not unlike a ballet, poem, or quartet for Steiner. Both the poem (for the poet and the reader) and the ideal (for the moral striver) involve enactments of meaning which are commitments to meaning. Meaning which is appreciated and not only understood "comes home" to us. We become its executant, responsible for it and answerable to it.

The final paragraph of "Desire and Intelligence" unashamedly and unabashedly sounds the triumphant note for the transfiguration of the ordinary and everyday. In art and religion, the "appreciations and intimations" of the ideal are called forth and "wrought into the texture of our lives."[60] Notably, Dewey does not attend to artistic/aesthetic meaning but instead focuses solely on the religious. Also notable is Dewey's term "intimations." Ideals invite and require appreciation, which in turn invites commitment and enactment. The appreciated ideal must be bodied forth. But Dewey has not forgotten the shadowy nature of the ideal, its reach into a poorly defined infinity. Thus, we have intimations of the ideal, not declarations of it.

The paragraph is, then, a remarkably condensed formulation of what I call, with no hesitation, pragmatic grace. Purposes are good, definite purposes are even better, and methods are not to be despised. But these energies and instrumentalities of "moral and intellectual consciousness" do not tell the whole story. Dewey agrees that "religious consciousness" begins where these leave off: "In the sense that definite purposes and methods shade off of necessity into a vast whole which is incapable of objective presentation this view is correct." He does not, however, believe that the "shade off" occurs after or subsequent to the deliberations of thought, the specification of purposes and ends-in-view, and the refinement of methods. The shading and fading occur in, not after, deliberation: "But there is a point in *every* intelligent activity where effort ceases; where thought and doing fall back upon a course of events which effort and reflection cannot touch. There is a point *in* deliberate action where definite thought fades into the ineffable and undefinable—into emotion."[61]

Dewey has not simply introduced into deliberation an element of uncertainty, revisability, temporality. At least partly constitutive of "an experience in which striving, resolution and foresight are found" is a "course of events which effort and reflection cannot touch." The shadow of the ideal, which, as he said earlier, "outruns the seen and touched," lifts our striving and our sights toward that of which we can have only an intimation.

There is no substitute for effort and will, but neither is there a substitute for what Dewey calls "this effortless and unfathomable whole." The point of contact between effort and effortlessness is not easily described or characterized. Frontier? Intersection? Combination? Dewey is clear that the effortless and the unfathomable are *in* the striving, the strain, the staking of self, the struggle: "The religious experience is a reality in so far as in the midst of effort to foresee and regulate future objects we are sustained and expanded in feebleness and failure by the sense of an enveloping whole. Peace in action not after it is the contribution of the ideal to conduct."[62]

In 1891, Dewey made much of the phenomenological fact that our acts of consciousness can intend meanings which range expansively, indeed infinitely, beyond their "point" or end. Such extensions of meaning are prompted by a certain kind of desire, the desire for a "possible ideal good." Such desire requires effort and struggle, but these pragmatic thrusts or interventions into the world are part of a larger life, a "life of *aspiration*, and of *faith*." By 1922, Dewey has succeeded in refining and elaborating the deliberative machinery necessary for pragmatic intervention. But he also has refined and elaborated the transcendental aspiration and faith of the moral life. Having thoughtful ends-in-view to help "regulate future objects" is a fine thing, for it properly balances the actual and pragmatically realizable ideals. For Dewey, however, there is something much finer than this. It is the faith to stake oneself on, and to be sustained by, a transcendent reference — shadowy, ineffable, indefinable, unfathomable — in other words, in 1891 words, it is faith in a "possible ideal good."

·CHAPTER 3·

"In the Midst of Effort"

There are various ways in which the transcendence located "in the midst of effort" can be lost, neglected, forgotten. In this chapter, I wish to look at some of the ways—in literary criticism, philosophy, and art history—in which the shadows cast by the transcendent ideal in Dewey have simply dropped out of discussion, consideration, attention. It could be argued in each instance that it was not the purpose of the authors to analyze what "outruns the seen and touched" in Dewey. Their analyses, it might be argued, are concerned in one way or another with practice, activities of inquiry, purpose, democracy, contingency, in short, with intelligently guided effort. Such analyses are, I suggest, misleading and unreliable because they omit what occurs "in the midst of effort": the staking of self in action on appreciations and intimations of the ideal. Failing to grasp the interior spaces of action, effort, and desire—infinities, shadows, unfathomables, aspirations, and duties—Dewey's pragmatism loses its elevation and its mystery.

I turn first to Jonathan Levin's *The Poetics of Transition: Emerson, Pragmatism, and American Literary Modernism*. Levin begins, boldly and loosely, with the claim that "the pragmatists reject all explicitly supernatural trappings while retaining and cultivating a naturalized, immanent idealism." This "de-divinizing" follows the

> Emersonian pattern by which habitual and therefore degraded forms of spiritual and imaginative experience are rejected in order to open the space for a more authentic experience of spiritual and imaginative ideals. In a sense, the pragmatists are never more "spirited" than when insisting on the wholly secular dimension of the pragmatist project.[1]

Pragmatists like movement, change, and transition. The habitual as an arrest or stop is "degraded." Ideals are fine, so long as they are natural and immanent. Thus, effort is secularized, purged of any transcendent referent. The purge is completed boldly, loosely: "What matters most to a pragmatist is not the object of that experience (be it Art, God, or Spirit), but rather the process the experience sets in motion. This process infuses life with deeper (but never definitive or absolute) meanings."[2] In other words, the pragmatist does not attend to the "object of experience," to something the experience may be "about." The pragmatist attends to process, to transitions transitioning, all of which occur this side of immanence.

Dewey would be surprised. Habit degraded? That some habits become degraded is, of course, obvious to Dewey. How, though, can habit in general be a degradation when habit *is* the self and will, the basis of observation, memory, judgment, thinking? The capacities Dewey attributes to habit in *Human Nature and Conduct* are not simply numerous, they are fundamental and basic, grounding and forming, and inventive: "The medium of habit filters all the material that reaches our perception and thought. The filter is not, however, chemically pure. It is a reagent which adds new qualities and rearranges what is received."[3]

Lacking sufficient appreciation of the different kinds of forming energies of habit, their drive and insistence as well as their playfulness and lightness, Levin simply puts the self in motion. The endurance of habitual meaning, along with its claims and privileges, as well as the creativity of habitual meaning, with its claims and privileges, is absorbed by process— no, by Process. Meaning endures but only for the moment, until further notice. Meaning comes into being, but the effort, the struggle on behalf of the meaning undertaken by the person who means, need not be dwelt upon too long. Meanings and persons, properly understood, are in transition.

For Levin, the pragmatic self, without let or hindrance from habit, need not even concern itself with objects of experience. Such a view, of course, is not Dewey's:

> A self having habits and attitudes formed with the cooperation of objects runs ahead of immediately surrounding objects to effect a new equilibration. Subjective morals substitutes a self always set over against objects and generating its ideals independently of objects, and in permanent, not transitory, opposition to them.[4]

Habit-grounded intentional acts and processes have intentional objects, those available to mind and consciousness without participation of the senses and those brought to mind through the senses. "What matters" to

Dewey is meaning, and life cannot be infused with the "deeper" meanings Levin has in mind without an environment of objects—physical, imagined, remembered, written, spoken. Dewey recognized that the intentional existence and inexistence of objects often merged in ways which eluded social scientific statement but which could be expressed through painting, literature, and poetry, that is, through art. Through our experience of these expressive objects, our habits are set in motion: some are set aside, some are set running and screaming ahead. There are indeed transitions in such motions.

But not indefinitely and without end or fulfillment. There are transformations, consummations, realizations. Transitions are not ontologically ultimate: "In art as an experience, actuality and possibility or ideality, the new and the old, objective material and personal response, the individual and the universal, surface and depth, sense and meaning, are all transfigured from the significance that belongs to them when isolated in reflection."[5] The meaning intensified and consummated in aesthetic experience is not simply a disengaged remnant of what Levin calls, in connection with Emerson, "the ecstatic, flowing whole." The times of transfiguration occasioned by the objects of art are occasions of spiritual fulfillment. Dewey, phenomenologically far more sophisticated and demanding than Emerson, understood that transition, even a poetics of transition, requires a transcendence appropriate to it. Dewey could not treat aesthetic transfigurations as transitional. Transitional to what? The next transfiguration borne along on the stream of experience? The very thought of such restlessness is too impertinent for Dewey, too discourteous.[6] In an odd way, it is unempirical, for it is inattentive to what this experience promises and fulfills. It is spiritual ingratitude.

Levin's view of Dewey's aesthetics, as well as the place of ideals and ideality in it, continues to work the theme of transition at the expense of any other interpretive possibility: "Dewey's discussion of art should be recognized as another variation of the Emersonian poetics of transition. Instead of focusing on the aesthetic finality or autonomy of the work of art, Dewey looks to art as an agency of continuous re-creation and renewal."[7] A closer look, however, at what Dewey says about fulfillments and consummations warrants the claim that for Dewey the aesthetic experience is the most intense expression of the creation and growth of meaning as well as the lastingness of meaning:

> In the process of living, attainment of a period of equilibrium is at the same time the initiation of a new relation to the environment, one that brings with it potency of new adjustments to be made through struggle.

The time of consummation is also one of beginning anew. Any attempt to perpetuate beyond its term the enjoyment attending the time of fulfillment and harmony constitutes withdrawal from the world. Hence it marks the lowering and loss of vitality. But, through the phases of perturbation and conflict, there abides the deep-seated memory of an underlying harmony, the sense of which haunts life like the sense of being founded on a rock.[8]

The "struggle" here is not simply a practical one of overcoming obstacles and prevailing over a resistant environment. The struggle is a moral and spiritual one: what ideals will motivate the struggle, give it—and the agent—potency, elevation, depth? In other words, "in the midst of effort," in the midst of the perturbation and conflict, what is there? In *Human Nature and Conduct*, Dewey calls it "the sense of an enveloping whole." And it is in *Art as Experience* that he calls it "the deep-seated memory of an underlying harmony, the sense of which haunts life like the sense of being founded on a rock." Being in transition and "being founded on a rock" may not be wholly incompatible, and undoubtedly dialectical maneuvering could reconcile them. The reconciliation would show the stresses and strains of attempting to unify what does not call for unification. No, this is not "another variation of the Emersonian poetics of transition."

When transition is all, the force of ideality is provisional, tentative, contingent. Ideality is another word for transition, and thus pragmatic occasions of transcendence toward the ideal, including aesthetic transcendence, are Big Transitions. The artist is the manager, the overseer, of such Big Transitions and not surprisingly the artist becomes a transition, a frontier, between subjective and objective. Levin quotes the following passage from *Art as Experience*:

> The artist is driven to submit himself in humility to the discipline of the objective vision. But the inner vision is not cast out. It remains as the organ by which the outer vision is controlled, and it takes on structure as the latter is absorbed within it. The interaction of the two modes of vision is imagination; as imagination takes form the work of art is born. It is the same with the philosophic thinker. There are moments when he feels that his ideas and ideals are finer than anything in existence. But he finds himself obliged to go back to objects if his speculations are to have body, weight, and perspective. Yet in surrendering himself to objective material he does not surrender his vision; the object just as an object is not his concern. It is placed in the context of ideas and, as it is thus placed, the latter acquire solidity and partake of the nature of the object.[9]

A few points deserve mention before I comment on Levin's treatment of this passage. In chapter 1, "The Pragmatic Struggle for the Good," I considered the import of Dewey's 1891 claim that "to surrender the actual experienced good for a possible ideal good is the struggle." The "possible ideal good" does not have a counterpart in the actual, physical world. Thus, we "stake ourselves" on what is not "of sight." In a very loose manner of speaking, one can say that Dewey is seeking to integrate the "actual experienced good" and the "possible ideal good" to show the interdependence ranging through their transitions. But such language dramatically distorts the phenomenology of surrender. There is a transcendence of one state of being, and the degree and kind of continuity it permits, if any at all, cannot be decided by the comforts of a poetics of transition. Transcendence is more precarious than that.

Likewise, in *Human Nature and Conduct,* in the chapter "Desire and Intelligence," one could say that Dewey was seeking to integrate emotion and thought, infinitude and finitude, shadow and light. And again it is apparent that such transitioning/unifying zeal distorts the phenomenology of transcendence which occurs "in the midst of effort." Dewey says: "But there is a point in *every* intelligent activity where effort ceases; where thought and doing fall back upon a course of events which effort and reflection cannot touch." "Effort ceases," striving ceases, and for that time while we are not trying, we "fall back upon"—surrender to—what Dewey calls appreciations and intimations of the ideal. The moral struggle is the expression of faith in the ideal, and it is intellectual and practical: I act in accord with, and thereby stake myself on, an ideal which "outruns the seen and touched."

The denseness, as well as delicacy, of the passage quoted above from *Art as Experience* is now more evident, as is Levin's extreme simplification of them. The "inner vision" of ideal meanings of the artist, opening out to the "encompassing infinity of connections," "remains" not simply as coparticipant in a friendly interaction between inner and outer visions. The inner vision is "the organ by which the outer vision is controlled, and it takes on structure as the latter is absorbed within it." Dewey is in something of a mess here, one glossed by Levin as well as many other commentators (sympathetic and critical). The artist must not merely "submit" to objective vision, but in "humility." Submission and humility do not alter the basic phenomenological stance of Dewey: the inner vision controls the outer vision. If Dewey intends "interaction" to mean parity, then clearly something is conceptually out of joint. To control and to be controlled is not a state of ontological equivalence. To control is to determine, to determine the terms and conditions of that state of being which is controlled.

The capacity to control is a victory of the most fundamental kind: certain freedoms are won or lost at its boundary. For this reason, Dewey's idealism is softened or blurred beyond recognition in this comment from Levin: "This disciplined submission constitutes a victory for neither the subjective ideal nor the physical world, since the aesthetic process makes each responsive and responsive to the other."[10] Levin claims that in imagination we do not have "one mode set over and against the other," that is, the inner "over and against" the outer. This is not what Dewey says. He says that the inner has control over the outer, and whether it is against the outer will depend on how distantly the outer strays from the inner's intimations and appreciations of the ideal.

The simplifications of Dewey by Levin are numerous, but their common root is worth mentioning again. Ideals are temporal events or moments, de-divinized moments at that: "Dewey . . . would see ideals (and aesthetic appreciations) as transitional agencies, extending or otherwise developing material circumstances."[11] The desire which Dewey addresses in 1891, the desire for a "possible ideal good," is basically unchanged in the desire which he addresses in *Human Nature and Conduct* in 1922: the desire to place the "little island" of "foreseen" plans and purposes in the "infinite sea" of ideals of which we have whispering appreciations and shadowy intimations. The aspiration and hope summoned by ideality is not transitional, nor are ideals "transitional agencies." And they certainly are not extensions or developments of "material circumstances."[12] Ideal meaning is not "of sight"; it "outruns the seen and touched." Levin simplifies both Dewey and Wallace Stevens when he says: "Like the pragmatists, Stevens was skeptical of any effort to posit hidden or ideal realities somewhere behind the actual appearances and processes of the material social world."[13] In chapter 9, "Dewey, Wallace Stevens, and 'The Difficult Inch,'" I consider some of the ways in which Dewey and Stevens struggle with appearances which invite and resist the augmentations and appropriations of imagination. The hiddenness and ideality of meanings present to imaginative consciousness does not prompt skepticism in Dewey and Stevens; rather, it moves them to some of their most worthy efforts as philosopher and poet.

For thirty-five years, Richard Poirier's literary criticism has paid careful and wonderfully discerning attention to the crossings of American poetry and literature and American pragmatism. Thus, his contribution to *The Revival of Pragmatism* asks a question which he is indeed very well qualified to answer: "Why do pragmatists want to be like poets?" Both, he argues, are concerned with action, but not action *simpliciter*. Poets and pragmatists are pledged to action which involves struggle. The struggle for the poet/creator is what Lawrence calls the "struggle for verbal consciousness."

Again, it is not simply consciousness finding suitable verbal expression, but rather "some unexampled expansion of human consciousness."[14] The aspirations of heroes in Cooper, Emerson, Thoreau, Melville, Hawthorne, Twain, and James are, we may say, excessive. They—aspirations and the selves aspiring—exceed what "existing environments" can comprehend, even endure. Standards are at stake:

> Works like *Moby-Dick* or *The Ambassadors*, for example, are *designed* to make the reader feel that his ordinary world has been acknowledged, even exhaustively, only to be dispensed with as a source of moral or psychological standards. They are written so as finally not to be translatable into those standards, and their extravagances of language are an exultation in the exercise of consciousness momentarily set free.[15]

The imaginary "environment in language" created by the writer/poet "excludes the standards" of the real environment. The cost of "exultation" is not inconsiderable: conventional standards and environments must be excluded, dispensed with, displaced.

Now, imagining such displacements in language is not easy work. It is a matter of style and effort, stylistic effort, in short, linguistic struggle:

> The result is a struggle to create through language an environment in which the inner consciousness of the hero-poet can freely express itself, an environment in which he can sound publicly what he privately is. Emphasis on the element of struggle in giving even a temporary existence to this environment means that the archetypes, images, themes, or ideas that have been the main concern of most recent studies of American literature are in this study only of incidental or procedural use.[16]

This outlook sets a critical course for Poirier, and it provides the beginning of his answer to Cavell's question asked in *The Revival of Pragmatism*: "What's the use of calling Emerson a pragmatist?" Cavell has two reasons not to call Emerson a pragmatist. The first is that whereas Emerson (like Wittgenstein) is "in struggle with the threat of skepticism," neither James nor Dewey took "the threat of skepticism seriously."[17] Not so for Poirier:

> Consider: the emphasis on action, on transitions as a valuable form of action, both in Emerson and in James; the need stressed by both of them for movement *away* from substantives or "resting-places" or settled texts; Frost's definition of a poem as only "a momentary stay against confusion," and the virtue attached by Stevens to becoming "an ignorant man again"—these are evidences of a special Emersonian form of skepticism

that seems to me worth promoting in the life of the world no less than in the world of books.[18]

Cavell's Emerson struggles against skepticism; Poirier's Emerson struggles on behalf of at least a restricted type of skepticism, linguistic skepticism.

The second reason not to call Emerson a pragmatist is that he counseled patience, a patience distinct from practice, even if the patience is "exercised aggressively, as an agent of change."[19] For Cavell, the "apparent difference of practice and patience, action and passion," argues against the alignment of Emerson and pragmatism. For Poirier, practice, action, and performance are places of conceptual alliance for Emerson and pragmatism:

> "Action" is a key term which American pragmatism, especially William James's version of it, took over from Emerson, along with the word "transition," which is equally central. Both words, as I hope gradually to make clear, point to an alliance of pragmatism with the workings of language in literature, with poetic making.[20]

The act of expression requires patience and receptivity. Indeed, it may express patient attention in one or several of its forms. Nonetheless, for Poirier the expressive act is a deed, a working, an activity: "Literary study can thus be made relevant to life not as a mere supplier of images or visions, but as an activity; it can create capacities through exercise with the language of literature that can then be applied to the language of politics and power, the language of daily life."[21] The "workings of language in literature" work; that is, they actively, almost aggressively, make and remake orders of meaning and sensibility. And if such "poetic making" is successful, if it works, it frees and liberates us, not just in the imaginary world of literature and poetry, but in "daily life":

> When a writer is most strongly engaged by what he is doing, as if struggling for his identity within the materials at hand, he can show us, in the mere turning of a sentence this way or that, how to keep from being smothered by the inherited structuring of things, how to keep within and yet in command of the accumulations of culture that have become a part of what he is.[22]

The action and practice of the writer (and reader), "the turning of a sentence this way or that," pace Cavell, are expressions and vindications of what Poirier likes to call Emersonian pragmatism.

The "alliance" Poirier believes exists between pragmatism and "poetic making" is problematic because he claims too little on behalf of pragmatism, perhaps because he takes Emerson (and his interpretation of Emerson) as equivalent to pragmatism: "A pragmatist, by which I mean some version of Emerson . . ."[23] Cavell would like to find transcendence in pragmatism; he does not find any and on that basis wishes to detach Emerson from pragmatism. Poirier is glad that pragmatism makes no transcendental claims, and on at least that basis, he wishes to attach Emerson and pragmatism. Both positions fail to do justice to Dewey's phenomenology of the intangible, the supersensible, the ideal. To put the point as simply as possible: "in the midst of effort," in the midst of Dewey's kind of struggle and effort, there is transcendence toward the ideal. In the midst of Poirier's kind of Emersonian effort and struggle, or rather in their fulfillment, there are "moments when language and the person using it reach a point of incandescence."[24] Incandescence minus transcendence is as far as Poirier is willing to go in the direction of transformation. In short, the benefit, the good, of a well-turned sentence does not require or promise the turning of a soul.

The relationship of art to life is ultimately at issue, and Poirier is clear that literature and poetry should not be expected to be a "supplier of images and visions," a resource for exploring what Benjamin DeMott calls "life's problems." The relevance of well chosen and well written words to life is indirect, allusive, playful. Poirier puts his entire argument on the table and the line when he rejects Louis Kampf's contention that if a physicist's love of Proust was real, he would stop working on missiles: "I'm afraid I don't see why this should be so. If the physicist hadn't already stopped out of love for his family or his dog, why should he stop for Marcel Proust? Are we to believe that literature's relevance to life is finally a matter of its being more relevant *than* life?"[25] This is brilliant, wrong (with respect to Dewey's pragmatism, James's, and I think Emerson's), and extremely important. The reason it fails as an account of the life effects or consequences (not too onerously called, perhaps, the life-worldly effects) of literary experience, is that Poirier simply neglects what occurs "in the midst of effort," in the midst of writing and reading. Why should we *not* believe that literature is "more relevant *than* life"? Why should the novelist's or the poet's struggle be construed only as a Laurentian "struggle for verbal consciousness"? Is literature not also a moral struggle and effort precisely because it invites, with insistence, attention to meanings which liberate or confirm, unsettle or settle, *in some direction?* I, the reader, to be like *that*, to do *that*, to think *that*? How is it possible? Is it possible? Poirier would balk, I think, at such self-regarding possessions of literary works. The poet's and writer's struggles, their possibilizing in language, ought not, and probably will not, establish comforting equivalences between the poem's or story's meanings and my meanings. Meaning may come and go before I have had a chance to "identify" with it and to catalog it as a resource for exploring and dealing with life's problems. Literature is too dispossessing for that kind of disguised narcissism.

Poirier's view of literature's relationship to life is inadequate not because he has a faulty view of the nature of mimesis (the fault line depending on one's theory of mimesis), but rather because he reduces the scope and depth of struggle and what it is good for. I see little difference between the writer/reader's struggle and the moral struggle described by Dewey in 1891: "To surrender the actual experienced good for a possible ideal good is the struggle."[26] The ordered intentionalities of meaning set loose in the literary experience are decidedly impractical and practical, sometimes simultaneously. How is *that* possible, not only for me, but for anyone, not as a possibility to be enacted in the next five minutes or five days, but simply and wonderfully as a meaning to be entertained? The answer to that question tends to blur the line between the writer's problems and the reader's problems. It requires precisely what Dewey says if the possibility is dramatically distant from what Poirier often calls the inherited structurings of things, that is, surrender of an "actual experienced good." Of course literature occasionally is "more relevant *than* life," more compelling than my present self-definition and self-understanding. It occasions a struggle which might not be occasioned by life, my present, actual life.

These occasions of struggle, effort, and striving do not have for Dewey any hope of reaching a "once-and-for-all" disposition, a conclusion. But newness, change, reinvention, movement, happy instabilities were not the cause or effect of Dewey's disavowal of "once-and-for-all." A "possible ideal good" moves us and moves us further. And, quite important, these struggles take hold of us in ways which are not fully, or relevantly, incorporable in words. What words do in and to our experience often takes us, as Poirier says, "outside the writing" even outside our selves. Poirier recognizes this, but he still requires a certain temperance when it comes to transcendence. If what he calls "the actions of words" manages to be so wonderful and so liberating that the self is eradicated, extinguished, or transcended, we should not expect such self-disposal to be a prelude to self-redemption. "Writing off the self," surrendering the self, is "*un*sanctified and *un*sponsored." We do not know what good will come of surrender, so there is some wisdom in treating it cautiously, perhaps skeptically; and if one is a pragmatist, "opportunistically as a chance in these instances to analyze language in order to learn something about its limitations as a cultural artifact."[27] Dewey, I suggest, thought otherwise.

Before noting the distance between Poirier's Emersonian pragmatism and Dewey's pragmatism, let us recall a central point from Dewey. He says that "the consciousness of this encompassing infinity of connections is ideal," and thus "the *meaning* of a present act is seen to be vast, immeasurable, unthinkable."[28] Dewey's claim is not that an act is open to infinite interpretations, of meaning attributions. And neither is his interest simply that of opening up the present act to its own possibilities by finding a place for it in an "indefinite context" of infinite meanings. His concern is with a "possible ideal good" and its relationship to the present act. We must care for the ideal, strive and struggle for it, as much as we care for the immediate situation or circumstance. And our reward for such effort is small. Ideals (though perhaps not idealities) are thought to be the most visible and tangible of things, but they are not. We catch glimpses of them. They come to us not as declarations or announcements, but rather in quite sensibility-dependent ways. Historically, we have relied particularly heavily on two ways: "It is the office of art and religion to evoke such appreciations and intimations; to enhance and steady them till they are wrought into the texture of our lives."[29] In the midst of effort, specifically, the efforts customarily associated with art and religion, we have intimations and appreciations of a "possible ideal good." Transcendence.

What we miss in Poirier's pragmatism is the ideal and the good. When either does appear, it is usually part of the resistance program offered by pragmatism's interest in freeing things up, moving things around. Poirier remarks: "What is centrally important is the evidence almost everywhere in American literature of an idealistic effort to free the heroes' and the readers' consciousness from categories not only of conventional moralities but also of mythopoeic interpretation."[30] Freeing consciousness is not necessarily a bad thing, but it is not necessarily a good thing. It depends on the direction of the freeing, of the "possible ideal good" under consideration and, perhaps, cultivation. It is not clear what "idealistic effort" comes to in Poirier other than "a special Emersonian form of skepticism."[31] Thus, it is hard to make out the force of a statement like this: "To be such a master of the inward richness of words is to take visionary possession of the things to which the words allude."[32] The writer's struggle pays off with a "visionary possession." Why, though, ought not the reader's struggle pay off with images and visions, ones which might be, in Dewey's words, "wrought into the texture of our lives" and which quicken our capacities to appropriate and transcend what he calls "past satisfaction"? Might the writer's struggle draw our attention to a "possible ideal good," not as a direct lesson in moral self-cultivation, but through quickened appreciation of what is at stake when the writer chooses certain literary ends, chooses as good, certain literary ends?

Perhaps the ideal is performance, modes of performance, the phenomenon of performance—and then, not simply performance, but the struggle inherent in it. But it is an odd kind of performance from Dewey's perspective. It desires very little, having sealed itself off from "life's problems." Further, it turns in on itself but not on its meaning: "We must begin to begin again with the most elementary and therefore the toughest questions: what must it have felt like to do this—not to mean anything, but to do it."[33] A doing which does not "mean anything"? It is hard to determine whether such a stricture represents the fullest realization of the desires of the toughminded or the tender-minded. But meaning does not remain a distraction too long in Poirier, and in *The Renewal of Literature* language and the person using it can reach "a point of incandescence." Not simply words, but the meanings of words become luminous, bright, occasions for us to see more clearly what we had not seen before. But once again ideality is tempered. Such seeing does not fix anything, either in the sense of repairing (for instance, the soul) or stopping anything (for instance, transitions).[34] For this reason, literature ought not be thought of as an occasion of transcendence. In the study and experience of literature, we can do without what Poirier calls the "heroism of transcendence."[35]

Poirier's fine phrase, "heroism of transcendence," catches something of the tone and attitude of the moral struggle for Dewey. The self at stake in moral struggle is striving for self-definition, such defining being profoundly indebted to, but not circumscribed by, inherited definitions. For Dewey, the artistic struggle, including the poet's and novelist's struggle, is a moral one very much like what we have already heard Poirier describe: "When a writer is most strongly engaged by what he is doing, as if struggling for his identity within the materials at hand, he can show us, in the mere turning of a sentence this way or that, how to keep from being smothered by the inherited structuring of things, how to keep within and yet in command of the accumulations of culture that have become a part of what he is."[36] Poirier may resist thinking of such struggle as an instance of "heroism of transcendence" (and his "as if" provides his needed touch of resistance), but Dewey does not. The artistic struggle is heroic and is an occasion of transcendence, one which may even endure into the aesthetic experience of the perceiver. For the "strongly engaged" reader, no less than the "strongly engaged" writer, the communicable meanings of well-ordered words can move and stir us to struggle for our identity. Such struggles can be, and often are heroic, even revolutionary. Ultimately, then, Poirier does not advance our understanding of Dewey when he says that he "does not ever talk about the writing of poetry as a struggle with words, a difficult, potentially revolutionary effort to change language on the way toward possible changes in cultural concepts of reality."[37] As Poirier notes, Dewey says a fair amount about language, poetry, and work, just not specifically "poetry as a struggle with words." What Poirier fails to mention is how much Dewey has to say about heroic effort and struggle and what occurs in its midst.

Poirier gives us something very important to consider with respect to Dewey when he says: "It is possible to confer value on moments of transformation or dissolution without looking ahead toward a narrative of fulfillment. The moment is endowed with something as vague as wonder or beauty, empty of the desire to translate these into knowledge." Poirier would prefer that such "moments of transformation"—transcendence, if one must—not be "a mere prelude to the re-entry of an enhanced self into already existing 'arrangements of knowledge.'" In concert with Emerson, Nietzsche, James, and Foucault, Poirier considers it "presumably possible to experience such an interlude without calling for any of the religious and humanistic sanctions at work in life around it and without contributing to these sanctions."[38] For the self at stake in Dewey, the aspiring self, "the *meaning* of a present act is seen to be vast, immeasurable, unthinkable."[39] Thus, a "narrative of fulfillment" cannot be promised by moral and artistic struggle. The endowments of meaning and value found in words and sentences and paragraphs are results of artistic struggle, moving through—and with—doubt, affirmation, relief, turmoil. As I discuss at more length in chapter 6, "The Undeclared Self," to abbreviate and index the sometimes tattered results of these struggles, to make them handily thinkable as endorsements or resources for the improvement of character, tends to make these conferrals of meaning more certain than they are, more visible and tangible. To appreciate the endowment, to respond to the beauty and wonder it occasions, may require us to be "empty of the desire to translate these into knowledge." Dewey would agree. But, for Dewey, we are not empty of all desire, least of all the desire for "a possible ideal good." Such a good may be present to consciousness as luminous and incandescent, or it may be shadowy. It may be stably presented or tremulously. No matter. We are stirred, desire and effort are awakened, and a "possible ideal good" stirs our aspirations and the transcendence solicited by them.

In 1944, Dewey contributed the lead chapter to *Naturalism and the Human Spirit*. The title of this essay was "Antinaturalism in Extremis." The titles of the book and the article define the context for my comments on Richard M. Gale's characterization of Dewey's naturalism in an appendix to his book *The Divided Self of William James*. This appendix, "John Dewey's Naturalization of William James," seeks to show that Dewey's essays on

James "gave a blatantly distorted, self-serving account of James's philosophy, the basic aims of which were to despookify and depersonalize it so that it would agree with Dewey's naturalism and socialization of all things distinctively human." For Gale, "Dewey's naturalism" is straightforward and unproblematic, easily formulated in two tenets: first, "there is no ontological dualism between the mental and the physical, be it in the form of an irreducible mental/physical substance or a mental/physical event dualism, psychological states and processes being reducible to certain distinctive ways in which an organism interacts with its natural environment." The second tenet is that "the sciences alone give us knowledge of reality, and they accomplish this by use of an objective common pattern of inquiry."[40] Dewey's naturalism is not, I believe, this monolithic or consistent. It is porous and sufficiently so that philosophical intersections of naturalism and the human spirit would not have struck him as romantic or unfounded. On the level of experience, nature and spirit cross or intersect, not only in art and religion, but even in everyday experience, even in the midst of our most mundane efforts. We have intimations of nature opening toward spirit and ideality, an opening properly characterized as transcendence. In short, Gale wholly neglects not merely the various senses in which there is more *to* Dewey's naturalism than antidualism and science; he neglects the way in which "more" functions *in* Dewey's naturalism.

The porousness of Dewey's naturalism is inseparable from his phenomenology of habitual meaning. His naturalism makes certain claims on his phenomenology, and in turn, his phenomenology of habitual meaning makes certain claims on his naturalism. Habit so broadly and deeply pervades every aspect of his philosophy that it is no artificial enlargement of its importance to call it an ontology of habit. Dewey did wish to naturalize as much of existence as he could, but his naturalism was not of one color, painting everything in terms of causal explanations, hypotheses, inquiries. Dewey was not content with James's physiological account of habit. Habit requires its physiology, but it also demands a phenomenology. James was better at the first than Dewey, Dewey considerably better at the second than James. But if James could not manage the phenomenology of habit, neither could Husserl. If James splits the world into, as Gale says, many worlds and many selves, so does Husserl. Some brief reflections on James, Husserl, Dewey, nature, and habit will suggest how Dewey's philosophy of experience maintains substantial naturalistic credentials while simultaneously incorporating a theory of consciousness which resists a fully naturalistic explanation. Rather than distorting James's account of mystical experience, as Gale claims, Dewey's habit-based philosophy of experience gives us some hints how it might be respected for more than what Gale calls its "spookiness." He was trying, similar to James (and often, to Husserl), to follow the intentional arcs of meaning stretching from the most sensibly visible and tangible to the supersensibly invisible and intangible. But, advancing beyond James, he was concerned to attend to the intangible in the midst of the visible efforts of the Promethean self.

We turn first to Husserl, who presents a very elaborate discussion of nature in *Studies in the Phenomenology of Constitution*, book 2 of *Ideas Pertaining to a Pure Phenomenology and to a Phenomenological Philosophy*. It is clear that his ontology of nature is unambiguously negative. Transcendental phenomenology is a refutation of naturalism and the naturalistic attitude. A naturalistic ontology, Husserl believes, is founded upon the thing, hence consciousness is a thing for naturalists, a psychophysical unity. And for naturalists, relations are causal. This negative view of naturalism is of course one of the central themes in the well-known essay "Philosophy as Rigorous Science." In the long section titled "Naturalistic Philosophy," he says that for the naturalist "whatever is is either itself physical, belonging to the unified totality of physical nature, or it is in fact psychical, but then merely as a variable dependent on the physical, at best a secondary 'parallel accompaniment.'"[41] Clearly, for Husserl naturalism has everything backward. Nature does not condition consciousness; consciousness is a correlate of nature. Nature is not absolute; consciousness is absolute. Natural science cannot isolate its objects from absolute consciousness because the relation of self and world is intentional, not causal.

For James, Dewey, and, I might add, Merleau-Ponty, it simply will not do to argue "the ontological priority of the spiritual world over the naturalistic."[42] The subject is undoubtedly the center or seat of meaning in the sense that the subject experiences the meaning, but as Dewey and Merleau-Ponty recognized, the subject is not the sole source of meaning, not the solitary condition for meaning to be. If nature and naturalism actually accorded with Husserl's description of them, then his antinaturalism would be understandable and worthy of support by all self-respecting philosophical humanists. However, it is clear that Husserl conceives of nature as the totality of realities that are of a material or physical nature or founded upon a material or physical nature. Thus, in a section titled "The Personalistic Attitude versus the Naturalistic" (section 49), he says:

> As we know, it pertains to the essence of this nature—which consequently emerges here as the *pure sense* of the acts that make up the natural attitude, as their constitutive correlate—that a thorough grounding is accomplished as the positing of nature in the first sense, that of

physical nature, in which everything else that is called nature has the source of its sense, as something founded therein.[43]

There are naturalisms of this sort, but there are naturalisms which are not of this kind. Speaking of antinaturalists, Dewey remarks that they

> identify naturalism with "materialism" and then employ the identification to charge naturalists with reduction of all distinctively human values, moral, aesthetic, logical, to blind mechanical conjunctions of material entities—a reduction which is in effect their complete destruction. The identification thus permits antinaturalists to substitute name-calling for discussion of specific issues in their own terms and in their connection with concrete evidence.[44]

While Husserl is not engaged in "name-calling," perhaps Gale is. In both cases, one is not convinced that they have done justice to the possibility that nature and spirit may speak to each other. Gale's argument that Dewey naturalizes James wholly glosses the matter of how Dewey retains "distinctively human values" through a theory of meaning as intentional and habitual. Mindful of Dewey's invitation to the antinaturalist to consider "specific issues," let us briefly look at such an issue, that of habit.

Husserl relies quite heavily on the concept of habit to characterize the pure ego. This is apparent in section 29, "Constitution of Unities within the Sphere of Immanence: Persistent Opinions as Sedimentations in the Pure Ego." Husserl, talking about enduring intentions, says:

> Now within the absolute stream of consciousness of a monad, certain formations of unity occur, but ones which are thoroughly different from the intentional unity of the real Ego and its properties. To those formations belong unities such as the persistent "opinions" of one and the same subject. They can, in a certain sense, be called "habitual," though there is no question here of a *habitus* as what has become customary, the way the empirical subject might acquire real dispositions which would then be called customary. The habitus that we are concerned with pertains not to the empirical, but to the pure, Ego.[45]

In an unpublished paper titled "Husserl's Understanding of Body and Spirit," Richard Cobb-Stevens asks a telling question: "How can the pure ego be both a pure and detached spectator and also a habit-laden life?" Cobb-Stevens asks another, even more telling question: "What status may we attribute to 'habits' that are somehow neither psychological nor subjective characteristics, but that belong to a primal process of 'togethering/

othering'—a process which does not occur within the form of subjective time, but rather makes the form of the present and of presence possible?"[46] Habit for Dewey is the middle term between presence and absence, the visible and the invisible, the empirical and the spiritual. Dewey is not interested in materializing the spiritual.[47] He is concerned to show that the subject—the habitual subject—can intend meanings which are larger, broader, looser, tighter, narrower, than the intentional object which solicits the subject's response. He says that "a self having habits and attitudes formed with the cooperation of objects runs ahead of immediately surrounding objects to effect a new equilibration."[48] When the self runs ahead of what is present or presentable to the senses, Dewey occasionally shrinks back from such invisibility and asks for a visible accounting. Nearly as often, though, meaning grows beyond the visible point or end created for it by the empirical self. With the help of habitual meaning, meaning runs ahead of "tried and tasted" meaning. We have arrived at an empirical entrance to transcendence.

Husserl believed, and I think with good reason, that your average, run-of-the-mill naturalist simply could not make the jump, not easily, from causality to intentionality. But James and Dewey were not average, run-of-the-mill naturalists. Their respective theories of meaning were theories of intentionality. This led them to want to know how it is that, if we are in the world as intentional beings, the natural world is in us. To the extent that they both wanted to give their answer in terms of habit, it is apparent that Dewey's theory of habit is the much more successful of the two. James's theory of habit is conservative, phenomenologically as well as socially and politically. Gale is not interested in the former aspect of James's conception of habit, but he does appear put off by the following remark of James to his sister Alice: "The boy has acted so far as cabin boy. His blue black hair falls over his eye brows, but he is a real willing young savage & we hope, by keeping him low and weak to make an excellent servant of him for all the time we are on the Amazons."[49] In many respects, James and Dewey radicalized Husserl's theory of passive genesis. James, however, never thought of habit as anything other than a passive registration device, and certainly not as a device or mechanism for the genesis of disruptive or novel meaning. Through prereflective habit, I establish an accord with the world, with the natural world, and this accord endures and influences further acts of consciousness, including reason's attempts to understand its own activities. James and Dewey are in accord up to this point. For Dewey, however, the influence is not a constant or a fate. What seems natural with respect to a cabin boy (social class, status, rights) can be changed and improved, transcended, by a discordant ideal.

A single sentence summarizes a large part of Dewey's philosophy of experience and clearly aligns him with the existential phenomenologists who cannot accept Husserl's ontological priority of the mental world over the natural world (or James's desire to keep the cabin boy "low and weak"). Dewey says: "Through habits formed in intercourse with the world, we also inhabit the world."[50] For Dewey, the empirical self does indeed gain "real dispositions," as Husserl calls them. One such disposition is to perform the *epoche*, another is write about eidetics, and yet another is to be worried about naturalism. Husserl felt that criticism, the critical habit of mind, could be secured only by annulling the natural world and its naturalisms. Dewey believed that the understanding of lived meaning, meaning-for-a-subject, is not secured by annulling the world in a quest for certitude, but by bringing reflective and imaginative habits of mind to the world as it is lived by human beings. Things make sense, or at least a certain kind of sense we find desirable. They fit together better, or at least fit together in ways we find desirable. Sometimes the sense and fit are so luminous or beckoning or awesome that the world as actual is bracketed, but involuntarily. It loses some of its authority. Dewey would not, however, neglect the fact that the natural world has pushed its way into the habitual self, has insinuated itself into the habitual self, has been coaxed into the habitual self. Dewey follows the natural world into James's mystical self, not to reduce the latter to the former, but to better understand transcendence, not transcendence *of* the worldly or the practical, but transcendence *in* the practical.

Quentin Lauer, in his introduction to "Philosophy as Rigorous Science," provides a useful insight into Husserl's need to establish a good or pure habitual self and a bad or natural habitual self. Speaking of the ideal that inspired Husserl, Lauer says: "Only in consciousness is being not infected with the 'facticity' that is an impediment to absoluteness."[51] Husserl was after, in other words, absolute certainty, absolute knowledge, and in order to assure that the problem of *bleibende meinungen* would come out on the side of the pure I, Husserl split the empirical I and pure I so that the latter would not be, as Lauer calls it, "infected" by the former. Judged by a standard of purity, naturalism and pragmatism are serious and unfortunate infections which obstruct not only the attainment of spiritual purity but even the search for it. For Dewey, however, we do not have much of a choice about whether we are world-infected, "facticity"-infected. We simply are. On occasion, though, meaning runs ahead of nature and its facticities to such an extent that terms like invisibility, spirit, even ineffability, have their empirical justification. When these terms appear in Dewey, which is often, they are not conceptual lacunae or mystical weakenings of the naturalist's stiff knees. It is simply that, in his view, meaning is grounded in both reason and nature, idea and experience. Nothing eidetic, certain, or eternal is likely to come from such an alliance. What may come from such intersections is, though, quite wondrous. We can hope for more than what Gale envisions, namely, "a taking-turns solution of the first-I'm-this-and-then-I'm-that sort."[52] The large and small openings to transcendence in Dewey all occur through world-infected habit and its capacity to occasionally intend meanings which point beyond the sensible but which sometimes invisibly reverberate "in the midst of effort" and the practical.

I should like to offer one more example of the loss of the intangible, transcendent ideal in Dewey. In "When Mind Is a Verb: Thomas Eakins and the Work of Doing," Ray Carney offers an intriguing argument that "Eakins deserves to be regarded as a pragmatist." The basis for such a claim is relatively simple: in paintings such as *The Gross Clinic* and *The Agnew Clinic*, Eakins bridges, connects, combines thinking and doing; even more, being and doing. The paintings are not expressions solely of successful bridgings and combinations. They also draw our attention to occasions when the combination "is flawed or absent in various ways."[53] Carney's elaboration of this central claim is crisp and clear. The figures in these two paintings

> are defined not simply in terms of states of *being* (which might be said to be the expressive mode of most other portraits), but in their practical mastery of forms of *doing*. In Eakins' definition of who and what we are, consciousness is not a merely private, internal state, but is required to externalize itself in a concrete course of action. The shift from the one definition of identity to the other might be called the pragmatic turn. We *are*, at least in large part, what we *do*. We are our hands as much as our minds.[54]

To link hands and mind in what he calls "a disciplined, productive relationship" is, for Carney, a good to be desired. And certainly the consensus interpretation of pragmatism finds this erasure of the distinction between "manual and mental dexterity" to be a good thing. No surprise, then, that one of the quotations with which Carney begins his article is from *Art as Experience*: "Mind is primarily a verb."[55] It says too little about action, practice, and the mind to simply assert that consciousness "is required to externalize itself in a concrete course of action." But Carney means more than externalize; he means realize, translate into practice, fulfill in action. But even realization is an inadequate account of the "pragmatic turn" because it omits what occurs in the nicely integrated mental and physical actions of a surgeon or a rower. It displaces what occurs in the midst of actions which are efforts, that is, actions which are for the sake of ideal meanings perfectible in, and also perfectible beyond, this context, this time.

To speak of pragmatically "realizing" ideal meanings, bodying them forth in the tangible, material world, says very little of interest about pragmatism, action, or ideals. Dewey's pragmatism can be held to a higher standard than simply one of realm-joining, repeating again and again the good of combining mind and hand, the good of their "contact," the good of merging "seeing, being, and doing," and so on. Why should we care about handiness or mindfulness apart from the ideals they serve? The pragmatic question is thus infinitely more vexing than how ideals are translated into practice. The translation quite predictably becomes a doing: how are ideals done in experience, what are we to do with them, how are they done up in experience. Let us imagine something different. Rather than the expected pragmatic to-and-fro movement between ideal and practice, practice and ideal, imagine a commitment to vigilance, to doing justice to the phenomenon of, say, dedication, authority, mortality, or pain. How do we attend to such matters with and without the help of ideal meanings? How are ideals there, in a "real" clinic, say, in New Brunswick, New Jersey, or in the clinics portrayed by Eakins's paintings? What sort of effort of attention is needed to do justice to the "appreciations and intimations" of transcendence in both?

The scalpel cuts through flesh, the oar through water. What do these acts, these practices, mean in Eakins? Are they evidence that "the subject of almost all of his work is the intimate connection between ideas and acts, impulses and executions."[56] "Connection"? What sort of "connection"? Is it that of having an idea or goal and seeking the means of attaining it? The goal might be to excel as a surgeon or as a rower. Thus, the pragmatic axiom takes charge of Eakins's art: these ends, which acts? Or these ideals, which performances? To move from idea to act is not simply to be efficient or practical, that is, a good pragmatist. It is to be heroic:

> As both the Gross and the Agnew portraits demonstrate, the essence of this distinctively American conception of heroism is its stunning equation of mental and practical power, as if there were no inherent obstacle in converting the one into the other. That daring leap of faith from mind to matter is the heart and soul of the pragmatic position and the deepest connection between Eakins' work and pragmatic philosophy. Seeing, being, and doing merge.[57]

There is something heroic about pragmatism, and Carney has it briefly in sight here: "that daring leap of faith." Why, though, is the movement from mind to matter a "leap of faith"? Why is it "daring"?

Let us recall what Dewey says about the ideal and infinity:

> The consciousness of this encompassing infinity of connections is ideal. When a sense of the infinite reach of an act physically occurring in a small point of space and occupying a petty instant of time comes home to us, the *meaning* of a present act is seen to be vast, immeasurable, unthinkable. This ideal is not a goal to be attained. It is a significance to be felt, appreciated.[58]

In Eakins's two clinic paintings, we certainly have acts "physically occurring in a small point of space." In both paintings, the low wall encircling the operating theater marks center and periphery. The luminous centers are, though, physically small compared to the unbounded recession of the encompassing. The auditorium or amphitheater has a wall, but it is not in sight. The center of attention has an indefinite background. What can be fixed with more precision is surgery's place in time: when it takes place, how long it lasts, how long it will take to recover. It is, however, what is not precisely present in these paintings which makes them interesting and important. This act of surgery, occurring in this time and this space—what is the meaning of this act?

The meaning—let us be clear, the *pragmatic* meaning—of this act of surgery is "vast, immeasurable, unthinkable." Surgery is not only an occasion for the demonstration of humans' ability to merge "our mental and our manual 'grasp,'" to "bridge the realms of thinking and doing," to connect "being with doing," to combine "mindfulness and handiness," to "masterfully inject mind into the world." The "daring leap of faith from mind to matter" which Carney so admires in Eakins and the pragmatists draws its potency and importance from another faith, what Dewey called "faith in the moral order": "this faith is not a mere intellectual thing, but it is practical—the staking of self upon activity as against passive possession."[59] Surgery is the occasion for a good that is vaster, larger, more encompassing than the good of mind/hand bridges and connections. The Eakins paintings afford, I think, intimations of transcendence which have their beginnings and endings in practice.

The practitioner, a surgeon, does not know or think for its own sake or for the knower and thinker's own good. The practitioner thinks in order to do, to practice an art or technology, a science or a craft. In other words, the world of practice is not simply a sort of display case for knowings and thinkings; it is the place where ideas and ideals are put to use, actually practiced rather than only contemplated. It would be mistaken to say "merely" contemplated or "simply" contemplated. Such formulations suggest that contemplation which does not seek to go beyond itself is flawed, deficient, of questionable importance. This does not do justice to contemplation, since not all thinking asks to be useful or practical and the self which often is concerned with practice is not always interested in practice. In other words, there are a fair number of goods external to practice or at least irrelevant to practice. Let us entertain the possibility that the Eakins clinic paintings ask something like this: interior to practice, inside the useful, where is one to find transcendence?

Transcendence which is an aspiration — toward the sublime, the sacred, the Good, God — must occasion something more than what James Wood calls "mystical goose bumps."[60] Well, there are no "goose bumps" evident in the clinic paintings. Things are more deliberate, studied, and practical than such mystical expressions. In both paintings the viewer attends to others' attending, but not just any attending. It is practical attention, and that is a particular kind of attention and a particular way of focusing that kind of attention. When we seek to be practical, we attend with care to the finite. To care about the practical, to *be* practical, is to care about finitude. To care about finitude is to recognize human limitation, limitation in all its varieties: physical mental, spiritual, emotional. And finally, we come to transcendence. Recognizing our limitations, as well as the limitations imposed by the world, we push against them; we desire to transcend them. In its longest arc, this longing for transcendence is the longing for the unlimited, the infinite, the perfect, the Good. Stirred by a shorter arc of transcendence, we long for the improved and better, not the Good, but the Good Enough. In either case, practice attends to the finite and particular.

What pragmatism cannot do and still be pragmatism, it is argued, is aspire to transcendence interior to practice. In other words, for pragmatism, transcendence is a temptation which we should outgrow because there is not, and cannot be, transcendence internal to practice. It is fruitless to deny the finitude we meet in the world of practice. We chip away at it, we try this or that, in short, we progress. Progress which is a result of intelligent practices does not hope for perfection but rather satisfactory resolution of the problem at hand. "If we lived in a perfect world, it would be nice to . . . but we do not live in a perfect world." In other words, cut out the transcendence talk and get back to the task at hand. In short, get practical. The small and momentous tasks at hand for any surgeon, and certainly for Eakins's surgeons, would seem to support Carney's aim to place "practical mastery of forms of *doing*" at the center of the operating theater.

This aim, this attitude, is more sophisticated than it initially appears to be. In a chapter titled "The World of Practice," Irwin C. Lieb considers the claims of reason, art, and faith to be vehicles of transcendence, pathways beyond practicalities. But the person who considers practice to be primary, to be the ground rather than itself grounded, will not gladly accept talk about transcendence which is internal to practice. We can attend to matters other than the practical, and in those forms of attention we certainly do transcend the practical. This, however, is transcendence external to requirements of practice and probably is not properly regarded as transcendence. Practice must guard its integrity, guard what makes practice distinctly practice. Lieb says:

> Practice, on this view, has . . . always to be attentive for the perversions which might occur when we withdraw from thickest practicalities. Thought, art and religion can move from practice and then, aberrantly, seem to lose all touch with it. They may even turn against it, or so it seems, and then practice will override them. . . . Theorists of practice, alert to unsound departures, try to make clear just where and how far from practice thought and art and faith can go and still stay within reach of it. Their injunction is that practice is primary and that except as thought bears on practice, it is not thought at all, and that art and religion can also become vaporous.[61]

Internal to practice there is not, and cannot be, a longing for transcendent "departures." The requirements of practice are met practically, and whatever other modes of attention to the world may offer to practice, they must be used practically. Might it be, though, that "thickest practicalities" quicken or stir in us a responsiveness to what exceeds our finitude? In such departures—momentary or prolonged—the requirements of practice have not been thinned or compromised or perverted. Something quite different is possible: the good of practice is made more perfect and praiseworthy by practitioners' intimations of an intangible ideal, perhaps only vaporously present, somewhere, in the midst of "thickest practicalities."

Surgery is an art. Surgery is a science. Or it is a combination. But it is also, considered from the viewpoint of its meaning, a struggle. To consent to surgery—routine or difficult—involves "the staking of self." To perform surgery involves "the staking of self." Healer and healed are motivated by a "possible ideal good." The pragmatic meaning of the good of surgery may appear to be precise, limited, specifiable: to be able to walk, breathe, see, live. In their surgical efforts, Gross and Agnew hope for "good results," that is, determinably good results. But one looks at their faces, and again at their faces, and Dewey comes to mind: "There is a point *in* deliberate action where definite thought fades into the ineffable and undefinable—into emotion."[62] Is it possible that Gross and Agnew have been caught at the moment when, no longer touching the patient, their efforts have touched what Dewey calls the "shadowy background," the "ineffable and undefinable," the ideal? Carney says that each surgeon "has momentarily taken a meditative step off to one side of the heaving sea of activity around him."[63] Meditative? Why meditative? Richard Selzer gives us a pragmatically better picture, a better idea, of the phenomenology of the "step off to one side": "To do surgery without a sense of awe is to be a dandy—all style and no purpose. No part of the operation is too lowly, too menial. Even when suturing the skin at the end of a major abdominal procedure, you must operate with piety, as though you were embellishing a holy reliquary."[64] The mind may be, as Carney is pleased to remind us, a verb. But he presses the point too hard: "Where mind is a verb, there can be no resting place, no end to the activity of expressive realization."[65] Dewey says: "But there is a point in *every* intelligent activity where effort ceases; where thought and doing fall back upon a course of events which effort and reflection cannot touch."[66] For Dewey, the intimation and appreciation of transcendent ideals allow us to cease effort, to steady faith and aspiration, and through our best efforts, to take up the struggle. To miss, as I think Carney does, the intersection of effort and transcendence in pragmatism, one might even say their desire for each other, is an inattentiveness with a very large consequence. We fail to see how practical matters, such as cutting open a body, invite—and morally require—appreciative responses like awe, piety, and reverence. When the mind is a verb, especially *because* the mind is a verb, it can aspire to such enlargements and transcendences of its motions and efforts. It is no easy matter, though, to attend to the intangible in the midst of the attention-draining demands of tangible and "thickest practicalities." Vigilance is necessary.

· CHAPTER 4 ·

Humanism and Vigilance

In response to Jean Beaufret's question whether we can "restore" meaning to the word "humanism," Martin Heidegger responds in his "Letter on Humanism" by asking, "I wonder whether that is necessary."[1] He then proceeds to criticize what might be called the arrogance of "subjectism," that is, the view that the human being or the subject is the measure of truth and Being. In opposition to this view, Heidegger argues that "what counts is *humanitas* in the service of the truth of Being, but without humanism in the metaphysical sense."[2] Although my view of what "counts" in an effort to "restore" meaning to the concept of humanism is somewhat different than Heidegger's, I do share his belief that we cannot accept conventional interpretations of its meaning, particularly the idea that humanism is a celebration of the centrality of the human—"man the measure." If meaning is to be restored to the concept of humanism, it must be freed from the evaluative roles it typically has played. It must be recognized that humanism has become a tired concept, perhaps because its meaning seems so obvious and unproblematic and yet at other times its meaning seems so personal and relative. The excellence to which humanism refers must be recovered; it no longer can be taken for granted.

I believe the excellence or virtue to which humanism refers is vigilance. This chapter is an attempt to establish some conceptual and phenomenological features of vigilance. These analyses will reveal that vigilance impedes or slows the natural momentum of our habits of mind in order to bring to presence possibilities of meaning and interpretation not immediately suggested by our habits of mind. It will be shown why vigilance—the desire to "do justice to the phenomenon"—requires us ceaselessly to question the confidence and sureness of our principles, values, and commitments, as well as the habits of mind upon which they are founded. It follows from this that humanism cannot be entirely identified with a commitment to a set of "humanistic values" or "principles." It will be shown that although vigilance does not provide a set of universalizable "directives" or "principles" with which to guide one's conduct, it is the habit of mind which makes our values and principles worthy of our commitment. Thus, to restore meaning to the concept of humanism requires that we suspend conventional notions of humanism which identify it with a set of commitments, and instead seek to understand what sort of response humanism's appeal to vigilance calls forth.

"To Do Justice to the Phenomenon"

Speaking of liberal or humanistic education, Henry David Aiken says that these are

> attempts, all too feeble, to make teachers and students aware of human concerns, as well as responsibilities and rights, more ultimate and more pervasive than those defined by any special job of work, academic or otherwise. And it has been the endless, often thankless, task of college and university teachers committed to liberal education to illuminate and, if possible, to strengthen all those primordial forms of action, of speech and art, of sympathy and passion that serve to offset the myriadic sources of alienation of men from their lives and from one another which the term "specialism" symptomizes.[3]

Humanism requires awareness of concerns, responsibilities, and rights, more ultimate and pervasive than those characteristic of any "special job of work," academic or otherwise. What Aiken's remarks begin to point toward is the necessary pluralism of humanistic education. Humanism is the enemy of the limited perspective, the absolute perspective which limits our awareness of more ultimate and pervasive perspectives. Humanistic education values the plurality of perspectives, their capacity for improvement, revision, and rejection, as well as their potential for being communicated and shared through "those primordial forms of action, of speech and art, of sympathy and passion." Liberal and humanistic education see the plurality of perspectives as a resource, not a refuge. But isn't the "specialism" which Professor Aiken wishes to "offset" through humanistic education a perfectly natural expression of the pluralism of perspectives? Are humanists simply specialists of a certain kind, namely, those who concentrate on "ultimate" and "pervasive" perspectives? A deeper understanding of the meaning of specialism is required in order to restore meaning to the concept of humanism. This is not because humanistic education offsets the effects of specialism and therefore by understanding humanism's negative condition we can come to grasp its positive nature. Rather, specialism reveals something essential about the structure and functioning of consciousness: its natural tendency to form itself into unities or configurations of meaning, into habits of mind.

In the concluding section of *Craft and Consciousness*, titled "The Narrowing and Extension of Craft Horizons," Joseph Bensman and Robert Lilienfeld significantly expand upon Aiken's point concerning the narrowing of concerns and perspectives which "specialism" too often promotes:

> It is unfortunate that individuals who start their work with self-consciously created points of reference lose, in the process of doing the work, their awareness that they are viewing only a limited aspect of the world. When they do this, they are making a reduction of sorts—all phenomena are reduced to something that can be seen only from a very limited perspective. It is correct to criticize the materialist reduction, the psychological reduction, sociologism, logical, linguistic, and epistemological reductions, even reductions to the "thing itself." In the latter case the reduction consists of refusing to entertain alternative possibilities. This stricture does not apply to Edmund Husserl, for whom an unlimited horizon of further determinations was an essential aspect of any object of experience. The reproach is more applicable to studies which call themselves phenomenological, but which appear to be subjectivistic. No reduction is in itself "incorrect" so long as the observer or analyst is aware that, in using a restricted perspective or method, he is describing a limited aspect of experience. If the observer or analyst maintains such awareness he is likely to ask: How much of the phenomenon that I wish to explain is explained by the use of the methods that I have employed? How much remains unexplained? What other perspectives, or "reductions," need I employ in order to do justice to the phenomenon? If he asks such questions, he is more likely to employ a wide variety of perspectives or reductions. In fact he is likely to rotate perspectives as his mode of analysis, asking always how much is left unexplained by his use of various reductions. Since the world of experience is infinite, subject to an unlimited number of perspectives, there is little likelihood that one will be able to ascertain a true image or absolute knowledge of any one thing, but rather by the use of such methods, it would seem to us that the probability of error is diminished. Moreover, it might, by such efforts, be possible to achieve a truly humanistic image of the world, and to

escape the blunders that often appear to be the hazards of occupational attitudes.⁴

The authors argue that every craft, discipline, and profession embodies attitudes and habits of mind. These habits of mind enable the practitioner not only to see the world, but to see it *as* a particular kind of world. The world is seen and experienced as roles, spaces, words, distances, power statuses, measurements, economic indicators, caregiving, God, precedents, inputs-outputs, and so on. Since no occupation or profession incorporates all possible habits of mind, each represents a necessary reduction to those habits of mind characteristic of that craft or profession. Habits of mind and the reductions they permit become natural, taken-for-granted; at times some may be subjected to scrutiny, but then within a context still taken-for-granted, still conventional. On one hand we have the subject matter, *die Sache*, the phenomenon, and on the other, consciousness, which tries "to do justice to the phenomenon." Hence, the centrality of Bensman and Lilienfeld's "contention that major 'habits of mind,' approaches to the world, or in phenomenological terms, attitudes towards everyday life, and specialized attitudes, are extensions of habits of thought that emerge and are developed in the practice of an occupation, profession, or craft."⁵

Clearly, it must not be thought that habits of mind are simply ruts or grooves worn in our experience and recorded in our mind or consciousness. Habits of mind are sources of blindness, but they are also vehicles of vision; they attune us to certain possibilities of meaning and exclude us from others. This attunement is not merely a matter of having certain concepts, paradigms, values. Habit describes *how* we have these; that is, we have them so deeply, so naturally, that they create for us our fundamental accord with the world. They form our sensibility, establishing our "sense" of something as distinguished from our conception or definition of that thing. Habits do not merely conserve our experience and its meanings; they create or constitute our experience. Paul Ricoeur says that "to acquire a habit does not mean to repeat and consolidate but to invent, to progress."⁶ Habit is a power, a capacity which should not be judged by its fall into automatism. What Ricoeur calls "the flexible habit" is the foundation of our skill and "know-how," regardless of whether this "know-how" involves our ability to swim or to care for the patient in cardiac arrest. Humanism has its roots in the tension between the conservative and inventive qualities of habit.

Habits of mind limit or narrow the world to what George Kelly, in connection with concepts and constructs, calls their "range of convenience."⁷

A specialist operates within a certain "range of convenience," the contours of which are set by the depth and extensiveness of the specialist's habits of mind, as well as their availability for readjustment and reorganization. Specialization can be and perhaps must be viewed as a natural and inevitable feature of the organization of consciousness, if it is conceived as the mind's natural tendency to make distinctions. This tendency to make distinctions John N. Findlay calls one of the "essential 'drifts' of consciousness":

> If conscious experience thus involves a *nisus* towards the eliciting of relations, we may with the same justice recognize in it a *nisus* towards the *eliciting* and ever sharper *distinction of parts and aspects*. To be aware of anything is, as we saw, to be aware of it *as* something or other; the life of consciousness, like that of journalism, involves a perpetual quest for "angles," and, if one may so put it, an endeavour to make these *more* angular. To draw ever finer and more numerous distinctions, and to remove all vagueness and borderline overlap from among them, is merely to carry farther a process essential to consciousness, it is merely to be *more* conscious in a certain direction.[8]

This "drift" is not the only one which characterizes consciousness; it is important to recognize that among the other "drifts" of consciousness the tendency to "bring out *wholes* of various sorts" is as basic as the need to make distinctions. Nevertheless, it is very helpful to see the specialist habit of mind—the desire to "be *more* conscious in a certain direction"—not as a narrowing of consciousness which is somehow unnatural to it, but rather as a quite natural and essential "drift" of consciousness. Thus, habits of mind which have been arrived at through what Findlay calls the "perpetual quest for 'angles,'" that is, distinctions, reflect the natural tendency of consciousness to turn from "all," to "some," to "this." I believe it is misguided to criticize specialism, not merely because we need specialist knowledge in a utilitarian sense, but also because specialism displays one of the ways in which consciousness fulfills and celebrates itself.

Thus, the specialist habit of mind—to have turned from all, to some, to this—is not the natural enemy of humanism. Rather, it is humanism's constant reminder that the tension between the inventive and conservative nature of habit is never concluded, never settled. What part can or should specialization play in helping us see how things "hang together" as Richard Rorty says?[9] Indeed, what are the consequences of specialization for the conversationalist who likes to see how things "hang together": in an age of multiple and specialized perspectives, how does one see how things "hang together" without resorting to metaphysical landscapes? In Rorty's case, one practices being a "name-dropper" whose "specialty is seeing similarities and differences between great big pictures, between attempts to see how things hang together."[10] There appears to be no way around specialization, even if your specialization is "great big pictures." I think specialization is a profound demonstration of the fact that human beings develop habits of mind, that these habits of mind enable us "to be *more* conscious in a certain direction," and that these directions tend to become certain, that is, the way we see the world. Specialization is humanism's constant reminder that habits of mind are our epistemological square roots. Recent discussions of relativism are closely related to the meaning of specialization and humanism, for I think relativism is consciousness caught in the process of specializing itself and then living with the results of its own and other specializations. Although recent criticisms and defenses of specialization rarely have had as their main purpose the rethinking of the meaning of humanism, I nevertheless believe that this ought to be one of the most important consequences of any philosophical consideration of the meaning of specialization. Specialization invites us to reflect on our ability to "do justice to the phenomenon" and our readiness to alter or preserve our habits of mind in order to do so; these concepts greatly help us in understanding the excellence to which humanism refers. Before considering more directly the notion of vigilance, we must first determine how commitment and value may hinder efforts to restore meaning to the concept of humanism.

Commitment and Value

Humanism's meaning cannot be restored by trying to derive it from some preconceived, authorizing idea or image of the human—the human being as rational thinker, language user, tool maker, social animal, and so on. Humanism's perspective is *in* as well as *of* history, events, sociality. These contexts seem to have a way of requiring definitions of "man as . . ." to be continually amended, revised, and discarded. Merleau-Ponty says of humanism that

> it begins by becoming aware of contingency. It is the continued confirmation of an astonishing junction between fact and meaning, between my body and my self, my self and others, my thought and my speech, violence and truth. It is the methodical refusal of explanations, because they destroy the mixture we are made of and make us incomprehensible to ourselves.[11]

The contingency and ambiguity grounded in the "astonishing" junctions of fact and meaning, and so forth, preclude any perspective of man gaining a privileged status, one which would demonstrate that Being and intelligibility coincide. The closer humanism moves toward becoming an absolute ground, the further away it moves from all those phenomena of experience which elude absolutizing perspectives.

Humanism cannot secure its meaning and truth from a preconceived idea of man. Isn't, though, its meaning derived from man? Since all meaning is connected with, rooted in man, isn't man the principle of intelligibility—man-the-measure? Such a view is tempting, and of course in a certain sense it is true. The human being is the giver of meaning, though not the only condition of meaning. Meaning presupposes man, but is man self-explanatory? Is man's meaning unquestionable, clear, without doubt? Apparently not. If man is the measure, it is not an absolute measure but instead a measure of contingency that solicits wonder, not merely explanation. The human cannot be an absolute explanatory principle since it is the human which prompts the greatest wonder. This is why Merleau-Ponty believes humanism is "the methodical refusal of explanations." He is not proposing obscurantism, mysticism, or a mushy romanticism at the expense of intelligibility. He is simply emphasizing the radical contingency and wonder of meaning coming into being, whether in the form of a poem, a clinical diagnosis, or a memory. Such wonder detracts nothing from these phenomena, but positions them in the context of human finitude.

The excellence, then, to which humanism refers cannot be derived from some capacity or characteristic of the human which is taken to be man's "essence"; we do not seek to restore meaning to the concept of humanism by locating "models" and "images" of the human which are taken to be distinctly or essentially human and from which we can deduce what is "humanistic" and what is not.

Because of the "astonishing junction between fact and meaning," meaning cannot be restored to the concept of humanism by locating certain "humanistic values" or "principles" to which we ought to commit ourselves as a result of some necessity thought to inhere in them. Nevertheless, virtually all forms of contemporary humanism advance a set of "central" values and commitments which are felt to be compelling because they most fully represent or characterize the ideal or telos implied in a certain "image" of man. Thus, if man is free, then respect for freedom and dignity is a "humanistic value." If man is a whole, then "holism" is a "humanistic value." If man is rational, then choice and responsibility are "humanistic values." And so on. Certain "values" and our commitment to them are universalizable because they follow from and most profoundly express the flowering and perfectability of our human nature; they are the very condition for any discussion of our human nature. Thus, John N. Findlay defends the thesis that "universally pursuable" values of pleasure, satisfaction, success, power, freedom, knowledge, love, justice, and virtue are "valid in that they can and must be a basis for practical discussion among persons, as no object of factual liking must necessarily be."[12] These values are necessary if we wish to imagine what we can, or ought to become. Given such an eloquent formulation of "universally pursuable" values and their desirability, it is no wonder that under the influence of such visions humanism has become a search for values to which we can commit ourselves. In fact, it is not unusual to define humanism as the concern with values.

Although less common than the view which finds a necessity in the universal, there is another form of necessity which sometimes is associated with humanism. This is the view that the concrete situation imposes a certain necessity upon our interpretation of it. According to this view, the general and universal must accommodate themselves to the authority of the concrete. Without such accommodation, we do "violence" to the situation by forcing it to express itself in a language which, no matter how general and universal, is not *its* language. I shall consider an example of this in the next section. I simply want to note here that humanisms derived from universalism or particularism, despite their differences, are predicated upon the presupposition that humanism is a commitment to a value or principle. To be humanistic is to be *for* something, presumably something good and desirable. To be humanistic is to be committed to certain values and principles, and since commitment is worthy only if its objects are worthy, humanism necessarily becomes a court of appeals ruling in favor of some values and against others. However, humanism is not a court of appeals. If meaning is to be restored to the concept, it must not be identified solely with the content of our commitments but also with the manner in which we have and hold them. No value or principle is worthy if it is held without vigilance; as the appeal to vigilance humanism is the appellant; it is humanity's insistent appeal to keep a vigilance over origins, ultimate concerns, the Encompassing. This vigilance is kept not in the hope of once and for all determining which commitments are good and which bad, but rather in the hope that we may "do justice to the phenomenon," a hope solicited by, embodied in, and menaced by the obviousness and ambiguity of experience.

The novelty of the view of humanism I wish to present, then, is that it is not based upon the assumption that in order to "do justice to the phenomenon" you simply must have the "right" commitments in order to get the phenomenon "right." The conception of humanism I want to describe takes its beginning not from the authority and necessity felt to reside in a certain principle or commitment, but rather from the manner in which we experience what is present and absent from any principle or commitment. To restore meaning to the term humanism, then, requires suspension of the creedal attitude, that is, the view that humanism is a particular set of principles and values. We must instead turn our attention to the nature of the awareness which gives character to a particular value or principle. It is the quality of vigilance we keep over our field of awareness or consciousness—our habits of mind—which sets the limits to the depth and imaginativeness of our responses to the world, including moral, practical, aesthetic, and religious ones. A creedal view of humanism destroys what is most essential to humanism—the appeal to vigilance.

Vigilance

Vigilance has no a priori commitment to the particular or universal; it stands in opposition to formulations of humanism which seek to "ground" themselves either in universal values or the requirements of the "here and now." The claims of the general and the particular are not decided or reconciled by vigilance. Through vigilance, though, we gain a clearer view of what is missing or absent from the general and the particular. Humanism refers to the generalized habit of vigilance which enables us to experience the presence of things, their visibility, through keeping us heedful of what is absent from their presence.[13] The intelligibility of a phenomenon, its presentability to consciousness, is always a dialectic between what is present to consciousness and what is absent from it. Absence is not a nothingness, a lack of being, nor is it a deficient or imperfect mode of being. Absence is a positive mode of being which influences and qualifies our lives occasionally in very direct ways, but most often in much more subtle and elusive ways. The thoughts of John Dewey are instructive here:

> Herbert Spencer sometimes colored his devotion to symbolic experiences with a fact of dire experience. When he says that every fact has two opposite sides, "the one its near or visible side and the other its remote or invisible side," he expresses a persistent trait of every object in experience. The visible is set in the invisible; and in the end what is unseen decides what happens in the seen; the tangible rests precariously upon the untouched and ungrasped. The contrast and the potential maladjustment of the immediate, the conspicuous and focal phase of things, with those indirect and hidden factors which determine the origin and career of what is present, are indestructible features of any and every

experience. We may term the way in which our ancestors dealt with the contrast superstitious, but the contrast is no superstition. It is a primary datum in any experience.

We have substituted sophistication for superstition, at least measurably so. But the sophistication is often as irrational and as much at the mercy of words as the superstition it replaces. Our magical safeguard against the uncertain character of the world is to deny the existence of chance, to mumble universal and necessary law, the ubiquity of cause and effect, the uniformity of nature, universal progress, and the inherent rationality of the universe.[14]

Humanism is a protection against the exaggeration of "the immediate, the conspicuous and focal phase of things." Humanism is a reminder of those "indirect and hidden factors which determine the origin and career of what is present." Dewey was not saying that with a better positioning or perspective we are assured of touching the untouched and grasping the ungrasped. As the second paragraph clearly shows, the absent for Dewey was a fact of experience having the force of a metaphysical principle. Science and technology have replaced superstition as safeguards against hiddenness and absence, they are our sophistication, but so too, increasingly, is creedal humanism. By embracing "humanistic values" we try to assure ourselves that we are not missing something, that we are bringing ever larger bits of our humanity and that of others to fuller realization or actualization. Creedal humanism, by focusing so intently on bringing to presence certain "humanistic values," suffers a diminished vigilance, for vigilance is the middle term between presence and absence, the play of presence and absence made habitual. Humanism is this habit of vigilance, the habit of holding in focus what is present by what is absent. The humanistic appeal to vigilance is not easily reconciled with well-intentioned though nonetheless dogmatic declarations of "humanistic values," "humanistic principles," and "humanistic practices."

It is tempting to interpret vigilance as an "expanded awareness" or an "expansion of consciousness." It must be noted, however, that awareness can be broadened without necessarily establishing a tendency to seek expansion in the future. Instead of a circle ten feet in diameter, I now move within the confines of an eleven- or twenty-foot circle. My consciousness includes *more*, but it may be uncertain whether this acquisition establishes the habit or disposition to continue *including* more. Actually, an expanded awareness may have the effect of making me *less* rather than more vigilant, depending upon other things, the degree of satisfaction I take in my new awareness and the extent to which I experience what Jaspers calls the "need to avoid a harmonizing world view." The hope, of course, is that what is included in a new "awareness of" is not merely a new content but a continuing disposition to imagine what may be absent from my present awareness, however new and exciting it may be.

If vigilance is not "raised consciousness" or "expanded awareness," neither is it a quality of all our ways of being present to the world's phenomena. Feeling, intuition, memory, imagination, thinking are ways in which we bring the world's meaning to presence. It does not make much sense to talk about "vigilant anger" or "vigilant memory." However, these ways of experiencing the world may serve vigilance. Empathy may make me more heedful of a person's fears and concerns (and thereby move me closer to the person); my literary imagination may present the person to me in his similarity to the self-pitying character in a novel or short story (thereby moving me away from him). To some extent my vigilance may be armed with certain beliefs and convictions, yet such an armed vision may too strongly direct and therefore constrain vigilance's tense play between presence and absence, the belief or "value" forcing a presence that does not want to come. So too, feelings, "gut feelings," intuitions, and hunches may be expressions and vehicles of a vigilant attitude, or they may signal the embrace—the total embrace—of a certain perspective, one appropriate for a "true believer."

The end or purpose of vigilance, and the unique satisfaction it gives us, is not that of bringing an experienced phenomenon to a certain completion, that is, bringing it to fullness, to full being and presence, whether it is knowledge, truth, happiness, or commitment. Nor is vigilance a choice to refrain from gearing into the world, a passivity, a "wait and see what happens" attitude. Neither is vigilance radical doubt. Vigilance permits us to "do justice to the phenomenon" by quickening and improving our sense that consciousness is not exhausted by its object, that is, what is absent from consciousness sustains what is present to it. Yet even here there is a tendency to make vigilance into a kind of Easter egg hunt—if absence is not here, then perhaps it is present somewhere else. Absence is not an object, you do not find it by looking harder under the bush or behind the porch. Absence is not remedied by presence, as if absence were a flaw or imperfection of presence. Vigilance is the proper presencing of a phenomenon within a context of absence; humanism is vigilance become habitual. So-called humanistic values—dignity, respect for persons, equality—name what is absent as much as they name what is present. This does not mean that we simply wish to bring them into existence in some situation. It means that the manifestation or presence of any of these values or principles is only one or some of the ways it may be available to, present to, consciousness and experience. "Humanistic values" and "principles" do not ease the tension caused by the play between presence and absence; they simply name the ways in which the habit of vigilance permits us to see whether we are coming closer to or moving further away from the ideal to "do justice to the phenomenon." To "do justice to the phenomenon" does not mean, then, making it fully and immediately present; rather, it means properly presencing the phenomenon in absence. It is never self-evident that a certain "humanistic" principle or practice is the decisive mode of presencing for a certain situation. Vigilance attunes us to possibilities of presencing not immediately envisioned or encoded by general principles and values.

It may be instructive at this point to view vigilance in connection with the more familiar concept of "thinking," though given a rather special formulation by Hannah Arendt. She was concerned to distinguish between knowing and thinking, intellect and reason. Although our desire to know may arise out of practical problems, theoretical issues, or simple curiosity, all knowing fulfills itself by reaching its goal or termination in the object known. Our "thirst for knowledge" may be "unquenchable," yet it is satisfied at least provisionally when we have come to know what we desire to know. The activity of knowing results in knowledge—a product or accomplishment. Arendt says, however, that

> the inclination or the need to think, on the contrary, even if aroused by none of the time-honored metaphysical, unanswerable "ultimate questions," leaves nothing so tangible behind, nor can it be stilled by allegedly definite insights of "wise men." The need to think can be satisfied only through thinking, and the thoughts which I had yesterday will be satisfying this need today only to the extent that I can think them anew.[15]

When thinking, I solicit a world of meanings that are not at hand and this soliciting is done for its own sake. When seeking to know, I introduce a condition external to meaning—evidence—so as to establish certain meanings as true. In this case, thinking is a means to an end, for example, knowledge, truth. Arendt puts the issue boldly: "The need of reason is not inspired by the quest for truth but by the quest for meaning. And truth and meaning are not the same. The basic fallacy, taking precedence over all specific metaphysical fallacies, is to interpret meaning on the model of truth."[16] To reason is to understand the meaning of something; it is to move beyond appearances as present to the senses so as to realize the mind's capacity to make present to itself what is absent from the senses, that is, possibilities of meaning.

The connection between Arendt's analysis of thinking and my discussion of vigilance can now be made more explicit. Speaking of thinking, she says that "if Kant is right and the faculty of thought has a 'natural aversion' against accepting its own results as 'solid axioms,' then we cannot expect any moral propositions or commandments, no final code of conduct from the thinking activity, least of all a new and now allegedly final definition of what is good and what is evil."[17] Similarly, vigilance does not "ground" or authorize a commitment or judgment by subsuming it under a certain axiom. Thinking and vigilance prohibit one from pronouncing a certain value or principle to be final and exhausting the realm of the possible. Thus, in the sense that thinking and vigilance frustrate the "quest for certainty," for axioms and maxims, they are as Arendt says, "resultless." By according as much ontological dignity to possibility and contingency as to actuality and necessity, thinking and vigilance also frustrate any effort to make further thinking and vigilance unnecessary.

Seen in this light, it is certainly wrong to view vigilance as the first step to the "liberalization" of values and conventions and as the final step to moral and conceptual nihilism. Vigilance would contradict itself if a priori it ruled out the possibility that there may be absolutes. Yet even absolute truths require care in order to discern when a supposed absolute truth is on the fringe of its absoluteness, its "range of convenience." The need for such discernment—such vigilance—springs from the possibility that if there is one absolute, there might be two absolutes, or three, and then with no assurance that they are so well coordinated that their claims shall never conflict or contradict each other. There are, after all, Ten Commandments. Particularly in this theological context, where claims to absolute truth are not uncommon, it is pertinent to note Hans Küng's observation that theologians, like natural scientists, aspire to definitive truth, but

> do not possess this truth definitively. They must also constantly seek the truth afresh, they can only approach closer to it, learn by trial and error and must therefore be prepared to revise their standpoint. In theology, too, the scientific interplay of project, criticism, counter-criticism and improvement should be possible.[18]

This preparedness for revision of which Küng speaks is clearly a complicated phenomenon. If we are too quick to change our fundamental convictions, it is not clear in what sense they were convictions or why they were fundamental. If we are totally unprepared to modify our basic convictions, if we persist unmindful and uncaring of alternative possibilities, then conviction hinders rather than helps our ability to "do justice to the phenomenon." Being a "person of convictions" is never a guarantee that we will "do justice to the phenomenon," nor is having the "courage of one's convictions." What makes my convictions worthy of my courage and continued affirmation is not confidence in their truth and absoluteness but my vigilant attention to what is present and absent from their perspectives.

Thus, humanism as the appeal to vigilance is not the enemy of devotion to a principle, doctrine, or value. It is the habit of mind which enables us to take exception to the ease or confidence with which a certain value or principle would presume to pronounce the "real" meaning of a phenomenon, and it is through vigilant adoption of a certain value or principle I assume responsibility for what that value does to me and to others. The habit of vigilance is the way we care for and tend our habits of mind. As I suggested earlier, it is not the case that left to themselves habits are destined to become automatic and routine. The "flexible habit," as Ricoeur calls it, is not turned in upon itself, requiring constant inspection to assure that habit has not become an unthinking reflex. We must maintain a vigilance over our habits of mind not simply because they may tend to draw the world too narrowly into their compass, but because their compass becomes too vast, too expansive. The work of vigilance would be relatively easy if all it had to do was spring us loose from the dead spots of habit. However, vigilance must also keep watch over habit's creativity, what Ricoeur beautifully calls the "exuberance of habit." Vigilance is habit's reflexivity upon its inventive nature as well as its conservative nature. Such reflexivity may deepen one's commitment to a principle or value, or it may cause us to disown it. Through vigilance we come to see that some perspectives are more interesting and compelling than others, some habits of mind more fruitful, virtuous, and beautiful. Our responsibility is to "do justice to the phenomenon," not merely to be "true to our principles." The effect of such vigilance is to reduce arbitrariness, not increase it.

This reduction of arbitrariness is not achieved through a decisive reconciliation of the claims of the general or universal and the particular brought about through the power of vigilance. It is important to note Alasdair MacIntyre's argument that "not all, but only some, moral valuations are universalizable."[19] Only conventional morality works on the basis of universalizable maxims or principles; when there is real moral perplexity "all that can be done is to exhibit the passage of the moral agent through perplexity." MacIntyre continues:

> To offer us a maxim on which or in accordance with which the moral agent finally acted is to tell us what the resolution of perplexity was but not how the perplexity was resolved. In this clear-cut sense then the maxims of morality do not guide us, nor do they prescribe conduct to us.

And to describe the function of moral valuation in general or of "ought" in particular as prescriptive is highly misleading unless this is made clear. The catalogue of possible uses of "ought" needs to be supplemented by a catalogue of those moral purposes for which "ought" and words like it and sometimes any words at all can be of little or no use.[20]

What or whom can guide us? MacIntyre is clear and brief: "Only the phenomenologist can help us here and the kind of phenomenology we need is that supplied by the novelist."[21] Whether we get our phenomenology from novels or philosophy seems to me less important than whether we do in fact develop a phenomenological habit of mind. Although such a habit of mind is certainly not the only source of vigilance, it is a most powerful inducement to "do justice to the phenomenon." The "oughts" which we so naturally bring to experience — this is the way it ought to be done, this is what it ought to look like and so on — are suspended in order to allow possibilities of the phenomenon to come to presence which are not anticipated by our "oughts." Phenomenology's "return to experience" is a return to the ought-laden character of experience. It is not an attempt to somehow see experience without "oughts" but rather to take the activity of these "oughts" less for granted. For the same reason that MacIntyre wishes to free morality from an identification with commitment to universalizable principles or maxims, I wish to free humanism from its present identification with commitment to "values" and "principles," however commendable and universal they may be.

"Oughts" can be authorized by the universal; they also may be authorized by the concrete. In a chapter titled "A Concrete Humanism?" Arthur Brittan develops his formulation of a Marxist criticism of "abstract humanism," that is, humanism authorized by the abstractions of universals. Humanistic values like "wholeness," "autonomy," "respect for the individual," and so on, have no meaning unless they are grounded in the actuality, the concreteness of everyday life. Concreteness must be the criterion of humanism if it is to be a defensible position, not abstract categories like the "condition of man." What does this criterion of concreteness entail? Brittan says:

> If we are to speak of the concrete individual, then this must of necessity entail the totality of his situation, including his experience of that situation — that is, his subjective definition of the reality of the world as having a degree of immutability. In short, the alienated worker in capitalist society cannot be described independently of his consciousness of that society. In concretising his situation we are saying something about

his total environment in the total situation including his consciousness of this involvement. But alienation is also about false consciousness—hence, in concretising the individual, we are not merely saying that consciousness is an integral part of his life-situation, we are also saying that this consciousness is located in a historical situation in which his view of himself is false and distorted.[22]

Concrete humanism sets the task of totalizing the situation or phenomenon, that is, striving to bring to as full presence as possible the way it is for the concrete individual in the concrete situation. This may, and probably should involve close attention to the body and to linguistic practices, but most important, humanism cannot be a "speculative metaphysics or some vague commitment to 'the individual.'"[23] It must speak to individuals in "real concrete situations," or else "be relegated to the scrap heap."

Thus, instead of commitment to abstract and universal values like the individual, concrete humanism proposes a commitment to concrete social relationships, concrete consciousness of these, and the problems of political economy. Neither universal humanism nor concrete humanism would, of course, concede that in the view of Bensman and Lilienfeld "they are viewing only a limited aspect of the world." Whereas universal humanism is always faced with the problem of adjusting its universal principles to the particular situation, concrete humanism is always grounded in particular situations for it "tries to catch the here and now of experience." Thus situated, the effort to characterize the "total situation" becomes a matter of thoroughness, a task in principle capable of completion so long as one begins on the right side of the track—the concrete. Concrete humanism sees absence as a temporary obstacle on the way to emancipation. Vigilant humanism asks how the concrete is to be properly presenced in the context of absent yet possibly pertinent perspectives. The concrete is *not* the foundation, principle, or commitment which underwrites humanism. Humanism as the appeal to vigilance must dispute the view that there is no way of going beyond the concrete particularity of everyday life. The concrete is not a magnet which draws whatever is of value from the absent. The essentialism of universal humanism is not overcome by making the concrete into the principle of intelligibility. To seek new descriptions of things, to find new and more fruitful ways of talking, to benefit from a tradition, to sharpen criticism, all may require going beyond the concrete particularity of the phenomenon. Thus, even phenomenology's appeal to "lived experience" as an authorizing base or foundation is not exempt from vigilance and the attempt to "do justice to the phenomenon."[24] What is absent may hold riches not realized in the presentations of the concrete and lived, though nevertheless realizable in concrete, lived experience. Theory, imagination, and hypothesis are just some of the ways in which we move from the presently concrete to absent possibilities not imaginable on the basis of a prior commitment to the primacy of the concrete. The vigilance which makes it possible to "do justice to the phenomenon" is always a tense adjustment of the present and absent, the success of which cannot be prefigured by a "criterion of concreteness."

Vigilance is often quiet and gentle; to be watchful or heedful is not an engrossed or absorbed attention, although vigilance may at times reach such levels of intensity. Yet even when most quiet and gentle, vigilance is a struggle of the person with him- or herself. It is the struggle to use one part of experience against another in order to secure an opening for possibility. Vigilance requires, phenomenologically, a certain level of continuing tension, a preparedness for exception. Creedal humanism promises more than vigilant humanism: its "oughts" seem powerful, urgent, authoritative. Vigilance by contrast seems so uncertain, nervous, and, well . . . noncommittal. Vigilance almost seems designed to introduce stress into a person's life by introducing one doubt after another concerning a person's deepest commitments and convictions. Nevertheless, I believe certain forms of stress are critically important to the full and growing life, the healthful life. Vigilance increases a person's freedom *and* health, for in Ernest Becker's view health should be seen as a synonym for liberation, "a liberation *for values yet unknown, yet to be ushered into the world.*"[25] Vigilance does not guarantee the birth of new values, nor does its lack set the impossibility of the emergence of new values. Vigilance, though, gives us our first view of what we have won or lost in the birth or death of a value; such a viewing is rarely a casual matter. Thus, if humanism is vigilant rather than creedal, its impact will almost always be somewhat discomforting, transforming the naturalness of our commitments, regardless of whether these taken for granteds are embodied in policies, customs, practices, or habits of mind.

To fully appreciate the quality of struggle implicit in vigilance, we must return to Hannah Arendt's discussion of thinking. She has described thinking as the "habit of examining and reflecting upon whatever happens to come to pass, regardless of specific content and quite independent of results."[26] Further, Arendt believes that "thinking inevitably has a destructive, undermining effect on all established criteria, values, measurements for good and evil, in short on those customs and rules of conduct we treat of in morals and ethics."[27] In my conception of vigilance I have tried to soften the "destructive" element in Arendt's notion of thinking but not wholly to eliminate it. Thinking and vigilance are "dangerous to all creeds" not because they are destined to always have an "undermining effect" on what is, but rather because their insistence upon the ontological importance of the absent requires that we take heed of the plurality of existence. It is precisely in connection with this plurality of existence that the struggle implicit in vigilance takes on its special significance.

Through vigilance, as with thinking, "a difference is inserted into my Oneness."[28] Contrary to creedal holism which insists upon the "wholeness" of the person:

> It is this *duality* of myself with myself that makes thinking a true activity, in which I am both the one who asks and the one who answers. Thinking can become dialectical and critical because it goes through this questioning and answering process . . . whereby we constantly raise the basic Socratic question: *What do you mean when you say* . . . ? except that this *legein*, saying, is soundless and therefore so swift that its dialogical structure is somewhat difficult to detect.[29]

Vigilance and thinking actualize and then reduce the plurality of the world to the duality of the vigilant dialogue between me and myself. The difference, otherness, and plurality which characterize the natural world are actualized in thinking, and "only in this humanized form," says Arendt, "does consciousness then become the outstanding characteristic of somebody who is a man and neither a god nor an animal."[30] Vigilance attunes us to difference, otherness, and plurality, not so as to destroy what we presently affirm but rather to assure that our affirmation is able to "do justice to the phenomenon." Such justice may require one to see beyond the affirmation, to see possible or essential otherness. Plurality is not merely a condition for the existence of things; it is a condition for the existence of consciousness.[31] Vigilance and thinking necessarily involve some degree of struggle, for in "being-conscious-of-myself, I am inevitably two-in-one."[32] Vigilance actualizes the difference, the plurality, given in consciousness. Humanism is the recognition and appreciation that I am—we all are—"two-in-one." Without this split between me and myself—the dialogue of myself with myself—I would never experience the tension or insufficiency which leads me to new possibilities of meaning, to "values yet unknown," to vigilance.

Although it is rather late in this analysis to introduce a distinction fundamental to an understanding of vigilance, it is one which could only be made after the basic outline of vigilance was presented. Arendt's discussion of thinking prompts the obvious question: how is vigilance different than "open-mindedness"? To have an "open mind" would seem identical to vigilance so far as both states are concerned with what is absent from my consciousness. In a fine book on the subject (one of the very few on the subject), William Hare says that "a person who is open-minded is disposed to revise or reject the position he holds if sound objections are brought against it, or, in the situation in which the person presently has no opinion on some issue, he is disposed to make up his mind in the light of available evidence and argument as objectively and as impartially as possible."[33] My mind is open to the degree that it is disposed to be corrected or changed by reasons, objections, and counterarguments absent from its current consideration. Further, this capability may be an enduring capability, a disposition to continue including more reasons, objections, and so on. Hare makes a helpful distinction between a willingness to "look at" objections and a willingness to "look for" objections.[34] The open-minded person does not wait for objections to his or her viewpoint (objections being signs of absence), but rather seeks out objections, seeks out what is absent. Is vigilance simply a fancy word for open-mindedness?

The phenomena open-mindedness attends to are matters of evidence and belief, of conceptual schemes, of reasons and arguments. In other words, open-mindedness is the vigilance of the knowing subject, the way in which we take heed of our epistemological habits. Open-mindedness is aimed at getting better reasons, better justifications, greater impartiality; vigilance includes such efforts to "do justice to the phenomenon" but does not stop with them. Vigilance looks to all the sorts of habits we are, not merely to the ideas we have. A sunset, a recurring anxiety, a melody from a Haydn quartet, a two-year-old's hands occasion vigilance, not open-mindedness. I seek to presence these phenomena not through absent contexts of objections and counterarguments, but rather through absent images, moods, feelings, attitudes, memories, reveries, musings, sensibilities, impressions, and so on. Through vigilance we rein in the inventive nature of habit and relax its more conservative nature. Vigilance focuses difference and otherness in consciousness, but not all differences and othernesses appear to consciousness as beliefs, arguments, and good reasons. In short, open-mindedness is a specialization of vigilance, the means whereby we render strange our epistemological habits of mind. Open-mindedness may even borrow some of the wonder-evoking power of vigilance, transforming what we know and our relationship to what we know. Open-mindedness cannot, however, supplant the more encompassing work of vigilance.

Thus, whereas open-mindedness commonly results in, or at least is a prelude to, fuller knowledge, the interrogations of vigilance and Arendt's "thinking" are "resultless" by comparison. Yet vigilance focuses the difference and plurality given in consciousness, and through it "a difference is inserted into my Oneness." These apparently "resultless" accomplishments of vigilance have a most startling result: through vigilance we can perhaps more deliberately "usher" into the world "values yet unknown" by seeking to "do justice to the phenomenon." Such "justice" is inseparable from the possibility of *other* perspectives and the necessity to seek them. Thus, it will not do to disparage the importance of vigilance by smug acknowledgment that "of course there are other perspectives, values, and habits of mind; but, this should not hinder investigation into this perspective." Indeed it should not: favored perspectives and habits of mind, intellectual, commonsense, aesthetic, religious, and moral ones, should be pressed and pursued not in a hesitant and limping manner, but with conviction and determination. We should not seek to be corrected too soon. Yet if we are truly heedful of the one-sidedness of our perspectives, if I truly respect difference and plurality, if I have cultivated a "readiness" for a possible defeat of my perspective, then the "two-in-one" which I am will focus and honor this otherness. We will come to sense with William James the extent to which otherness infects our lives and commitments: "Our mind is so wedded to the process of seeing an *other* beside every item of its experience, that when the notion of an absolute datum is presented to it, it goes through its usual procedure and remains pointing at the void beyond, as if in that lay further matter for contemplation."[35] Perhaps because the insistence of the "other" is so great, we base estimates of our intellectual sophistication on our ability to exclude it: "Of course I know there are other perspectives, but . . ." James's view of intellectual maturity was quite different than this one, for he deeply believed that "in reflecting men it is just when the attempt to fuse the manifold into a single totality has been most successful, when the conception of the universe as a unique fact is nearest its perfection, that the craving for further explanation, the ontological wonder-sickness, arises in its extremest form."[36] It is this "ontological wonder-sickness" in the form of vigilance which I believe forms the purest meaning of humanism and which is the most compelling basis for any effort to restore meaning to the concept of humanism.

What solicits our vigilance, our "ontological wonder-sickness," is the pluralism of existence, its resistance to inclusion in what James calls "all the great single-word answers to the world's riddle, such as God, the One, Reason, Law, Spirit, Matter, Nature, Polarity, the Dialectic Process, the Idea, the Self, the Oversoul."[37] If we wish to restore meaning to the word humanism, we might consider abandoning the attempt to unify and authorize our "oughts" under the name of a commitment to "humanistic values" and "principles." With James, we will

> confess that when all things have been unified to the supreme degree, the notion of a possible other than the actual may still haunt our imagination and prey upon our system. The bottom of being is left logically opaque to us, as something which we simply come upon and find, and about which (if we wish to act) we should pause and wonder as little as possible.[38]

Fortunately, many do wonder and in this wonder is the excellence to which humanism refers. A "possible" haunts our imagination and preys upon our commitment, and unsure whether we have come to the "bottom of being," our habits tense and we are vigilant.

· CHAPTER 5 ·

The Rationality of Conduct: Dewey and Oakeshott

Vigilance keeps watch over the mind, reminds us what to keep in mind. In this respect, it might be said to make up the mind by keeping what is relevant and important before it. Vigilance does not, however, choose or decide. For this, deliberation is required. The general topic of this chapter concerns the rationality of conduct, or more precisely, the rationality of deliberated conduct, conduct that is the outcome of reflective consideration of alternate courses of action. This topic organizes itself into two questions. First, how is reason present in deliberation? Second, what should deliberative reason accomplish? I want to characterize the views of reason found in the theories of deliberation of Michael Oakeshott and John Dewey. Reason sees but often is not and cannot be seen. It prevents blindness but itself may not be explicit or visible. Why this invisibility of reason? For Oakeshott and Dewey, the answer to this question is that deliberation is the reciprocal adjustment of habits and imagined outcomes. This adjustment can be made only partially explicit and visible because habits of mind are only partially formulable into propositions, rules, or principles. Oakeshott and Dewey reject the idea of deliberation as the self-conscious following of explicitly formulated rules. Instead of rule, principle, or proposition being the distinctive voice of reason, both philosophers substitute habit of mind as the source of reason's guidance. They would agree, I think, on what distinguishes deliberative reason from demonstrative, deductive, or calculative reason. Deliberative reason must maintain a phenomenological, and not merely logical, continuity with habitual meanings, that is, the prereflective, tacit, implicit structurings of meaning characteristic of everyday, practical life. In short, deliberation arises out of a life-world layered with visibilities and invisibilities, layered with objectivities and fleetingly glimpsed intimations of transcendence.

What does reason do in such circumstances? How is reason efficacious even when its presence is not announced or declared? I outline an answer to these questions based on the perspectives of Oakeshott and Dewey.

To be sure that the question motivating my analysis is clear, consider this from Oakeshott: "Everywhere we come back to the conclusion that concrete activity is knowing how to act; and that if 'rationality' is to be properly attributed to conduct, it must be a quality of the conduct itself."[1] What does it mean for rationality to be "a quality of the conduct itself"? The "quality" Oakeshott stipulates sounds quite accessible, discoverable, hence determinable. After all, it is in the "conduct *itself*." But the "itself" is not, I think, intended to focus our attention on something that is there for the seeing and telling. Practice may be aimed at what is modifiable, determinable, and in some sense, tangible, yet reason is not for Oakeshott itself determinably present, at least not in the form of premeditated rules, principles, and propositions. These are what he terms "abridgements" of, abstractions from, our conduct. Ultimately, the "quality of conduct itself" becomes for Oakeshott what he calls "a flow of sympathy, a current of moral activity."[2] I think Dewey is in substantial agreement with this idea, but his agreement eventually leads to a fundamental difference between himself and Oakeshott. Both philosophers are suspicious of a rule or principle that, as Oakeshott says, "comes from outside the activity,"[3] that is, outside the "flow of sympathy." For both philosophers, circumstance or context is important: reason's activities—its frustrations and its satisfactions—are activities which occur in a context. However, for Dewey context points to transcendence; for Oakeshott, it reinforces immanence. For Dewey, habits and reason's habits can be cultivated in such a way that we strive to surpass or exceed what we take to be our capacities or powers; that is, we grow by perfecting, by striving to transcend, our present level of responsiveness, imagination, rational power. For Oakeshott, the aim of a habit-grounded world is quite different: "It is to be equal to one's own fortune, to live at the level of one's own means, to be content with the want of greater perfection which belongs alike to oneself and one's circumstances."[4] So my central questions for this chapter return: how is reason present in deliberation and to what does it aspire?

This chapter has two sections. In the first, I consider a few of the central features of Oakeshott's theory of deliberation. In the second section, I present a very condensed version of Dewey's theory of deliberation against the background of Oakeshott's views.

I

Oakeshott presents in section 2 of "Rational Conduct" two accounts of the view of reason and deliberation that he wishes to criticize. A close look at the initial formulation of his target will provide a suitable starting point for drawing out the central and recurrent issues in his position:

> The view we are to consider takes purpose as the distinctive mark of "rationality" in conduct: "rational" activity is behaviour in which an independently premeditated end is pursued and which is determined solely by that end. This end may be an external result to be achieved, or it may be the enjoyment of the activity itself. To play a game in order to win (and perhaps to win a prize), and to play it for its own sake, for the enjoyment of it, are both purposive activities. Further, "rational" conduct is behaviour *deliberately* directed to the achievement of a *formulated* purpose and is governed solely by that purpose.[5]

Naturally, Oakeshott is not objecting to having purposes and ends or to the rational adoption of ends. He is objecting here, and in many other places, to what he variously calls premeditated ends, predetermined ends, preestablished ends.[6] On the view that Oakeshott is attempting to criticize, to be rational is to pursue an explicitly held or known end that governs the pursuing in an explicit, determinable manner. To be rational is to give an account of where one is headed, of what one is aiming to do. Most important, the account can be held accountable, can be put to the test through argument and dialectic. Thus, it is not merely to have a purpose, it is to have a formulation which can be defended and criticized. It is reason making an announcement or declaration of its intentions. Reason unannounced is not fully reason.

But rational conduct is not only this. Premeditated ends require explicit, premeditated means. Oakeshott says "there will be in 'rational' conduct not only a premeditated purpose to be achieved, but also a separately premeditated selection of the means to be employed."[7] If conduct is to actualize what already exists in thought, the predetermined ends of conduct must be served by predetermined means. A sloppy and imprecise means may tarnish an otherwise perfectly good end.

The above description of how Oakeshott does *not* believe reason appears in deliberation may seem a bit sketchy, so it might be well to provide some amplification of it. He says:

> The calculated choice of end and means both involves and provides a resistance to the indiscriminate flow of circumstances. One step at a time

is the rule here; and each step is taken in ignorance of what the next step is to be. The "rationality" of conduct, then, on this view of it, springs from something that we do *before* we act: and activity is "rational" on account of its being generated in a certain manner.[8]

Oakeshott is clearing the way for a view of rationality and deliberation that does not spring from something we do "before" we act, something prior and external to the act. While it makes the voice or light of reason much easier to identify if it is set off from the act, Oakeshott simply rejects this interpretation of reason's presence in deliberation.

Oakeshott's position is phenomenologically quite convincing. Robert Sokolowski, in his book *Moral Action: A Phenomenological Study*, says that "the core of the being of the moral act is not something that comes before or something that comes after, but the performance itself. The befores and the afters, the anticipations and the consequences, are derivative upon the activity itself."[9] I shall look at Sokolowski's analysis of moral action in more detail later in this chapter, but this brief passage serves to underline an essential claim in Oakeshott. My deliberation and the conduct accompanying it are not advertisements for a rule or a principle. Oakeshott would concur with Sokolowski's point that it is a mistake to think that deliberated conduct "publicizes what has already been achieved in privacy and inwardness."[10] In short, for both Oakeshott and Sokolowski, reason's presence in conduct is implicit and indirect; it is unpublicized.

Oakeshott repeats a number of times his contention that ends are determined in the course of an activity, not prior or antecedent to it. With each repetition, it becomes increasingly clear that he is abandoning the search for a privileged starting point for deliberation, a "before," so to speak, that shall all but guarantee the "after":

> It is an error to call an activity "rational" on account of its end having been specifically determined in advance and in respect of its achieving that end to the exclusion of all others, because there is no way of determining an end for activity in advance of the activity itself; and if there were, the spring of activity would still remain in knowing how to act in pursuit of that end and not in the mere fact of having formulated an end to pursue.[11]

At the risk of getting ahead of myself, I should like to note that this is virtually a summary statement of at least one aspect of Dewey's pragmatism. In the activity, the situation, the circumstance, the context, ends suggest themselves. Ends are, in Oakeshott's language, intimated; in Dewey's language, sensed. What we conserve from the past and use in the specification of the present situation are not previous aims or ends, uncut and unedited. Such memories can take us only so far into the present situation. The aims and ends of conduct in the present situation are of *this* time, not *that* time. This time may be like that time, but such a fact, and the determination that it is a fact, is a discovery of deliberation, not a premise.

Let us, then, suppose with Oakeshott that "there is in fact no way of determining an end for activity in advance of the activity itself." If deliberation is reflection in the service of action, reflection concerned with the choice and performance of actions, what ties the act of deliberation together, internally? Phrased slightly differently, what, precisely, is deliberation deliberating? Oakeshott says that

> what falls to be deliberated are alternative concrete performances, actions or utterances each of which is distinguished by a "meaning," a purposed outcome, exclusively its own. And deliberating cannot be (what it is often said to be) considering alternative means for achieving an independently premeditated end with a view to discovering the best, easiest, the most effective, etc., way of achieving it.[12]

What we deliberate are meanings, or more precisely, act-meanings or utterance-meanings. Deliberation seeks to determine what enacted or spoken meaning is called for here, in this situation. What meaning does justice to this circumstance, this context? Oakeshott's description of the meaning situation for the deliberator is, considered phenomenologically, fairly elementary, but its point is clear. As meanings are proposed with which to respond to the deliberative situation, provisional, tentative, possible outcomes or ends are imagined. In other words, as the meaning situation is *defined*, it is *refined*, and eventually it is *confined*. Some meanings are compelling and enlightening, others obscuring and what Oakeshott calls "clogging." Some meanings endure, some do not, and Oakeshott never tires of reminding us that the survivors are not the result of calculation or of demonstrative reasoning. Why some meanings survive and others do not is, of course, the central question for Oakeshott's theory of deliberation and for *any* theory of deliberation. Before considering his answer to the survival question, two points require further attention.

The alternative courses of action available to a deliberator are not given or fixed. Oakeshott says that the person deliberating is not in the position of a chess player "who has to choose between a fixed number of alternative moves. The alternative actions he has to consider are his own inventions, and deliberating is not merely reflecting in order to choose, it is also imagining alternatives between which to choose." Put somewhat differently, the person who deliberates is a creator and inventor. The number of meaning possibilities available to a deliberator as responses to a situation are, Oakeshott says, "limited only by the virtuosity of his imagination."[13] But are there no constraints on imagination and the alternatives it invents? Of course there are. The imagined alternatives are alternatives to *this* concrete situation. The situation applies pressure to our imagination and our imagination responds. Clearly, though, this is far from an adequate answer. Imagination may be responsible to the particulars of this situation, but what does that ultimately come to? We shall see that Dewey has something important to offer in connection with this issue, but if he is to have any relevance here, he shall have to be able to take account of a rather demanding theoretical specification of Oakeshott: of the unlimited number of alternatives able to be imagined by the deliberator, none, Oakeshott says, "may be deduced from the situation to be responded to."[14] The imagined meaning, in the form of an end or what Oakeshott calls a "wished-for outcome," must be a specification of this situation, but it cannot be deduced from this situation.

The second point I wish to make about ends in Oakeshott concerns the resources available to the deliberator in taking aim or imagining ends. Oakeshott says that "the materials at the disposal of an agent are beliefs about his own capacity to act, opinions about the world of *pragmata* he inhabits, expectations about the response a projected action is likely to meet with, about the incidental satisfactions it may bring with it, and about the likely cost in terms of satisfactions foregone or imperfectly enjoyed or dissatisfactions incidentally to be suffered." One is struck less by what is included in this picture of the deliberator, and more by what is left out. Where is reason's strongest announcement; that is, where is a truth or standard which can measure and is commensurate with the intimations of meaning produced by imagination? Oakeshott has not forgotten them, nor has he included them under another description: he simply has excluded them. Referring to the "materials" at the disposal of the deliberator, Oakeshott says:

> They may be more or they may be less reliable, but they are not flickering shadows of necessary truths or premises from which conclusions can be deduced. They are aids to reflection, guesses of varying generality, made with different degrees of confidence and drawing upon evidence of varying quality, which, in deliberation, are not subjected to the test of a criterion superior to themselves but are made to criticize and illuminate one another.[15]

Oakeshott is saying here that deliberation is not an argument or an account. Choice is not the reward of an argument. While it always *seems* perfectly appropriate to ask a person deliberating, "What are your reasons for believing that," Oakeshott has serious doubts whether the intellectual authority of such reasons derives from what they offer in the way of "flickering shadows of necessary truths." The rationality of deliberation for Oakeshott is not quite equivalent to an Aristotelian accommodation of the universal and particular effected through *phronesis* (though it is very similar), and it is not quite a Kantian accommodation of a principle and a case effected through judgment (though again it is very similar). For Oakeshott, the working tools of the deliberator cannot be "subjected to the test of a criterion superior to themselves but are made to criticize and illuminate one another." The process of deliberation is guided and regulated from within, illuminated from within. How, though, can such a seemingly circular and self-enclosed process result in anything other than blindness, self-deception, weakness of will? On what basis does deliberative reason narrow the field of relevant meanings, differentiating the poorest from the better, the better from the highest good? In short, on what basis do meanings survive for Oakeshott?

Oakeshott generally supplies his answer to this question in such condensed formulations that on first reading they may appear somewhat unsatisfactory. But in their essentials, they may be satisfactory. If rationality is a quality of the conduct itself, then what is this quality? Oakeshott says that it is

> *faithfulness to the knowledge we have of how to conduct the specific activity we are engaged in*. "Rational" conduct is acting in such a way that the coherence of the idiom of activity to which the conduct belongs is preserved and possibly enhanced. This, of course, is something different from faithfulness to the principles or rules or purposes (if any have been discovered) of the activity; principles, rules and purposes are mere abridgments of the coherence of the activity, and we may easily be faithful to them while losing touch with the activity itself.[16]

The knowledge Oakeshott is talking about here is very similar to the tacit knowledge described by Michael Polanyi, the life-worldly knowledge of the natural attitude described by Husserl, as well as the embodied knowledge in Merleau-Ponty's analyses of the prereflective intentionality of habitual meaning. The coherence of our conduct does not necessarily derive from an explicitly held rule, principle, or idea. Our conduct does not deflate like a balloon if explicit, self-consciously held principles escape from it. Conduct, as well as the "idiom of activity" to which it belongs, is coherent before, during, and after a reflective appeal to rule or principle because meaningful conduct is constituted and retained prereflectively in lived experience, in lived, *habitual* experience.

Oakeshott appears to reach what might be called his phenomenological bedrock in a formulation that sounds remarkably similar to William James's stream of thought. Oakeshott says that "no action is by itself 'rational,' or is 'rational' on account of something that has gone on before; what makes it 'rational' is its place in a flow of sympathy, a current of moral activity."[17] The "flow of sympathy" is, I propose, Husserlian lived experience, and what Oakeshott wishes to say about this "flow of sympathy" is that it is intentional, it can pronounce worth. As intentional, this flow or current does not wait for a principle to tell it what can be approved and what must be disapproved, what will survive in the flow, current, or stream and what will not. Oakeshott says that "this approval and disapproval does not spring from these principles or from knowledge of them. They are merely abridgements, abstract definitions, of the coherence which approvals and disapprovals themselves exhibit."[18] Deliberation may bring to light unseen or unnoticed aspects of my habitual, prereflective approvals and disapprovals. It does not, however, create approvals and disapprovals or impose upon a passive subject a structure of meaning which was either nonexistent prior to deliberation or inherently flawed. The "flow of sympathy," in short, is not blind; on the contrary, through it we see and understand even when we are not undertaking what Oakeshott calls "an express investigation of the situation to be responded to."[19]

Needless to say, Oakeshott's rejection of rule was a bit of bad news for Wittgensteinians like Peter Winch. Where Oakeshott uses habit, Winch prefers rule. In the chapter titled "The Nature of Meaningful Behavior" in his well-known work *The Idea of a Social Science,* Winch remarks that "Oakeshott appears to think that the dividing line between behaviour which is habitual and that which is rule-governed depends on whether or not a rule is *consciously* applied." Winch opposes this:

> I want to say that the test of whether a man's actions are the application of a rule is not whether he can *formulate* it but whether it makes sense to distinguish between a right and wrong way of doing things in connection with what he does. Where that makes sense, then it must also make sense to say that he is applying a criterion in what he does even though he does not, and perhaps cannot, formulate that criterion.[20]

Winch's criticism loses much of its force by virtue of its ambiguity. Oakeshott does not reject criteria; he rejects, remember, a criterion "superior" to the working ingredients, the intentional ingredients, of a deliberation. A rule or principle may be invited in, may function as a working ingredient in an act of deliberation, but that rule is itself put into question, is itself interrogated. I think this is the meaning of the following remarks of Oakeshott taken from his rather well known response to D. D. Raphael's review of *Rationalism in Politics*:

> I have no horror of principles—only a suspicion of those who use principles as if they were axioms and those who seem to think that practical argument is concerned with proof. A principle is not something which may be given as a reason for making a decision or performing an action; it is a short-hand identification of a disposition to choose.[21]

From Oakeshott's standpoint, to apply a criterion or principle in the way envisioned by Winch is to apply an axiom. Oakeshott does not think in terms of axioms. For him, a principle is an aid to reflection, an instrument to help us maintain a vigilant watch over the "flow of sympathy."

I think Winch's strongest criticism of Oakeshott, one which actually hints at Dewey's position, concerns the place of reflectiveness in managing change or novelty:

> Whereas Oakeshott maintains that the sort of change and adaptability of which he here speaks occurs independently of any reflective principles, I want to say that *the possibility* of reflection is essential to that kind of adaptability. Without this possibility we are dealing not with meaningful behavior but with something which is either mere response to stimuli or the manifestation of a habit which is really blind. I do not mean by this that meaningful behaviour is simply a putting into effect of pre-existing reflective principles; such principles arise in the course of conduct and are only intelligible in relation to the conduct out of which they arise. But equally, the nature of the conduct out of which they arise can only be grasped as an embodiment of those principles. The notion of a principle (or maxim) of conduct and the notion of meaningful action are *interwoven*, in much the same way as Wittgenstein spoke of the notion of a rule and the notion of "the same" being interwoven.[22]

Winch concedes that principles are not preexisting but rather "arise in the course of conduct." Further, he agrees that the sense or intelligibility of these principles derives from the action context within which they arose. But these concessions require Oakeshott to make one of his own. He must concede that these contextually determined rules are the source of the conduct's intelligibility. Oakeshott will not make this concession. The reflective embodiment of the lived experience is, as he says repeatedly, an abridgement of that experience, an abstraction from it. Oakeshott does not expect reflection to somehow duplicate lived experience. I do think, however, that he expects reflection to be an articulation of the lived. In Oakeshott's view, the rule to which we turn for clarification must be, if it is not to lose touch with the activity, faithful to the activity, not faithful to the rule. In other words, whatever light a rule or principle may throw, is a reflected light. In deliberation, it is a light interwoven with obscurity, uncertainty, and contingency.

In the context of Winch's criticisms of Oakeshott, it is easy to see how one might believe that Oakeshott is very close to saying that reflective consciousness, theoretical consciousness, is false consciousness. (This, incidentally, is reminiscent of the usual criticisms made of Dewey's pragmatism, namely, that it is "antitheoretical" or "antiteleological.")[23] I do not believe that this is a convincing interpretation of Oakeshott, though there certainly is a basis for proposing it. Oakeshott's basic contention, I believe, is that conduct is not an advertisement for a principle or a rule; it is no more "about" a principle or rule than a poem is "about" its title. This position does not commit him to the view that reflective awareness of rules and principles is false or inauthentic. It does commit him to the view that "principles are derived from the activity and not the activity from the principles."[24] Clearly, Oakeshott detaches or unweaves what Winch sees as interwoven. Principles may indeed illuminate experience, but they must be prompted by, suggested by, the experience, the idiom, the "flow of sympathy." Without such contextual intimations of meaning, we lose touch with "the activity itself."

These Oakeshottian phrases—"flow of sympathy" and "the activity itself"—sound more and more like Husserl's *die Sache Selbst*. But they also should cause us to think of the following two propositions from Wittgenstein in *On Certainty*:

> 94. But I did not get my picture of the world by satisfying myself of its correctness; nor do I have it because I am satisfied of its correctness. No: it is the inherited background against which I distinguish between true and false.
>
> 95. The propositions describing this world-picture might be part of a kind of mythology. And their role is like that of rules of a game; and the game can be learned purely practically, without learning any explicit [*ausgesprochene*] rules.[25]

A good part of the richness and elusiveness of Oakeshott's theory of deliberation is the reversal it effects. Because deliberation is concerned with choice among alternate courses of action, it is often supposed—by the philosopher and nonphilosopher—that reason is as tangibly present in deliberation as the deliberated action is tangibly there before our very eyes.

Oakeshott reverses this assumption. The explicit is not merely rooted in the implicit, in what Wittgenstein calls the "inherited background." What deliberative reason achieves, what it gains, are more like intimations than declarations.

I now turn to a very brief consideration of Dewey in order to gain a fuller understanding of how reason intimates as well as declares.

II

The basis of Dewey's theory of deliberation can be found in the 1902 essay "Interpretation of the Savage Mind":

> In conclusion, let me point out that the adjustment of habits to ends, through the medium of a problematic, doubtful, precarious situation, is the structural form upon which present intelligence and emotion are built. It remains the ground-pattern.... We have not so much destroyed or left behind the hunting structural arrangement of mind, as we have set free it constitutive psycho-physic factors so as to make them available and interesting in all kinds of objective and idealized pursuits—the hunt for truth, beauty, virtue, wealth, social well-being, and even of heaven and of God.[26]

Whether called custom, tradition, practice, common sense, form of life, or life-world, our habit-constituted everyday world is the background out of which the discriminations and distinctions of reflective life have their beginning. In Dewey's view, the everyday world of prehistoric man and the everyday world of modern man is at once a taken-for-granted world and a world shot through with the precarious and the dramatic. It is this precarious and stable world that is enlarged and enriched through the "idealized pursuits" of the "hunt for truth, beauty, virtue, wealth, social well-being, and even of heaven and of God." More simply, we could say that deliberation is shaped by the "ground pattern" of the dramatic habit of mind. Deliberation is, as Oakeshott calls it, an adventure. As we shall see shortly, it is an adventure or drama in which, contrary to Oakeshott, a regulative ideal makes its presence felt, though, in agreement with Oakeshott, more as an intimation than an argument.

As an aside, one might say that the postmodern condition abbreviates or truncates this equation: everything is precarious, tentative, mobile. Nothing can be, or should be, stable, taken for granted, held up, or held over. Loyalties are suspect. Custom is dogma. Everything is, or should be, in suspense, suspended, dramatic. One might say that certain versions of postmodernism suppress habit in the hope of freeing thought from a ground, a standpoint, a perspective. Dewey has no such interest in groundless thought or subjectless thought. He inquires into habit as visible and invisible in order to grasp the contingency of meaning . . . and the lastingness of meaning. "Idealized pursuits" can have no weight, no depth, no compulsion, no drama, no staking of self, without the intersection of the precarious and the stable.[27]

Let us return to the matter of deliberation. The thesis that is implicit and relatively undeveloped in "Interpretation of the Savage Mind" is made explicit in the 1905 essay "The Postulate of Immediate Empiricism": the experience of meaning is not equivalent to knowledge; being and being known are not equivalent. This is one of the central theses of Dewey's philosophy of experience, and it had a profound influence on the theory of deliberation that he developed for the next thirty years. He says:

> Now, this statement that things are what they are experienced to be is usually translated into the statement that things (or, ultimately, Reality, Being) *are* only and just what they are *known* to be or that things are, or Reality *is*, what it is for a conscious knower—whether the knower be conceived primarily as a perceiver or as thinker being a further, and secondary question. . . . By our postulate, things are what they are experienced to be; and unless knowing is the sole and only genuine mode of experiencing, it is fallacious to say that Reality is just and exclusively what it is or would be to an all-competent all-knower; or even that it *is*, relatively and piecemeal, what it is to a finite and partial knower. Or, put more positively, knowing is one mode of experiencing, and the primary philosophic demand (from the standpoint of immediatism) is to find out *what* sort of an experience knowing is—or, concretely how things are experienced when they are experienced *as* known things.[28]

It is here, in lived experience, that Dewey wishes to commence his inquiry into the nature of deliberation and reason's presence in it. I believe this is precisely the same move that Oakeshott makes in grounding deliberative activity in what he calls an idiom or tradition. If one is not careful, though, it is possible to mistakenly see Dewey and Oakeshott as opposed to each other here. Oakeshott advances "knowing how" to go about something as the basis of deliberation while Dewey rejects the idea that all experiencing is a mode of knowing. This clearly is a difference in formulation, not a difference in substance or intent. Both philosophers are concerned to establish a conception of reason that does not permit the undeclared achievements of reason to be construed as incidental to what can be announced and argued.

It is an interesting question—one I do not pursue here—whether Dewey in this essay comes closer to Husserl in such works as the *Crisis* and *Experience and Judgment* or to Heidegger in division 1 of *Being and Time*. Whatever the case, Dewey inquires into the constitution of the objects of experience as these are specified or made determinate through the ideas we have and the habits we are. To a surprisingly large extent, his theory of deliberation is heavily dependent on his theory of the qualitative immediacy: "By these words I want to indicate the absolute, final irreducible, and inexpugnable concrete *quale* which everything experienced not so much *has* as *is*. To grasp this aspect of empiricism is to see what the empiricist means by objectivity, by the element of control."[29] Knowing extends and deepens the objectivity and control in qualitative experience, but knowing is not the origin of such experience. Qualitative meanings are not blind feeling states which await the arrival of idea and judgment in order to attain cognitive significance; they are not as Dewey says of the achievements of the dramatic habit of mind, "merely sensuous indulgences." Qualitative understandings are intentional, and not intentional in a simple way, that is, as sources of liking, disliking, pleasure, pain. Qualitative understandings, appreciations, discern and pronounce worth.

How, then, are things experienced when they are deliberated? How is reason present in deliberation for Dewey? I should like to focus my remaining comments concerning Dewey on just one paragraph in the 1932 edition of *Theory of the Moral Life*. Dewey says:

> We estimate the import or significance of any present desire or impulse by forecasting what it will come or amount to if carried out; literally its consequences define its *consequence*, its meaning or import. But if these consequences are conceived *merely as remote*, if their picturing does not arouse a present sense of peace, of fulfillment, or of dissatisfaction, of incompletion and irritation, the process of thinking out consequences remains purely intellectual. It is as barren of influence upon behavior as the mathematical speculations of a disembodied angel. Any actual experience of reflection upon conduct will show that every foreseen result at once stirs our present affections, our likes and dislikes, our desires and aversions. There is developed a running commentary which stamps objects at once as good or evil. It is this *direct sense of value, not the consciousness of general rules or ultimate goals*, which finally determines the worth of the act to the agent. Here is an inexpugnable element of truth in the intuitional theory. Its error lies in conceiving this *immediate response of appreciation* as if it excluded reflection instead of following

> directly upon its heels. Deliberation is actually an *imaginative rehearsal* of various courses of conduct. We give way, *in our mind*, to some impulse; we try, *in our mind*, some plan. Following its career through various steps, we find ourselves in imagination in the presence of consequences that would follow, and as we then like and approve, or dislike and disapprove, these consequences, we find the original impulse or plan good or bad. *Deliberation is dramatic and active*, not mathematical and impersonal; and hence it has the intuitive, the direct factor in it. . . . *Many and varied direct sensings, appreciations, take place.* When many tendencies are brought into play, there is clearly much greater probability that the capacity of self which is really needed and appropriate will be brought into action, and thus a truly reasonable happiness result. The tendency of deliberation to "polarize" the various lines of activity into opposed alternatives, into incompatible "either this or that," is a way of forcing into clear recognition the importance of the issue.[30]

Failure to respect the continuity of the sensitive and the reflective has a predictable result: the dramatic is displaced by the engineered; judgment is replaced by rule. Such rationalistic abbreviations of what Dewey calls dramatic or imaginative rehearsal, and of what Oakeshott calls a "flow of sympathy," make them a mere prelude to the real deliberative work of evaluating and justifying, of arguing and accounting. But this is not how Dewey or Oakeshott sees deliberation. When Dewey says moral deliberation is dramatic, he means that in deliberation—in the play of appreciation and appraisal—perception and principle test each other and in various senses of "try," they try each other. The testing and trying occur within the "flow of sympathy," not in a cognitive stance external to it or another flow adjacent to it.

The agreement of Oakeshott and Dewey on the importance of this "flow of sympathy" sheds considerable light on their respective ethical theories. It also helps to call into question the calculative, criterial views of rationality which are often attributed to Dewey. For example, Jennifer Welchman believes that dramatic rehearsal is fine for description and discovery, but inadequate for evaluation. It cannot be Dewey's entire moral theory, for when habituated evaluations or appraisals falter or conflict, something else must be brought in, and explicitly brought in, that is, "rational criteria of evaluation." As Welchman argues in *Dewey's Ethical Thought*:

> When at the conclusion of a dramatic rehearsal of the opportunities of action open to us we have perceived which possibilities are good, a decision about what goods to pursue still has to be made. This judgment is

not immediate. Thus "dramatic rehearsal," as Dewey describes it, is not a method of making moral judgments. Dramatic rehearsal is a method of *gaining information necessary for moral judgment.* Moral judgment takes place when the incompatible goods giving conflicting reasons for action are evaluated in terms of the principles discussed above.[31]

So, while reason was at work in its appreciations, it was not yet evaluative, critical, judgmental. It found its way to some good possibilities, but no further, not to the goods which withstand testing in light of principles. It is considerably more convincing to say that for Dewey the context or background of qualitatively appreciated meanings, Oakshott's "flow of sympathy," is continuous with, not antecedent to, the dramatic situation and its rehearsal.

It is slightly odd how undramatic "dramatic rehearsal" sounds, compared to the evocative and subtly dramatic "flow of sympathy." Nonetheless, both theories of deliberation converge at the point of action and conduct. The doing is constitutive or creative of meaning, and because it is, it is dramatic. However, action should not be construed as if it were simply giving tangible expression to a ready-made, but intangible meaning. Consider this from Oakeshott:

> It may be said that in "doing" an agent casts off a mooring. He may be seeking a satisfaction, but what he *chooses* is an action; that is, the adventure of aiming at an imagined satisfaction. Hence the saying of Democritus that courage is the beginning of action: courage to put out to sea.[32]

The aiming as acting is constitutive of meaning. But the meaning does not have a terminus defined and delimited by *the* goal or the end-in-view. Also, the meaning does not originate in the sort of principled appraisal proposed by Welchman. As we saw earlier, intentional acts can intend meanings which expand or enlarge beyond the boundaries of their initial instigation or motivation. We do not "put out to sea" in order to navigate, but neither is the adventure of being at sea possible without navigation. Oakeshott expands the casting off and putting out to sea analogies. These are, I think, phenomenologically evocative, if not precise:

> Acting is making a bargain with an imperfectly imagined future. Choosing an action is an agent settling for a performance with which to put out to sea. And deliberating a choice is reflecting upon the only considerations capable of being deliberated; namely, the likelihood of uncertainties.[33]

Finally, what guides the performance, by what north star do we navigate? Oakeshott says: "Moral prescriptive principles and rules are not criteria of good conduct, nor are they primarily instruments of judgment; they are prevailing winds which agents should take account of in sailing their several courses."[34] In short, we put out to an uncertain world with less than certain resources. The metaphor may be a bit extravagant, but the point requires something grand or extravagant. Reason's contribution to action and practice, particularly moral action and practice, is not visible, argumentative, criterial. The "adventure of aiming" in moral action and choice is not corrupted or degraded by its acceptance that "neither changelessness nor perfection is a necessary condition of authority."[35] In other words, our intimations of what is needed, of what is good, do not require a mooring beyond experience.

Dewey is in almost full agreement with Oakeshott, even to the point of using the sea and wind analogy:

> What then is choice? Simply hitting in imagination upon an object which furnishes an adequate stimulus to the recovery of overt action. Choice is made as soon as some habit, or some combination of elements of habits and impulse, finds a way fully open. Then energy is released. The mind is made up, composed, unified. As long as deliberation pictures shoals or rocks or troublesome gales as marking the route of a contemplated voyage, deliberation goes on. But when the various factors in action fit harmoniously together, when imagination finds no annoying hindrance, when there is a picture of open seas, filled sails and favoring winds, the voyage is definitely entered upon. This decisive direction of action constitutes choice.[36]

This sounds a little more decisive than Oakeshott, a little more oriented to, or directed by, ends. But the ends are virtually identical to Oakeshott's; that is, they are internal or interior to the practice and hence their authority is interior to the practice:

> Ends arise and function within action. They are not, as current theories too often imply, things lying beyond activity at which the latter is directed. They are not strictly speaking ends or termini of action at all. They are terminals of deliberation, and so turning points *in* activity.[37]

Given the interiority of the ends, that is, of what we envision as an ideal outcome or highest good, one might think that they can be viewed with considerable clarity. The greater clarity might even contribute to a greater sense of certainty. Dewey denies this, at least the prospects for greater certainty:

Love of certainty is a demand for guarantees in advance of action. Ignoring the fact that truth can be bought only by the adventure of experiment, dogmatism turns truth into an insurance company. Fixed ends upon one side and fixed "principles"—that is authoritative rules—on the other, are props for a feeling of safety, the refuge of the timid and the means by which the bold prey upon the timid.[38]

Achieving coherence in the moral situation does not depend upon an early importation of impasse-breaking and conflict-resolving ideals, principles, or maxims. What we have "in advance of action" is an "adventure of experiment," what Oakeshott calls the "adventure of aiming."

Before noting a telling and consequential difference between Dewey and Oakeshott, let us be sure about the phenomenology involved in these accounts of adventure. Sokolowski is very helpful here:

> If I give you something in gratitude, it is true that I must have had a dispositional understanding, prior to my handing over, that you have been good to me and deserve something in return. But this prior appraisal and disposition are to be understood philosophically in relation to the performance of handing over; they are not somehow an efficient cause of my handing over. They become actualized in the formal cause of my grateful giving. Sometimes indeed there may be no prior anticipation at all; my understanding might develop along with a situation and its resources and along with my performance as it goes on in them (even though my character as one who will help others in danger must dispositionally precede the situation). Something threatens you and I defend you from it at some risk to myself; I act protectively and courageously, but right along with the situation. My understanding and decisions are not prior transactions, mental acts, causing my defense of you.[39]

Both Dewey and Oakeshott have been criticized for lacking principles, commitments, values, stabilizing virtues which outlast their operation or efficacy in a particular situation. In other words, no universals. Intimations in the case of Oakeshott, and hypotheses in Dewey's case, do not speak to the human's need for lastingness, for the everlasting. Why, it might be asked, would one not regard character as precisely that kind of prior state which brings about, occasions, or motivates such acts as gratitude or courageous defense of another person? Sokolowski even admits that character does not "come forth from a more basic root." It is, he says, "terminal," for "it qualifies us definitively as we take our moral position among others."[40] Where is the adventure in something "terminal"?

To practice a virtue, or as Sokolowksi says, to "crease" the world this way or that, is to practice not a rule but rather a desire. What is desired is something good. The good, though, requires refinement, and he distinguishes moral categorials from judgmental categorials. The former "simply serve to establish a moral transaction and to define, redefine, and confirm the relationship between the agent and the patient, for good or for ill." Sokolowski's example is helpful:

> If, as a way of showing that I hold you in low regard, I take something bad for you as my good, that would be an act of contempt; but establishing the act as an act of contempt is all that the moral categoriality does. It does not address the question whether I should be contemptuous or cruel or courageous or patient. It does not *judge* the act at all, it only establishes it as an action, as a deed.[41]

In this respect, the moral categorial is what Sokolowski calls "value-free." But judgmental categorials are "value-laden":

> Every statement and every moral term belonging to this reserve has approbation or disapproval built into itself. When we apply any one of them to a situation . . . we bring out the good or bad quality of the action being judged, and we display to others why we see the action as good or bad.[42]

This type of categorial is used to evaluate and judge. Our reserve of them — bravery, generosity, cowardice, the whole list of virtues and vices — constitute what he calls a "kind of corporate memory of what good and bad actions have displayed as the excellence that agents can achieve and the corruption they can fall into."[43] We pause. Corporate memory? What has this to do with adventure, intimation, with the rejection of truth as an "insurance company"?

Sokolowski's response starts in a rather restrained manner: "Our ready reserve of moral propositions thus seems to contain the sheer truth about moral behavior." Codify the judgmental categorials, distill them, cross-reference them, publish them. But there are two problems with such an ambition. The first is unmistakably a practical question, namely, how the judgmental categorialities are to be applied. How do we tell ourselves, or students (if we should like to have character education programs), that this "now is a case of cowardice or generosity, or that this is a situation that calls for patience"?[44] That, however, may not be the strongest objection to systematizing the judgmental categorials. Sokolowski's aversion to such systematizing sounds very much like Oakeshott:

Judgmental categorialities simply are not the kind of categorial objects that belong in a system. They do not have their truth by virtue of being derivable from other statements or by virtue of their position and status in a collection of statements. A judgmental categoriality lives and has its truth not in a systematic network but in proximity to performances. Each judgmental categoriality remains in touch with the way we act, and it does so rather independently of other categorialities. What we say about courage and cowardice gets its force not primarily by being related to what we say about justice or temperance, but by living off what courageous and cowardly agents do.[45]

Recall Oakeshott's claim that "principles, rules and purposes are mere abridgements of the coherence of the activity, and we may easily be faithful to them while losing touch with the activity itself."[46] Sokolowski does not want to lose "touch with the way we act," and Oakeshott fears "losing touch with the activity itself." The adventure in Sokolowski is now considerably clearer: a categorial judgment "has its truth" not in an argument and its rebuttal, not in "what we say," but "in proximity to performances." This is good, but not quite good enough for Oakeshott. He envisions more adventure and uncertainty: "For an agent in conduct a practice is an instrument to be played upon, and to do this he must have the understanding of a performer."[47] The performer, when inspired, takes us closer to the good resident in the activity. Even when the performance is not perfect, it actualizes a possible perfection.

Where, though, is the adventure in Sokolowski's phenomenology which would attract Dewey's attention? It is not hard to find:

> All human communities have moral norms about issues that typically arise in human life and that are morally risky, ones in which the urgently desirable often overwhelms the truly desirable or the good. The judgmental categorialities make us remember the moral engagement that we can never leave behind; they also give us guidance for the situations we are in. However, the judgmental categorialities do not do our moral thinking for us. We ourselves must work out the difference between the desirable and the good in the situation we are in, and we ourselves, not the judgmental categegorials, will be the owners of the action we perform. The action will issue from our assessment of our situation; it will not descend from a judgmental category.[48]

Dewey's effort was magnificent: to construct a reflective morality rooted in habit, respectful of character and the virtues, mindful of the Good, and which did not inattentively live off what agents do even in their moments of greatest indebtedness to habit, virtue, character, and tradition. And how to attend to these resources for being moral agents? As I described in the chapter 4, vigilance is essential. It is the care I exercise over the intangibilities of meaning which hold me to the worlds of practice, of work, of labor, of struggle, of leisure, of love, and memory. But none of these loyalties to the world, including their foundation in habit, virtue, character, and tradition, none of these "do our moral thinking for us."

Herein is the adventure and drama for Dewey. It falls to the person to "work out the difference between the desirable and the good." We often want to be the kind of person for whom the virtuous life is so deeply rooted that the need for thinking is all but eliminated. Or, if thinking is required, it will produce propositions and arguments which will stand or fall based on what Sokolowski calls their "position and status in a collection of statements." Such attempts to either abort thinking or abbreviate it by instilling "good habits" leaves the person with little to think about, little to work out. Dewey could not be tricked by this counterfeit of the struggle for the good. This working out, this deliberative thinking (certainly not exhaustive of all thinking), how long is its reach? When is it satisfied?

The reciprocity of reflective principle and lived quality seems to help Dewey avoid what one might consider the more extreme Oakeshottian position. Remember that Oakeshott has said that "principles are derived from the activity and not the activity from the principles." This would, I think, strike Dewey as unnecessarily dichotomous or discontinuous. In order to establish the parity of the lived and the known, it is not necessary to argue that "principles are derived from the activity," the known from the lived. It is sufficient to show that the lived and the known suffuse each other. In this respect, it is not difficult to see why Dewey once said that his favorite reading was Hegel, *after* Plato:

> Nothing could be more helpful to present philosophizing than a "Back to Plato" movement; but it would have to be back to the dramatic, restless, co-operatively inquiring Plato of the Dialogues, trying one mode of attack after another to see what it might yield; back to the Plato whose highest flight of metaphysics always terminated with a social and practical turn, and not to the artificial Plato constructed by unimaginative commentators who treat him as the original university professor.[49]

For Dewey, reasoned deliberations are not theoretical proofs, but intimations—some of moral relevance and some not—of ideal meanings.

Because Oakeshott tends to keep principle so tightly bound by and to the activity, we should not be surprised by this affirmation from him: "The instrumental mind does not exist, and if it did it would always lack the power to be the spring of any concrete activity whatever."[50] Dewey disagrees: "To laud habit as conservative while praising thought as the main spring of progress is to take the surest course to making thought abstruse and irrelevant and progress a matter of accident and catastrophe."[51] As we have seen, Dewey does not quarrel with Oakeshott's insistence that meanings are intimated within a situation or activity. But Dewey would not agree that habit's projection of meaning is tethered by the practical situation even though its projected or possible meanings must ultimately have their purchase within the practical situation. Reason's stretch, its "arc" through experience is just slightly longer—and higher—than Oakeshott allows. The "instrumental mind" does indeed exist for Dewey, and he sees it as one spring of activity. But its struggle for the good depends on another spring if "concrete activity" is to win any victories on behalf of the good. The instrumental mind must imagine ideals which use, honor, and transcend the gravity of habit. Aims and purposes are stabilized by habit, and in that respect, habit is the vehicle of immanence. Habit also is the vehicle of transcendence, turning not only our practices and behavior, but our very selves, toward that atmospheric and intangible light cast by ideals.

At this point, the difference between Dewey and Oakeshott could not be more vivid or fundamental. The existential context which Oakeshott wishes to rely upon is what he calls a "tradition of behaviour" and of this tradition he says that "it is neither fixed nor finished; it has no changeless centre to which understanding can anchor itself; there is no sovereign purpose to be perceived or invariable direction to be detected; there is no model to be copied, idea to be realized, or rule to be followed."[52] This does not seem to challenge the common popular and scholarly perception of Dewey as the champion of change, adaptation, and so forth. Oakeshott continues: "Though a tradition of behaviour is flimsy and elusive, it is not without identity, and what makes it a possible object of knowledge is the fact that all its parts do not change at the same time and that the changes it undergoes are potential within it." Again, nothing surprising here for the contextual, immanent interpretation of Dewey.

Dewey's understanding of context, however, is *both* immanent and transcendent. To speak of *the* context of a problem, issue, event, idea, or action is to make more precise, local, and definite what is none of these. Dewey's context transcends the definite: "The sense of an indefinite context of consequences from among which the aim is selected enters into the *present* meaning of activity."[53] It is not immediately apparent how something indefinite "enters into" the present, indeed the "present meaning" of an activity. For Oakeshott, a "tradition of behaviour" is "flimsy and elusive" but not so much so that whatever changes knowledge may introduce are not determinably "potential within it." But Dewey's potentials are simply too encompassing to specify their location as being "within": "When a sense of the infinite reach of an act physically occurring in a small point of space and occupying a petty instant of time comes home to us, the *meaning* of a present act is seen to be vast, immeasurable, unthinkable."[54] Dewey's movement from context to the infinite to the "unthinkable" is certain to disconcert the conservative who, Oakeshott says, prefers "the limited to the unbounded."[55]

Seen in this perspective, Dewey's attempt to develop a theory of deliberation out of what he calls "the problems and experience of everyday conduct" has a far loftier goal than simply fashioning a "practical" theory of deliberation for a "practical" culture. In everyday experience—a May morning, an act of gratitude, the carpenter's or surgeon's skill—are to be found mysteries, dramas, revelations, Oakeshottian intimations of the extraordinary. These intimations may become luminous and consummatory when brought to expression in aesthetic and religious experiences. In such experiences, some requiring deliberation and others not, we are, Dewey says "introduced into a world beyond this world which is nevertheless the deeper reality of the world in which we live in our ordinary experiences."[56] This intimation is not only of the world's "deeper reality." It also points to the deliberator's search for his or her own deeper reality, the search for self-realization. Dewey says: "Superficially, the deliberation which terminates in choice is concerned with weighing the values of particular ends. Below the surface, it is a process of discovering what sort of being a person most wants to become."[57] Hence, deliberation, certainly moral deliberation, is concerned with what goes on "below the surface"—with what is most deep in experience and to a large extent, out of sight.

Simply because many activities of reason are out of sight does not mean that we are in the dark, courting chaos, anarchy, and destruction. Oakeshott says: "Human beings are apt to be disconcerted unless they feel themselves to be upheld by something more substantial than the emanations of their own contingent imaginations."[58] We are "upheld" by reason and imagination in many ways, not all of which are, or can be, declared. We do not fail ourselves, truth, or nature when we incorporate the promptings of undeclared reason in our declarations of intent and purpose. For Dewey—and for Oakeshott in "The Voice of Poetry in the Conversation of Mankind"[59]—it is just such promptings of undeclared reason that sometimes afford us intimations of transcendence in even so practical a matter as a choice or decision.

Let us have an example of the declared where we might find, or hope to find, such an intimation of transcendence. Wallace Stevens prepares us: "That will not declare itself / Yet is certain as meaning."[60]

· CHAPTER 6 ·

The Undeclared Self

William Arrowsmith says: "Education is a spiritual enterprise. We deal in intangibles and invisibles, or at least we still profess to do that, whatever else we may do in the name of certifying skills and competencies."[1] My intent in this chapter is not to defend Arrowsmith's proposition, or to elucidate it any further, at least not directly. It is to draw out the implications of the idea that students, teachers, and professors "deal in intangibles and invisibles" by elaborating a conception of the self that tells us what kind of being it is who can profit (and not profit) from "intangibles and invisibles." The conception is hardly new—the self is more than it knows, its being transcends its knowing—but it needs reaffirmation. But mere reaffirmation is not sufficient. The idea that the self is not fully specifiable, determinable, or investigable; that its accessible and inaccessible aspects are interleaved or concatenated; and that self-realization involves accessible and not so readily accessible dimensions must be situated in the present moment in public and higher education. In short, I am outlining a moderately romantic, decisively transcendental view of the self, one which is suggested as well as supported by Dewey's philosophy of experience and philosophy of education. What follows, then, is not an analysis of Dewey's philosophical views on experience and education, but rather an attempt to draw out some interpretive possibilities of these views.

At points it shall undoubtedly appear as if I am attempting to deconstruct the unitary self. I am not. The sources for my reflections on the self are rather more conventional than Lyotard or Derrida. There are some convergences with Richard Rorty. His essay "The Contingency of Selfhood" raises questions which I find interesting and important, but my answers ultimately are rather different from his.[2] With Rorty, I would agree that Dewey had a rather profound sense of the *Doppelbödig* or contingent character of reality. However, to permit this to be taken as the main achievement of Dewey is to miss what is deepest and most challenging in his philosophy of experience. I think the main effort of Dewey's pragmatism was something like this: to give the broadest outlines of a philosophy of experience which, beginning with what Peter Berger calls "entrance points in the world of the ordinary," opens to the extraordinary and the transcendent. In other words, where does the earthbound pragmatist, Rorty's dedivinized self, stand to behold the "ethereal things" of imagination and the sublime? Where Rorty underemphasizes the importance of the transcendent and spiritual character of experience in Dewey, I shall underline its importance, possibly even overemphasize it.

What sort of center is the self, giving and receiving meaning according to the expectations and traditions of the professions, liberal arts, and humanities? What sort of self is it which invites self-knowledge? And what sort of self is it that underlies Dewey's conception of education as growth? Nietzsche, in *The Will to Power*, defines self as "the sphere of a subject constantly growing or decreasing, the center of the system constantly shifting." Can this be because the educable self, compressed by what is accessible and inaccessible in it, compressed by its surface and its depth, cannot be anything other than "constantly shifting"? Might its education consist of the fusion and difference of the specifiable and nonspecifiable? To think so would be to admit a rather unsettling possibility: that the good, the virtue, of broad ranges of educational influence are in principle inscrutable, or at least not manifest. Deductions about the effects of an educational endeavor can be made on the basis of the specifiable, but the specifiable is not necessarily the home or seat of what occurs most deeply and transformatively.

The self, then, cannot be wholly unlike the "intangibles and invisibles" with which it concerns itself in educational moments. The knowledge which forms a self at its deepest levels cannot be fully revealed and inspected as if it were like any other object, nor is the self that can learn from such knowledge formulable like any other object. Socrates cautions Hippocrates not to think so:

> For there is far greater peril in buying knowledge than in buying meat and drink: the one you purchase of the wholesale or retail dealer, and carry them away in other vessels, and before you receive them into the body as food, you may deposit them at home and call in any experienced friend who knows what is good to be eaten or drunken, and what not, and how much, and when; and then the danger of purchasing them

is not so great. But you cannot buy the wares of knowledge and carry them away in another vessel; when you have paid for them you must receive them into the soul and go your way, either greatly harmed or greatly benefited.[3]

Neither the knowledge that feeds the soul nor the soul that is so wonderously fed can be made wholly explicit or manifest. So the central question returns: how shall we think of the self if we are inclined to see education as a "spiritual enterprise," one concerned with "intangibles and invisibles"?

In order to see the self's intersections with "intangibles and invisibles" in a specific context or setting, I should like to focus on a quite familiar occurrence, namely, choosing or declaring a major in college. On the one hand, there is nothing special about this example. One might have focused on a high school graduate's choice of a job, the choice to continue to live with one's parents or to get an apartment, the choice between two political candidates, the choice to tell the truth or shade the truth, the choice to end a relationship, and so on. In short, I simply wish to look at the self becoming itself in everyday life. In another respect, though, the very everydayness of declaring a major (everyday at least for a college student) makes it an unusually interesting focus for discussing "intangibles and invisibles." Declaring a major is a rather revealing symbol: in a sense that shall become clear as I proceed, we are declaring a major throughout our life. What is important, central, worthy of attention and sustained effort? Just how spiritual is the declaration of what is major in college and life?

How mundane or modest a matter it is can be gathered from the answer to the question "When should I choose my major?" found in *Peterson's Guide to Four-Year Colleges 1990*:

> A major, or field of concentration, as it's sometimes called, is simply a series of courses designed to provide you with a strong background in the academic area you're most attracted to. No more, no less. Most of the time, declaring a major is a simple process. All you have to do is write in your choice on your registration form, and the administration takes it from there.[4]

Make your choice, write it on your registration form, and "the administration takes it from there." Let us put this bit of advice alongside the following characterization of today's undergraduates by Helen Lefkowitz Horowitz in her book *Campus Life: Undergraduate Cultures from the End of the Eighteenth Century to the Present*:

> Few college students ask existential questions about the meaning of life. As they compete for the grades that will get them into professional

school, they allow themselves little room to grow and become. College moves them along to a job or a career, but for most it no longer serves to liberate their souls.[5]

I want to suggest that if we have an interest in improving the prospects for an education—and a life—that sees itself as a "spiritual enterprise," then we might try to see what sort of self students are likely to find when they look for themselves by looking for a major. How is public and higher education to think of the self if "we deal in intangibles and invisibles"?

I

Despite persons (friends, counselors, parents, professors), despite paraphernalia (bulletins, catalogs, program and concentration overviews, orientation meetings), and despite commonsense principles ("study what you are really interested in," "major in something useful," "the professors in this department are really well known and respected"), it is likely that we greatly overestimate the extent to which the choice of a major is a considered, rational choice. The principal reason for this is that the self choosing the major is not a particularly stable, determinate, specifiable center, and not simply because the self at the "young adult" stage of its development is that way. The condition is broader, larger than a developmental stage; one might risk calling it ontological. Frithjof Bergmann puts it this way:

> The self crystallizes behind our back. Meanings attach themselves, experience is organized into new structures, and no announcements of the progress are made to us. It happens unobtrusively and in the background. To determine what we feel or want or hope or think is often hard enough, but these are ropes compared to cobwebs when the questions are: Is this feeling truly my own, or is it copied, borrowed from a book, invented or only a wish? Is this what I want, or is it a Pavlovian response, a knee-jerk of the brain? So the lines are blurred and seem to shift, only fragments come into view and then disappear.[6]

We grow, get wiser, meaner, less confident, more compulsive, less interested in astronomy and more interested in computers. These things happen and no announcements are made. The student choosing a major seems to be in precisely this situation, but with one profoundly significant difference. He or she is expected to make an "announcement" of the self's progress. This is called "declaring a major." And here, the problems begin.

In asking a student to declare a major, we are asking the student to declare or announce a self, an actual self and a possible self. The major will be the focus of the student's effort and attention. In what state, though, is the choosing, declaring self, that is, in what state of mind and being? In what state ought it to be in if its choices are to be "good" ones? A framework for answering these questions is found in one of the classic chapters from *The Principles of Psychology*, "The Stream of Thought." William James says:

> The traditional psychology talks like one who should say a river consists of nothing but pailsful, spoonsful, quartpotsful, barrelsful, and other moulded forms of water. Even were the pails and the pots all actually standing in the stream, still between them the free water would continue to flow. It is just this free water of consciousness that psychologists resolutely overlook. Every definite image in the mind is steeped and dyed in the free water that flows round it. With it goes the sense of its relations, near and remote, the dying echo of whence it came to us, the dawning sense of whither it is to lead. The significance, the value, of the image is all in this halo or penumbra that surrounds and escorts it—or rather that is fused into one with it and has become bone of its bone and flesh of its flesh.[7]

With the declaration of the major, the student steps into the stream and scoops up a pail or barrel of water and declares: "Here I am, this is me, or at least this is the closest institutional expression of me that I can find." This major or concentration is the institutional equivalent of James's focus, "topic," or "definite image in the mind." Remember, though, that James says the significance or value of the "definite image" is in the "halo" or "penumbra" that suffuses this focus. What is the institutional equivalent of the halo, the "free water of consciousness"? Distribution requirements? General education? Core curricula? How do these keep the "free water of consciousness" flowing? How do we keep the major from becoming all focus and no background?

If the self that declares a major is to a large extent, though certainly not entirely, undeclared—neither pails, pots, nor spoons of water—what can we expect a choice of major to be like for the undergraduate? This can be the undergraduate who has no idea what activates his or her interest and effort, or it can be the undergraduate who is interested in and pulled by a number of interests. In both cases, "interests" and "likes" are the basis for choice; they offer convenient, almost inevitable ways to focus the attention of the student and the adviser. "What are you interested in?" or "What are your pails, spoons, and quarts?" Interests and likes are the signs, the portents, the bones, that student and adviser as hermeneuticists attempt to read or decipher. Students seek to know themselves by knowing their interests and likes. In this respect, we are all more or less like students, most of our lives. We use one part of our self to inspect another part of our self. We make an object of ourselves to ourselves; we make an announcement of our self to our self. In so doing, we personalize the anonymous, undeclared self; we peek in on the self that "crystallizes behind our back." Maybe, too, we learn that the "free water of consciousness" can be only imperfectly known through its pots and pails.

Where does this leave our undergraduate who is declaring a major, announcing a self? In the language of recent literary criticism, one might say that the choice of a college major is usually either over- or underdetermined, depending upon how the "moulded forms of water"—likes and interests—are used. In the first case, students seek to know themselves by treating their likes and interests as if they were a list of topics and headings in a filing system. It is a big decision, full of the ambiguity and uncertainty that characterizes most big decisions. What is the student to do? Get information, a great deal of information, about majors. Make a list of goals and priorities. Get more information. Make a list of personal traits, likes, dislikes, strengths, weaknesses. Get more information. But the student is not in an enviable position. He is inexperienced in making consequential decisions; he is under the eye of parents, relatives, and friends who are interested in what he has done with his freedom; he is angry and possibly frightened that such an important decision has no guidelines, no syllabus. The student wants to know all about the color, the weight, the essential properties of the pots and pails he or she is considering as a major in the hope that the unannounced self's pots and pails will be teased out by these definitions and a perfect marriage made. The questions posed to oneself in choosing a major, the objectification of the self in such questioning and choosing, are of course deeply unsettling to the student. Calls to parents, adviser conferences, talks with roommates and friends, more calls, more conferences, more talks. These students give the impression that they really have been struggling, really trying to look in on the self forming behind their backs, but very often they simply have been tacking back and forth between one pot and another pot, one quart and another quart. Get the right pot and the "free water of consciousness" will be vanquished or at least safely contained. It is hard to tell how many of these "decision makers" believe they have reached, in James's magnificent phrase, "the bottom of being," but we should not be surprised if the number is quite large.

The situation may be otherwise. Here, the choice of a major is handled so directly, almost casually, that an observer would barely notice anything significant going on, and certainly not a struggle of any kind. For these students, the self and a major are formed behind their backs with a vengeance.

If the work of knowing the self for the "information processor" is that of a very ambitious but imperfect rationality, the "direct" choosers are astonishingly relaxed in their demands on rationality. "Liking" is necessary and nearly sufficient as a condition for choice. I liked history in high school, I really like my chemistry course, and so on. Certainly these likes may be "rational," but shunning much reflection on their likes, these students have little sense of what their likes mean beyond their sincerely felt attraction to a subject. Since, as Bergmann says, "only fragments come into view and then disappear," these students attend to the fragments, note which one seems to have the strongest valence for them, and go with it. There is little attempt to peek in on the self forming behind their backs, little inclination to feel that some aspect of the self, perhaps the contour of the whole self, is at stake. They "just" decide.

Despite the apparent difference or contrast between these two kinds of "choosers," they have something in common. Both set out from the same condition — a self that has crystallized "behind our back." Whereas the decision maker wishes to overcome the existential condition described by Bergmann by selecting his or her pots and pails with as much deliberation and precision as possible, the valence chooser simply bypasses it, feels an attraction to some pot or barrel, and goes there. It may appear that the overdetermined undergraduate is bringing more to the choice than the underdetermined student, more in the sense that at least he or she has sensed a problem or challenge. Maybe. And perhaps the relaxed students will ultimately make the wiser choice because they have not spent their energy on the hopeless task of making themselves transparent to themselves by engineering a perfect marriage of their "real self" and a "good major." Maybe.

What is the larger, general meaning of this sketch of the undeclared self; that is, how does this help us to grasp what is at stake when a student declares a major? First, it suggests that the self's choice of a major is, and should be, both a wedge and a bridge between two indefinites — the self and the major. Bergmann says: "In actual fact we never have a secure and settled sense of what our identity or real self is. It remains elusive and unstable, and is always seen as through a veil. We guess at it, suspect an error, and grope in a new place."[8] We guess at what our self is, and try to combat this indeterminacy with triumphant moments of rational decisiveness; or, we guess at what our self is, and surrender to this indeterminacy in noncombative moments of simply doing what we like. In both cases we are estranged from the unannounced self, as we must be. This estrangement is not an accomplishment or achievement of the self; it is its condition. This condition can be denied: we can attempt to stare at the undeclared self or we can look away; we can seek to encompass it or bypass it. But such dodges ultimately must fail, for we cannot live with the unannounced self in such artless ways, at least—or especially—not those persons who value the sort of growth that is both a condition for and outcome of self-knowledge and self-fulfillment.

And it is here that we perhaps expect too much and too little of education. What is the purpose of public and higher education, we ask, if not to help the student fashion a self, a whole self that has vanquished the diremptive tendencies of reconciliation and estrangement? J. Glenn Gray is very sobering on this point:

> Education does not eliminate these moods of reconciliation and estrangement. These poles between which human life is tossed are inseparable from the human condition. Education seeks rather to use them as a means for fuller self-understanding. Hence, education is something we suffer from before we can profit. Indeed, suffering in many of its forms seems indispensable to the educated person, however unwanted and ultimately undesirable it may be. The educated man must first be estranged before he can know reconciliation; he must be driven into the confines of his own skin, before he can experience that aspect of his being which is a part of the larger world. Or to put it another way, we must first experience the contrast of inner and outer being as a painful reality before any reconciliation is effected. And this does not happen once for all. Most of us never finally heal over this breach. To become fully at home in our world is an unrealizable and vain ideal, dreamed of by certain idealists. But to renew the struggle to achieve involvement and intimacy with this larger natural and human environment is surely the fuller meaning of the educational adventure.[9]

There is much to ponder here. If the student's choice of a major is a wedge driven between two indefinites—the self and the major—then the student ought to "experience the contrast of inner and outer being as a painful reality before any reconciliation is effected." But, unfortunately, students can be too quickly and too easily reconciled to the inherent estrangement involved in choosing a major by either trying to encompass it, treating it as a problem in information processing, or by trying to bypass it by going with the strongest valence, the strongest "like." In both cases the student has less chance of appreciating why "the educated man must first be estranged before he can know reconciliation." Such an experience is a profound instance of educational growth and offers the student a glimpse of the meaning of wisdom.

The second consideration to which our sketch of the unannounced self leads involves the element of chance, precariousness, or fragility. The endless cycling between estrangement and reconciliation does not have a stop or end. These poles, and our movement between them, are "inseparable from the human condition." This cycling is the basis of much that is tragic in life and the basis of much that is triumphant, specifically, when we come as near as possible to being "fully at home in our world." We would miss, however, the depth of the tragic and the triumphant if we saw estrangement and reconciliation as poles that simply alternated with each other. Their relationship is not so external or predictable because growth is not so predictable. In the midst of our most sublime moments of reconciliation we can be defeated, compromised, soiled. We can be shipwrecked, as Karl Jaspers says, and without warning. And too, we can be lifted up, suddenly and as if by a miracle, from despair and ruin. Estrangement and reconciliation suffuse each other, infect each other, ultimately qualify each other.

The second chapter of Dewey's *Experience and Nature* is titled "Existence as Precarious and Stable." It seems to me that the psychology, social theory, and educational theory Dewey developed throughout his life are embodied in the outlook presented in this chapter. The precarious and the stable he says "are mixed not mechanically but vitally like the wheat and tares of the parable."[10] This intertwining of the precarious and the stable means that uncertainty characterizes all our dealings, involvements, and stances. Our existence is perilous, subject to chance. So, too, is the growth that education properly seeks. "The Self as Precarious and Stable" is not the title of anything that Dewey wrote, but it is certainly the subject of much of what he wrote. And it is just this vital mixture of the precarious and stable self which helps move us in the direction of a deeper realization that in education we deal in "intangibles and invisibles."

The poles of the announced and the unannounced self are not less "vitally" mixed than the stable and the precarious, but we should be careful not to assume a symmetry between the announced and the stable, the unannounced and the precarious. The shadows cast by the undeclared self are delicately, playfully, solemnly present but unannounced. What we know of these shadows and signs cannot be fully calculated and exposed and hence they can wither and die from neglect or inattention. Or, still resisting calculation and revelation, they draw us to them and exhausting us, exhaust themselves. The intersection of the declared and the undeclared self unearths the contingencies and internal vulnerabilities which establish our finitude as well as the capacity for heroic transcendence of our finitude. It is precisely this remarkable blending and blurring of the announced and the unannounced which makes Dewey's conception of education as growth so risky, so Nietzchean.

Can we expect undergraduates to take their education seriously as an opportunity for self-discovery, in particular, to be moved by the humanities as heroic ventures into the depths of a largely unillumined soul, when their own experience, exemplified by their choice of a major, denies the precariousness, fragility, of the unannounced self? How shall they respond to, indeed, even recognize, the shadows cast by the undeclared self onto the appearing and accessible self? What shall be their motivation for the pursuit of wisdom? What shall be the meaning of wisdom in an environment where reconciliation follows no prior state of chance, drama, or estrangement? Dewey says: "A purely stable world permits of no illusions, but neither is it clothed with ideals. It just exists."[11] Ideals are born in the dramatic, uncertain union of the announced and unannounced self. Without the union, and without the drama, the world "just exists," without ideals. Without the union and without the drama, a major "just exists," equally barren of ideals.

Our third, and final, general point draws out the meaning of the precarious and dramatic union of the undeclared and declared self. The student's choice of a major ought to be what Gray called "an educational adventure." Choosing a major, and the education to which it leads, ought to be an adventure because the student has grown into a person who reasons, who reasons about the self. However, precisely because, in Gray's words, "education does not eliminate these moods of reconciliation and estrangement," the student realizes that neither does reason. These poles are "inseparable from the human condition." Reason is only partially successful in announcing what the self is up to, in clarifying what Bergmann says "happens unobtrusively and in the background." If the student is not content to encompass or bypass the unannounced self, the prospects for an "educational adventure" exist.

Very few writers have given us a better view of what this adventure looks like than has Nietzsche. In his essay "Schopenhauer as Educator," Nietzsche says:

> But how can we find ourselves again? How can man know himself? He is a dark and veiled thing; and whereas the hare has seven skins, man could skin himself seventy-times-seven times and still not say, "This now is you yourself, this is no longer skin." Besides, it is an agonizing, dangerous enterprise to dig down into yourself, to descend forcibly by the shortest route the shaft of your being. A man may easily do himself such damage that no doctor can cure him. And again, why should it be necessary, since everything bears witness to our being — our friendships and hatreds, the way we look, our handshakes, the things we remember and

forget, our books, our handwriting? But there is a way by which this absolutely crucial inquiry can be carried out. Let the young soul look back upon its life and ask itself: what until now have you truly loved, what has raised up your soul, what ruled it and at the same time made it happy? Line up these objects of reverence before you, and perhaps by what they are and by their sequence, they will yield you a law, the fundamental law of your true self. Compare these objects, see how one completes, enlarges, exceeds, transforms the other, how they form a ladder on which you have so far climbed up toward yourself. For your true nature does not lie hidden deep inside you but immeasurably high above you, or at least above that which you customarily consider to be your ego. Your true educators and molders reveal to you the true original meaning and basic stuff of your nature, something absolutely incapable of being educated and molded, but in any case something fettered and paralyzed and difficult of access. Your teachers can be nobody but your liberators.[12]

"It is an agonizing, dangerous enterprise." Is this not an echo of Socrates' warning to Hippocrates that there is "far greater peril in buying knowledge than in buying meat and drink"? When Platonic peril, Nietszchean danger, and Deweyan precariousness are spread throughout a life, we may think of it in terms of adventure.

What we notice about such a life is not solely its moments or episodes or risk and uncertainty, nor is it an outlook or stance formulated as a credo praising the "adventurous life." A life which has the look and feel of an adventure makes the less conspicuous claim that what we are and what we know are not symmetrical, or more generally, that being and being known are not equivalent. Can "the fundamental law of your true self" be disclosed through knowledge of those "objects of reverence" that one truly loves, objects whose power is nothing less than to have "raised up your soul"? No, because what I am and what I know do not coincide. To know these "objects of reverence" is to know "what until now have you truly loved"; it is to climb up a ladder "on which you have so far climbed up toward yourself." My being, however, transcends such knowledge: "your true nature does not lie hidden deep inside you but immeasurably high above you, or at least above that which you customarily consider to be your ego." Thus, the necessary premise of any attempt to "find ourselves again" must be that the human being "is a dark and veiled thing." Our being transcends our knowing, for, as Karl Jaspers says, "no matter what I think, my own being as a whole is not contained in any thinking or thought."[13] So too, the undeclared self transcends the declared self. A life that perfects these conditions of existence approximates an adventure. An undergraduate life that perfects these conditions approximates what Gray calls an educational adventure and what Dewey calls educational growth.

A choice of major is a fit or match, a bridge between two indefinites—self and major. It is also a wedge between the unannounced self and its possibilities as shaped by a particular major. The choice of a major is a homecoming and an embarking. It estranges and reconciles. The choice of a major—as the beginning of a series of estrangements and reconciliations—is something far more consequential than the choice of a set of courses and graduation requirements. Administratively or institutionally, declaring a major is, as *Peterson's* says, "a simple process." You just "write in your choice on the registration form, and the administration takes it from there." (The unintended, multiple meanings of this sentence would not have been missed by students in the sixties: it evokes the idea of foul-ups in the registration process as well as the various political senses in which an administration "takes" a student's choice.) I have suggested why the choice of a major is not, or at least ought not to be, a "simple process." Is a major a place to form oneself, shall we say existentially or humanly, or is it a place to define oneself as a pot or pail? These are not mutually exclusive. It is a great mistake, though, to think that they are unproblematically reinforcing. If the student tends toward the former, then the "free water of consciousness" must flow; if the latter, then pots and pails will do. What sort of situation does the undeclared self find in today's public school and college environment? Is there much "free water of consciousness" or is it all pots and pails?

II

To reflect on the proper place of "intangibles and invisibles" in education is not an indictment of the central place of the transmission of knowledge in public and higher education. That there is knowledge that must remain clear of "the shaft of one's being" in order to have its proper place in the world is one of the facts of existence which may occasion an initial estrangement in the student just discovering the discipline and authority inherent in the subject matter of a major. But such estrangement may grow into a kind of reconciliation—self-discipline. Glenn Gray says: "Self-discipline is acquired precisely where the material permits no concessions to subjectivity."[14] The "definite images" of transmissible knowledge do not make any particular or necessary claim on the unannounced self; that is, they do not depend upon the unannounced self for their authority, and, vice versa, the unannounced self can make no claim on the "definite images" of transmissible knowledge, that which permits "no concessions to subjectivity." Gray is right when he says that such knowledge "can represent something of the necessary austerity involved in all self-discipline." Of all the contents of consciousness, the "definite images" of transmissible knowledge offer the most resistance to engulfment by penumbral consciousness. They may be "steeped and dyed" by the free water that flows round them, but they are nonetheless specifiable independent of such colorations; they make "no concessions to subjectivity."

What such self-discipline—such "austerity"—might mean to the unannounced self poses a difficult question to defenders of the self-sufficiency of the rational will. If, as Bergmann said earlier, "only fragments come into view and then disappear," if, as Nietszche said, the self is "difficult to access," if, as Arrowsmith said, "we deal in intangibles and invisibles," and if, as Dewey believed, the precarious and stable are vitally mixed, then self-discipline cannot be the sole route "into the shaft of one's being." E. M. Cioran says:

> I live in expectation of the Idea; I foresee it, close in upon it, get a grip—and cannot formulate it, it escapes me, does not yet belong to me: might I have conceived it in my absence? And how, once imminent and vague, to make it present and luminous in the intelligible agony of expression? What conditions should I hope for if it is to bloom—and decay?[15]

How rational will illuminates the chiaroscuro world of the undeclared self, how, in other words, the austerity of self-discipline metamorphoses into the "agony of expression," is a worthy topic for public school and university curriculum committees and for conferences devoted to the future of public and higher education.

The one part of the curriculum where we have expected more than incidental attention to soul-making or at least self-making is the humanities. The humanities may have their own professionalized pots and pails, but there is also a presumption that they will have an improving, humanizing effect upon the undeclared self not usually expected of a course, say, in intermediate accounting. If all the great writers and all the great books resident in a high school or college humanities curriculum do not help in this humanizing effort, who or what will? In the great books of the humanities, students have available truly great models, teachers who are greater than any institution's teachers—Plato, Aristotle, Homer, and so on. This massive confrontation with greatness, mediated through the skills of a great teacher, will help students discover the bases of their own attempts at greatness.

Inspired by the authority of greatness, curricular pots, pails, and barrels in the form of great books and ideas are sent down the shaft of students and we await reports on the improvement of the soul. If there is little or no evidence of improvement in the state of the soul, we reorganize the curriculum. In the last two decades, there has been much curriculum reorganization.

This certainly is no objection to greatness, particularly as expressed in Whitehead's conviction that "moral education is impossible apart from the habitual vision of greatness." It is an objection to an astonishingly confident assumption in many of the great books proposals, core of common knowledge proposals, "our common heritage" proposals, and other prescriptions for steadying the rocky state of public and higher education, for example, the assumption that we truly understand how "a dark and veiled thing" makes use of greatness or benefits from greatness. That it often does, I do not doubt. Neither do I doubt that the "shaft of one's being" can be clogged with past greatness, as Emerson noted in "The American Scholar." The objection that the classics are hardly pots, pails, and barrels if properly taught—an objection as easily made as accepted—still does not adequately respond to Karl Jaspers' belief that "no matter what I think, my own being as a whole is not contained in any thinking or thought." When indeed the student is deeply "engaged" with a great text, is it self-evidently the case that the "intangibles and invisibles" with which we deal through it are somehow as nearby as the text or the declared self?

A failure to grasp the intersections of the precariousness and stability intrinsic to the undeclared self will almost certainly lead to a view of greatness which ignores the adventure essential to it. Whitehead says:

> A race preserves its vigor so long as it harbours a real contrast between what has been and what may be; and so long as it is nerved by the vigor to adventure beyond the safeties of the past. Without adventure civilization is in full decay.
>
> It is for this reason that the definition of culture as the knowledge of the best that has been said and done, is so dangerous by reason of its omission. It omits the great fact that in their day the great achievements of the past were the adventures of the past. Only the adventurous can understand the greatness of the past.[16]

Self-realization is not just one encounter-with-greatness away, or a series of such encounters. As greatness meets the penumbral world of the unannounced self, shadows may loom up, echoes may reverberate in unsettling ways, mirages may engulf us. To be engaged with a great book is not a moment of pure illumination which brings the unannounced self to heel, purging it of darkness and lifting the veil. Greatness which has become entangled in the penumbral world of human beings, greatness permeated by the peril involved in "a real contrast between what has been and what may be," is usually something more and less than textbook examples of greatness.

When one deals with what Walter Kaufmann called "life at the limits," a fitting modesty is required. Greatness in these regions involves a dimension of transcendence, what Arrowsmith called "turbulence,"[17] which unsettles as much as it settles and harmonizes. The "intangibles and invisibles" that may be taken "into the soul" are sturdy . . . and fragile. Such mixing and mingling of the precarious and stable is a necessary condition of heroic greatness . . . and tragedy.

III

The uninvestigable self, what I have been calling the undeclared self, is not, contrary to Kant, beyond experience but rather its center and horizon. The unannounced self underlies appearance but does not itself appear. No wonder that Nietzsche concluded that man is "a dark and veiled thing" and, as a corollary to this, that the basic material of our being is "absolutely incapable of being educated and molded, but in any case something fettered and paralyzed and difficult of access." How can the unannounced self be educated? Our best recent thinkers on higher education—including Henry David Aiken, William Arrowsmith, Jacques Barzun, F. R. Leavis, Michael Oakeshott, Philip Rieff, Harold Taylor—differ on many issues, but on one point I think they might agree: education concerned with what can be received "into the soul" necessarily deals with what Arrowsmith called "intangibles and invisibles." In periods of history aligned to such a spiritual enterprise, the task is difficult. In periods not inclined in this direction, it is virtually impossible.

Our present situation seems to be a turbid mixture of these two tendencies. The university is governed by vocational/professional values, and so predictably "intangibles and invisibles" are in retreat. The antidote? Core curricula, strong and weak versions of the great books, cultural literacy, and so forth. These really are not, however, responses to the professionalization of the student's consciousness, but to its emptying. In public education, our national attention is even more explicitly focused on what our students do not know and cannot do, accompanied by a very unmistakable focus on what is tangible and visible. Do these students know the presidents? Can they write a modestly coherent paper? Can they reason and think? Critically reason and think? These questions inevitably metamorphose into other questions: what should every graduate of a high school know? What should every graduate of college know? Literacy is in, ranging from computer literacy to moral literacy. In other words, what "pailsful, spoonsful, quartpotsful, barrelsful, and other moulded forms of water" should every student possess?

Further, how shall we—parents, students, and educators—be certain that our educational and humanizing efforts are not merely intellectual divertimenti? How shall we assess, evaluate, make sure that students are being held to the "highest standards"? Intellectual rigor and "intangibles and invisibles" are not incompatible but neither is their relationship an obvious one. That fact that "we deal in intangibles and invisibles" is simultaneously a confounding and ennobling condition of education, not an excuse for laxity and indulgence. Still, it must be acknowledged that it is vastly easier to determine what "high standards" might mean with respect to the mastery of pails, pots, and barrels than to things which enter "into the soul."

I think matters like this were on Dewey's mind in 1890 when he wrote a short article titled "A College Course: What Should I Expect from It?" In 1890 Dewey was still in his so-called idealistic period. What I shall simply assert here, but what I defend throughout the present work, is the proposal that Dewey never outgrew his idealistic period. His philosophical achievement is not to be located in his naturalism but in the frontiers along which the natural and the transcendental touch. In the last paragraph of the essay Dewey says:

> But all this is rather intangible, you will say, to one who wishes some definite instructions as to what he should expect from his college course. Undoubtedly; but the kingdom of heaven, in learning as in other matters, cometh not with observation. The general effects, the internal results, those which give the set and fix the attitude of the spirit, are the real effects of the college education.[18]

I do not think that one can understand what Dewey meant by "growth" twenty-six years later in *Democracy and Education* unless one sees its connection to the intangible and the "attitude of the spirit." Bill Arrowsmith would have like the idea of finding such intangibles and invisibles in, of all places, Dewey's pragmatism. He would join Dewey in affirming that the humility occasioned by a proper respect for the unannounced self provides no grounds for a cynical, ironic, or mystical posture with respect to the practices or policies of education. The vision of higher education shared by Arrowsmith and Dewey encourages a more sober and, simultaneously, a more wonderous appreciation of what education purports to do, at least in some settings and circumstances: to promote the examined life and the habits of mind essential to it. Such a vision of education requires a less grudging recognition that the self is not exhausted by the pots and pails surrounding it, whether or not those pots and pails are called majors, disciplines, or professions. The student is involved—and uninvolved—in his or her education as much through the undeclared self as the more apparent, declared self. Dewey and Arrowsmith would agree that precariousness, adventure, and turbulence attend whatever finds its way "into the soul." This is the drama of growth, in education and in life.

So it must be counted as a good for the undergraduate struggling (or not struggling) with the choice of a major to be reminded that as a spiritual enterprise, education deals in "intangibles and invisibles." Such a realization will not make the choice of a major easier, but it will encourage students to stay alert to what choosing a major means for "a dark and veiled thing," a condition of their humanity which some part of their education may speak to, but not eliminate.

> In memory of William Arrowsmith—"storm the intangible"
> A. R. Ammons

· CHAPTER 7 ·

"Meaning on the Model of Truth": Dewey and Gadamer on Habit and *Vorurteil*

> *The need of reason is not inspired by the quest for truth but by the quest for meaning. And truth and meaning are not the same.* The basic fallacy, taking precedence over all specific metaphysical fallacies, is to interpret meaning on the model of truth.
>
> Hannah Arendt, Introduction to *The Life of the Mind*

That "truth and meaning are not the same" was, I think, the central principle and vision of Dewey's philosophy. In habit Dewey believed he had found the concept best suited to challenge the view that meanings are apprehended only through actual or presupposed judgments about truth. For Dewey, not all meaning, certainly not all habitual meaning, anticipates truth; the intentionality of habitual meaning overflows truths and claims to truth at every turn. For Gadamer, on the other hand, reason and understanding are inspired by the quest for truth. I believe there is little doubt that Gadamer does, in Arendt's phrase, "interpret meaning on the model of truth." Truth for Gadamer is the standard or measure of understanding, and it is through *Vorurteil* that this measure is situated in the experienced world.

Now many would say that if Gadamer is read as a Heideggerian then not only is his interpretation of meaning on the model of truth acceptable but indeed it constitutes a major part of his philosophical achievement. In effect, this chapter challenges the view that Gadamer has gone beyond epistemology, that he has transformed or transfigured the standard conception of knowledge and truth built around theories of correspondence, validation, justification, and so on. Regardless of what he has extended or transfigured in Heidegger (itself not a wholly easy matter to determine), I do not think his rehabilitation of *Vorurteil* can serve him well in an attempt to "discover what is common to all modes of understanding."

In many respects my analysis deepens a criticism of Gadamer made by Hubert L. Dreyfus years ago. This criticism constitutes a very small portion of his article "Holism and Hermeneutics," so I should like to quote it in its entirety (including Dreyfus's own quotes from Gadamer's *Truth and Method*):

> Much of the confusion concerning hermeneutics in the current literature stems from the fact that Gadamer, who claims to be working out the implications of Heidegger's notion of hermeneutics, never seems to have taken a stand on Heidegger's claim that there is a level of everyday practice (the *Vorhabe*) beneath our theoretical presuppositions and assumptions (the *Vorsicht*). Gadamer often employs the right rhetoric, as when he says: "We always stand within tradition, and this is no objectifying process, i.e., we do not conceive of what tradition says as something other, something alien. It is always part of us . . . a recognition of ourselves which our later historical judgment would hardly see as a kind of knowledge." But at times he seems to side with cognitivists like Quine. In describing the hermeneutic pre-understanding, instead of speaking of *Vorhabe*, he speaks of *Vorurteil* (prejudice or pre-judgment), which seems for him to be an implicit belief or assumption: "The isolation of *prejudice* clearly requires the suspension of its *validity* for us. For so long as our mind is influenced by a prejudice, we do not *know* and consider it as a judgment."[1]

Dreyfus makes, I think, an important criticism of "Gadamer's claim to be expounding Heideggerian hermeneutics, when, in fact, he fails to distinguish practice and theory."[2] Gadamer is not consistent, in Dreyfus's view, in his portrayal of the background: Are the structures of preunderstanding more like belief (propositional knowledge, rules, representations) than practice (habits, customs, skills)? Dreyfus is sure that *"the background is not beliefs, either explicit or implicit."*[3]

While Dreyfus's criticism is sound as far as it goes, it does not go far enough. He is prevented from doing this for two reasons. First, his entire discussion of the nature of the background is in terms of practices, what he variously calls "background of practices," "cultural practices," "shared background practices," and so on. This is too narrow, even if it does accurately represent what Heidegger means by *Vorhabe*. As I hope my discussion of Dewey will make clear, there is no particularly good reason to limit primordial understanding to practical meaning. We must turn to Dewey the pragmatist to learn the limits of practice. Second, Dreyfus is simply mistaken when he asserts that "Heidegger is the first, as far as I know, to have noted this non-cognitive precondition of all understanding, and to have seen its central importance."[4] A decade before *Being and Time* was published, Dewey had already formulated his position that "the intellectual element is set in a context which is non-cognitive and which holds within it in suspense a vast complex of other qualities and things that in the experience itself are objects of esteem or aversion, of decision, of use, of suffering, of endeavor and revolt, not of knowledge."[5] My approach to deepening Dreyfus's criticism of Gadamer will not be to extend his brief analysis of Gadamer's flawed grasp of Heidegger, but rather to view Gadamer in the context of Dewey's theory of habit, a theory that is at least as powerful as Heidegger's in accounting for the "non-cognitive precondition of all understanding."

Thus, I wish neither to challenge Gadamer's Heideggerian credentials, nor to accept them as if the general understanding that Gadamer is extending Heidegger is above criticism. My argument will be that *Vorurteil* interprets "meaning on the model of truth." The result is that Gadamer's theory of *Vorurteil* shrinks or constricts the concept of understanding by requiring meaning to be fitted to the world in the interstices of truth and the promises of truth. In opposition to this view, Dewey would agree with Arendt that the "need of reason is not inspired by the quest for truth but by the quest for meaning." Habit, I think, better captures reason's inspiration than does *Vorurteil*.

A preliminary look at Dewey's and Gadamer's most basic starting points will help orient the following discussion and establish some of its outlines. Where one might expect Dewey to see understanding as a capacity of beings who have problems, test hypotheses, and seek scientific knowledge as the fullest expression of the cognitive significance of experience, one instead finds Dewey insisting that "what is really 'in' experience extends much further than that which at any time is *known*."[6] Where one might expect Gadamer to see understanding as a way of addressing the world freed not only from scientific standards of cognitive significance, but also from the epistemological tradition of limiting the experiencing of meaning to decisions about the tenability of a belief and its promise as a knowledge claim, one instead finds Gadamer insisting that "the primodial significance of the idea of understanding is that of 'knowing about something.'"[7] For Dewey, the world's meanings and its truths are ascertained independently of each other; habits are not recording devices for the retention and expression of truths. For Gadamer, meaning and truth come into being simultaneously because prejudices establish our initial "hold" on the world and these prejudgments—like judgments—are measured by their validity or legitimacy, their truth. The aim or desire of understanding is correctness, truth, knowledge. The correctness or truth of understanding depends upon the correctness or truth of the preunderstanding contained in one's prejudices. Thus, Gadamer's ambition is to show that true understanding—understanding wherein truth is distinguished from falsity—involves a range of truth more comprehensive than the scientific knowledge and truth provided by scientific method. Dewey's position is that the range of understanding is more comprehensive than that contained in knowledge and truth claims, scientific or otherwise, because habit's "hold" on the world cannot be measured simply or only by its truth or correctness. Habit and prejudice give us different versions of the nature and aim of understanding, because they provide very different accounts of the historicality of understanding, different accounts of the fore-structures of understanding, and generally different viewpoints on the kind of being it is who understands.

My procedure will be to focus on a limited number of texts relevant to habit and *Vorurteil*. From Gadamer, I will discuss section 2 of the second part of *Truth and Method*, "Foundations of a Theory of Hermeneutical Experience." I also will make use of two of Gadamer's essays, "The Universality of the Hermeneutical Problem" and "The Problem of Historical Consciousness." From Dewey I will rely primarily on two chapters from *Experience and Nature*: the 1925 and 1929 versions of the first chapter, "Experience and Philosophic Method," and the eighth chapter, "Existence, Ideas, and Consciousness." In none of these chapters is habit specifically analyzed by Dewey, yet they present some essential features of his understanding of how things are "'in' experience" prior to their presence as objects of knowledge. I shall first present Dewey's views on the habitual and then examine Gadamer's views on prejudice and understanding in the context provided by Dewey. I shall then draw out some of the implications of this comparison by examining an example of the hermeneutical experience offered by Gadamer: the reading of a letter. How do we understand a letter?

I

In *Human Nature and Conduct*, Dewey says:

> The word habit may seem twisted somewhat from its customary use when employed as we have been using it. But we need a word to express that kind of human activity which is influenced by prior activity and in that sense acquired; which contains within itself a certain ordering or systematization of minor elements of action; which is projective, dynamic in quality, ready for overt manifestation; and which is operative in some subdued subordinate form even when not obviously dominating

activity. Habit even in its ordinary usage comes nearer to denoting these facts than any other word.[8]

"We need a word" that will satisfy four conditions. First, it must express the historical character of human experience; it must allow for the endurance of meaning of "prior activity." Second, it must express the ordered, organized nature of human activity. Third, it must be active; it must establish not merely a level of readiness or preparedness, but must project a context. Fourth, the word must express a power that is "operative" though in "subdued form"; that is, the word must suggest both presence and absence, the manifest and the anonymous.

At least as early as 1902, in the remarkable essay "Interpretation of the Savage Mind," Dewey was using habit as the concept best suited to do justice to the historical, organized, projective, anonymous features of experience.[9] Habit is history naturalized, history become a nature. Habits record the outcomes of experience, organize the materials of present experience, and project the horizons within which present and future are specified or delineated, sometimes deliberately through critical reason and other times silently and anonymously. Our original access or opening to the world is founded on the creative, constitutive power of habitual meanings to prereflectively establish an accord between self and world. This primordial accord is taken up in many ways by human beings—labor, art, religion, everyday experience, science, and so on. All these forms of understanding the world depend upon habit for their sense, because none of them are possible without history, organization, projection, and the dialectic of presence and absence. Habit makes the world experienceable *as* laboring, appreciating, inferring, and so forth. Dewey nowhere better captured the centrality of habit than in his statement: "Through habits formed in intercourse with the world, we also inhabit the world."[10]

As late as 1949 Dewey was still advancing habit as the best "word" to account for the self and its world, objecting to Adelbert Ames, Jr., that "assumption" was "too *intellectual* a word to cover the active mechanism or apparatus" in perceiving rooms as rectangular.[11] We do not experience rooms as rectangular by virtue of acting on the assumption that they are; rather, we have the habit of perceiving rooms as rectangular. Dewey thus concluded that "the *assumption* that they are rectangular is in fact a net *intellectual* outcome of the habit."[12] Dewey wholly rejected any epistemological or metaphysical stance that substituted "intellectual outcome" for lived experience; this rejection is based upon his belief that habit's power to silently record, organize, and project a world cannot be limited or reduced to the knowing subject's organization and projection of a world.

Dewey's use of the idea of habit in *Experience and Nature* is particularly important not merely because it occurs at roughly the halfway mark of his half century use of the concept, but because it unmistakably shows that habit was the basis of his theory of experience and not merely a component of a more restricted area of inquiry, for example, in *Democracy and Education* or *Human Nature and Conduct*. Dewey does not devote a chapter to habit in *Experience and Nature*, yet chapter 1, "Experience and Philosophic Method," and chapter 8, "Existence, Ideas, and Consciousness," constitute the rudiments of what might be called a metaphysics of habitual being. These chapters develop a theory of consciousness, meaning, and understanding that is in effect an elaboration of Dewey's theory of habit. What Dewey explicitly says about habit in these chapters is in turn an amplification or deepening of his metaphysical intent to discover some of the "general features of experienced things," particularly those connected with consciousness, experience, and understanding. This conceptual reciprocity is fundamental to Dewey's entire philosophical effort. Habit as historical, organized, projective, and anonymous *is* experience, *is* consciousness, *is* understanding.

Perhaps the strongest claim made in the first chapter of *Experience and Nature* is that being and being known are not equivalent. We understand the world as habitual beings, and because we do, our relationship to the world is not primarily an affair of knowledge or intellect. Dewey was untiring in his criticism of epistemological and metaphysical positions that subscribed to this identification:

> *Being* and *having* things in ways other than knowing them, in ways never identical with knowing them, exist, and are preconditions of reflection and knowledge. *Being* angry, stupid, wise, inquiring; *having* sugar, the light of day, money, houses and lands, friends, laws, masters, subjects, pain and joy, occur in dimensions incommensurable to knowing these things which we are and have and use, and which have and use us. Their existence is unique, and, strictly speaking, indescribable; they can *only be* and *be had*, and then be pointed to in reflection. In the proper sense of the word, their existence is absolute, being qualitative. All cognitive experience must start from and must terminate in being and having things in just such unique, irreparable and compelling ways. And until this fact is a commonplace in philosophy, the notion of experience will not be a truism for philosophers.[13]

For Dewey, understanding "must start from and must terminate in being and having things in just such unique, irreparable and compelling ways."

The fore-structures provided by habit cannot be restricted to epistemological functions and values.

Heidegger was right: Understanding establishes my world openness in ways that go far beyond knowledge, information, and assertions. As Glenn Gray has so well said, "We are attached to the world in a thousand ways."[14] The fore-meanings projected by habit are not simply underdeveloped, incomplete beliefs, assertions, or propositions. What appears or presents itself in experience is not necessarily a belief seeking validation as a candidate for knowledge. The profundity of the following statement is disguised by its brevity: "What is really 'in' experience extends much further than that which at any time is *known*."[15] A metaphysics of understanding must from the beginning disclaim the "intellectualism" Dewey identifies:

> By "intellectualism" as an indictment is meant the theory that all experiencing is a mode of knowing, and that all subject-matter, all nature, is, in principle, to be reduced and transformed till it is defined in terms identical with the characteristics presented by refined objects of science as such. The assumption of "intellectualism" goes contrary to the facts of what is primarily experienced. For things are objects to be treated, used, acted upon and with, enjoyed and endured, even more than things to be known. They are things had before they are things cognized.[16]

The ways in which I "have" the world are not all modes of knowing. If a theory of understanding is not to be prejudiced from the outset in favor of objects of knowledge and judgment, and not even necessarily scientific knowledge and judgment, it must recognize with Dewey that "unless there is breach of historic and natural continuity, cognitive experience must originate within that of a non-cognitive sort."[17] Reflective experience is not the norm for all experience simply because reflective habits are not the standard or measure for all other habits.

The "being" and "having" that Dewey so respected are based upon habit; our "being" and "having" the world through habit compels us to acknowledge that "knowing is a connection of things which depends upon other and more primary connections between a self and thing."[18] The "primary connections" to which Dewey refers are established in and through habit; failure to attend to these knowledge-transcending "primary connections" is the result of what he calls "selective simplification" or "selective emphasis."[19] Dewey notes that "too often . . . the professed empiricist only substitutes a dialectical development of some notion about experience for an analysis of experience as it is humanly lived."[20] This tendency is not restricted to empiricists: "The commonest assumption of philosophies, common even to philosophies very different from one another, is the assumption of the identity of objects of knowledge and ultimately real objects."[21] Because the field of habitual meanings and its projected horizon is not simply an epistemological field, experience must be respected as a concatenated, complex field composed of an enormous variety of habitual meanings:

> Now the notion of experience, however devoid of differential subject-matter—since it includes all subject-matters—at least tells us that we must not start with arbitrarily selected simples, and from them deduce the complex and varied, assigning what cannot be thus deduced to an inferior realm of being. It warns us that the tangled and complex is what we primarily find; that we work from and within it to discriminate, reduce, analyze; and that we must keep track of these activities, pointing to them, as well as to the things upon which they are exercised, and to their refined conclusions.[22]

To see knowledge as a simplification of experience will seem strange as long as knowledge is separated from the "primary connections between a self and thing," connections founded upon habit. Habits fuse, dissolve, splinter, become stable and unstable, contradict and disagree with each other, confirm and agree with each other. Habit gives me a world of hues, intensities, shadings, hesitations, confidences, withdrawals, and openings. Habit's grasp of the world, its understanding of it, cannot be reduced to the "refined conclusions" of knowledge.

This tendency to confuse habit and its intellectual outcomes is a characteristic of many philosophical orientations, some with distinctly different and seemingly incompatible perspectives. The range of possibilities solicited by habit cannot be restricted to the offerings of reflective experience, yet the tendency of philosophy is to do precisely this. Dewey says of the philosopher that

> instead of seeing that the product of knowing is *statement* of things, he is given to taking it as an *existential equivalent* of what things really are "in themselves," so that the subject-matter of other modes of experience are deviations, shortcomings, or trespasses—or as the dialectical philosopher puts it, mere "phenomena." The experiential or denotative method tells us that we must go behind the refinements and elaborations of reflective experience to the gross and compulsory things of our doings, enjoyments and sufferings—to the things that force us to

labor, that satisfy needs, that surprise us with beauty, that compel obedience under penalty.[23]

"The gross and compulsory things of our doings, enjoyments and sufferings" is not an epistemological foundation for Dewey, but rather the context within which historically situated practices can be interpreted in the light of the prevailing habits of mind that give these practices their sense and import. The historicality of understanding requires not merely a respect for context, practice, and purpose, but a grasp of how history is embodied in the individual: "A human being carries his past in his habitudes and habituations, and we can rightly observe and understand the latter only as we are aware of the history which is included within them."[24]

Habit and history motivate each other and embody each other. The selective emphasis on known objects — the decontextualization of knowledge — distorts the human condition, not because it omits feeling, intuition, and so on, but because it makes knowledge impossible: "Knowledge that is ubiquitous, all-inclusive and all-monopolizing, ceases to have meaning in losing all context; that it does not appear to do so when made supreme and self-sufficient is because it is literally impossible to exclude that context of non-cognitive but experienced subject-matter which gives what is *known* its import."[25] Because we are habitual beings and not simply epistemological subjects seeking to reach agreement about the objects of the world, philosophers must resist the "exaggeration of the features of known objects at the expense of the qualities of objects of enjoyment and trouble, friendship and human association, art and industry."[26] Habit's hold on the world — and understanding's — exceeds the grasp of "traits characteristic of objects known."

Because we are habitual beings, experience cannot be reduced to the known nor can it be reduced to consciousness:

> Experience is something quite other than "consciousness," that is, that which appears qualitatively and focally at a particular moment. The common man does not need to be told that ignorance is one of the chief features of experience; so are habits skilled and certain in operation so that we abandon ourselves to them without consciousness. Yet ignorance, habit, fatal implication in the remote, are just the things which professed empiricism, with its reduction of experience to states of consciousness, denies to experience. It is important for a theory of experience to know that under certain circumstances men prize the distinct and clearly evident. But it is no more important than it is to know that under other circumstances twilight, the vague, dark and mysterious

flourish. Because intellectual crimes have been committed in the name of the subconscious is no reason for refusing to admit that what is not explicitly present makes up a vastly greater part of experience than does the conscious field to which thinkers have so devoted themselves.[27]

To properly understand experience, one must understand "twilight, the vague, dark and mysterious"; one must understand, in other words, the sense-giving powers of the horizonal field of habitual meanings within which the "conscious field" has its life.

Precisely because habitual, prereflective meanings are already at work, already anticipating the outlines of my world prior to any form of conscious, deliberate regard, my world has a depth which transcends its particular states of consciousness:

> When disease or religion or love, or knowledge itself is experienced, forces and potential consequences are implicated that are neither directly present nor logically implied. They are "in" experience quite as truly as are present discomforts and exaltations. . . . Experience is no stream, even though the stream of feelings and ideas that flows upon its surface is the part which philosophers love to traverse. Experience includes the enduring banks of natural constitution and acquired habit as well as the stream. The flying moment is sustained by an atmosphere that does not fly, even when it most vibrates.[28]

The sort of background or horizon that habit provides is not simply a warehouse of sedimented beliefs or a stock of knowledge at hand, or for that matter, anything "at hand." The habitual background is a vibrating or resonating "atmosphere" that sustains the "flying moment" of determinate, conscious states. Dewey thus would agree entirely with Dreyfus that the background *"is not beliefs"* and further that it cannot be made the object of an objective analysis. In the same manner that atmospheric perspective presences by itself receding, habit brings meaning to focus by itself receding from focus. Thus, consciousness and the products of presencing consciousness—information, agreement, clarity, determinateness, coherence—cannot be identified with experience when its habitual and transcendent character is accorded proper weight. To understand experience, its depth in habitual meaning must be addressed and in a manner that does not selectively simplify the sustaining atmosphere. Experience has a "deep structure" governed by habit; a theory of understanding must account for habit's manner of understanding the world.

In "Existence, Ideas, and Consciousness," Dewey analyzes how habit understands the world. His first step involves consideration of the "subconscious" of human thinking:

> Apart from language, from imputed and inferred meaning, we continually engage in an immense multitude of immediate organic selections, rejections, welcomings, expulsions, appropriations, withdrawals, shrinkings, expansions, elations and dejections, attacks, warding off, of the most minute, vibratingly delicate nature. We are not aware of the qualities of many or most of these acts; we do not objectively distinguish and identify them. Yet they exist as feeling qualities and have an enormous directive effect on our behavior. If, for example, certain sensory qualities of which we are not cognitively aware cease to exist, we cannot stand or control our posture and movements. In a thoroughly normal organism, these "feelings" have an efficiency of operation which it is impossible for thought to match. Even our most highly intellectualized operations depend upon them as a "fringe" by which to guide our inferential movements. They give us our *sense* of rightness and wrongness, of what to select and emphasize and follow up, and what to drop, slur over and ignore, among the multitude of inchoate meanings that are presenting themselves. They give us premonitions of approach to acceptable meanings, and warnings of getting off the track. Formulated discourse is mainly but a selected statement of what we wish to retain among all these incipient starts, following ups and breakings off. Except as a reader, a hearer repeats something of these organic movements, and thus "gets" their qualities, he does not get the *sense* of what is said; he does not really assent, even though he give cold approbation. These qualities are the stuff of "intuitions" and in actuality the difference between an "intuitive" and an analytic person is at most a matter of degree, of relative emphasis. The "reasoning" person is one who makes his "intuitions" more articulate, more deliverable in speech, as explicit sequence of initial premises, jointures, and conclusions.[29]

We stand, Dewey says, in a relationship to the world prior to the predication of distinct objects of inferential, representational thought. "Feeling qualities" project before me a field of implicit and prethematic meanings that constitute the horizon within which "our most highly intellectualized operations" perform their task. "Formulated discourse" is a refinement, a specification and articulation of this pretheoretical understanding of the world. Without this anticipatory grasp of the world, one "does not get the sense of what is said; he does not really assent, even though he give cold approbation." We must have a "sense of" something in order to have a conception of it.

What constitutes this subconscious "sensing" power? "The subconscious of a civilized adult reflects all the habits he has acquired; that is to say, all the organic modifications he has undergone."[30] What Dewey calls "feeling qualities" are habitual meanings that are immediately had or lived; they provide that "context of non-cognitive but experienced subject-matter which gives what is *known* its import."[31] Positings, reflections, and knowings are contextualized by a habitual background—a horizon of implicit, sensed meanings that foreshadows and prepares their achievements. These habitual, sensed meanings are the sustaining "atmosphere that does not fly, even when it most vibrates." And it is these habitual, sensed meanings that must find a central place in an adequate theory of experience and understanding.

By referring to the background as "subconscious," Dewey was seeking to emphasize as strongly as possible that "context" and "atmosphere" cannot be called "conscious." Dewey prefers to call this habitual context or atmosphere "mind," and wishes to distinguish it as sharply as possible from consciousness. He says:

> There is thus an obvious difference between mind and consciousness; meaning and an idea. Mind denotes the whole system of meanings as they are embodied in the workings of organic life; consciousness in a being with language denotes awareness or perception of meanings; it is the perception of actual events, whether past, contemporary or future, in their meanings, the having of actual ideals. The greater part of mind is only implicit in any conscious act or state; the field of mind—of operative meanings—is enormously wider than that of consciousness. Mind is contextual and persistent; consciousness is focal and transitive. Mind is, so to speak, structural, substantial, a constant background and foreground; perceptive consciousness is process, a series of heres and nows. Mind is a constant luminosity; consciousness intermittent, a series of flashes of varying intensities. Consciousness is, as it were, the occasional interception of messages continually transmitted, as a mechanical receiving device selects a few of the vibrations with which the air is filled and renders them audible.[32]

The "organic modifications" of habit are denoted by "mind": "the whole system of meanings as they are embodied in the workings of organic life." The field of habitual meanings—mind—"is enormously wider than that of consciousness." The anticipatory and historical foundations of intentional life are located for Dewey in habits of mind.

The difference between mind and consciousness is crucial to Dewey's theory of experience and to my assessment of Gadamer's use of prejudice, so I should like to quote a rather long section wherein Dewey significantly deepens his analysis of mind and consciousness:

> The relation between mind and consciousness may be indicated by a familiar happening. When we read a book, we are immediately conscious of meanings that present themselves, and vanish. These meanings existentially occurring are *ideas*. But we are capable of getting ideas from what is read because of an organized system of meanings of which we are not at any one time completely aware. Our mathematical or political "mind" is the system of such meanings as possess and determine our particular apprehensions or ideas. There is however a continuum or spectrum between this containing system and the meanings which, being focal and urgent, are the ideas of the moment. There is a contextual field between the latter and those meanings which determine the habitual direction of our conscious thoughts and supply the organs for their formation. One great mistake in the orthodox psychological tradition is its exclusive preoccupation with sharp focalization to the neglect of the vague shading off from the foci into a field of increasing dimness.
>
> Discrimination in favor of the clearly distinguished has a certain practical justification, for the vague and extensive background is present in every conscious experience and therefore does not define the character of any one in particular. It represents that which is being used and taken for granted, while the focal phase is that which is imminent and critical. But this fact affords no justification for neglect and denial in theory of the dim and total background consciousness of every distinct thought. If there were a sharp division between the ideas that are focal as we read a certain section of a book and what we have already read, if there were not carried along a sense of the latter, what we now read could not take the form of an idea. Indeed, the use of such words as context and background, fringe, etc., suggests something too external to meet the facts of the case. The larger system of meaning suffuses, interpenetrates, colors what is now and here uppermost; it gives them sense, feeling, as distinct from signification.[33]

What do we do — or what happens to us — when we read a book? I think it is possible to argue that Dewey's answer presupposes the hermeneutic circle, but that he would consider this an incomplete response to the question. Yes, the "focal" meanings or the "ideas of the moment" contribute to an understanding of the whole, and this "containing system" determines the meaning of "what is now and here uppermost." The remarkable matter for Dewey was not the circular nature of understanding, but rather the fact that movement between part and whole—movement within the "contextual field"—was accomplished through having a "sense of" rather than through an explicit "knowing." This "sense of" is an expression and achievement of the silent workings of habit, and it is only through this "sensing" that the specification of distinct ideas is possible. What is projected and conserved in our "sense of" is not an idea or belief seeking confirmation. Having a "sense of" is not an anticipation of truth.

Dewey was not satisfied that the example of reading a book fully explained the dialectic between background and focus, habitual meaning and idea, so he offers another example:

> Change the illustration from reading a book to seeing and hearing a drama. The emotional as well as intellectual meaning of each presented phase of a play depends upon the operative presence of a continuum of meanings. If we have to remember what has been said and done at any particular point, we are not aware of what is now said and done; while without its suffusive presence in what is now said and done we lack clew to its meaning. Thus the purport of past affairs is present in the momentary cross-sectional idea in a way which is more intimate, direct and pervasive than the way of recall. It is positively and integrally carried in and by the incidents now happening; these incidents are, in the degree of genuine dramatic quality, fulfillment of the meanings constituted by past events; they also give this system of meanings an unexpected turn, and constitute a suspended and still indeterminate meaning, which induces alertness, expectancy. It is this double relationship of continuation, promotion, carrying forward, and of arrest, deviation, need of supplementation, which defines that focalization of meanings which is consciousness, awareness, perception. Every case of consciousness is dramatic; drama is an enhancement of the conditions of consciousness.[34]

In viewing a play, I do not "remember" or "recall" earlier parts of it. The "purport of past affairs" is present through a "sense of" rather than a "conception of"; this retentive and protentive "sense of" is the horizontal structure "which defines that focalization of meanings which is consciousness, awareness, perception." Because our habit-born "sense of" is projective and anticipatory, as well as retentive and conserving, their meeting in the present is essentially dramatic, indeterminate, open. The fusion of past, present, and future is suspenseful and uncertain; my "sense of" may or may not be fulfilled as expected or anticipated. The projections of habit are solicitations of possible meanings, meanings that exist more as a vibrating "atmosphere" than a set of hypotheses awaiting confirmation. Parts or episodes are contextualized against the background of habitual meanings; background is modified and reconstructed as it presses forward and is challenged by episode or part, giving these background, habitual meanings "an unexpected turn."

Dewey's theory of habitual meaning not only permits but requires a broadened conception of understanding. An adequate theory of experience, as well as its intelligibility in and to understanding, is not a theory of knowledge, truth, or method. The entire thrust and spirit of Dewey's conception of habitual meaning is antagonistic to the view that one understands the meaning of an object when one can see, know, establish its truth. The circle of anticipation and fulfillment proposed in Dewey's conception of background, habit, and sensing does not presuppose truth, though it *can* take a course of truth-seeking. When we understand something—a poem, a disappointment, an explanation, or a child's hurt feelings—we are not simply settling doubt, fixing belief, getting at "the truth." We can understand these sorts of objects because "every empirical situation has its own organization of a direct, non-logical character,"[35] an organization prepared by habit and our "senses of."

The historicality of understanding and its anticipatory/fulfilling organization of the world cannot be reduced to "objects of a cognitive regard, themes of an intellectual gesture."[36] Experience in which habit is at work is historical consciousness, and because habit makes possible being and having things in "ways other than knowing them, in ways never identical with knowing them," historical consciousness cannot be identified with knowing consciousness. Dewey questions the priority of the known because in a sense, he must: his theory of habit establishes the intelligibility of the world prior to acts of knowing consciousness. The world's intelligibility, its understandability, is not equivalent to knowledge and its lessons in "how to conduct doubt profitably."[37] My habitual understanding of the world is "not an affair of truth or falsity, certitude, or doubt, but one of existence."[38]

The fact that there is a "contextual field" joining background habitual meanings and focal ideas accounts for Dewey's opposition to the "reduction of experience to states of consciousness."[39] There is more in experience than what we know, and more in experience than what we are conscious of. Understanding cannot be restricted to a "conscious act or state," to what is present to consciousness. An adequate theory of understanding must recognize that "what is not explicitly present makes up a vastly greater part of experience than does the conscious field to which thinkers have so devoted themselves."[40] My understanding is a consequence, an outcome, of what is no longer explicitly present. This absence—the past—is present in my habits. The presence of the past is habit's accomplishment.

The horizons projected by habit are not necessarily explicit, are not necessarily seen *as* horizons waiting to be seized by conscious attention and harmonized with each other. Any account of how habits of mind are both validated and fulfilled, when mind is understood as "the field of mind—of operative meanings," must provide for the "continuum of meanings" joining implicit mind and explicit, focalizing consciousness. Failing this, one will have a truncated theory of understanding because the absent—"the larger system of meanings" which "suffuses, interpenetrates, colors what is now and here uppermost"—will be construed as a virtual presence, a virtual state of explicit consciousness.

The implicit horizon of habitual meanings is not constituted by assumptions, expectations, hypotheses waiting to come to validated presence in knowing consciousness. "The flying moment is sustained by an atmosphere that does not fly, even when it most vibrates." The ways in which I adjust, adapt, and respond to the world are not restricted to the validation of those habitual meanings which constitute the atmosphere of my world and my experience. The world becomes meaningful for me between and around criteria for validity and truth; similarly, the world is not intelligible to me solely or primarily through what is "explicitly present." In short, the full presence of meaning to consciousness, specifically, knowing consciousness, is not Dewey's norm or standard of intelligibility or understanding because it is not habit's norm of intelligibility or understanding.

II

Many of the main components of Gadamer's theory of prejudice are contained in the following passage from "The Universality of the Hermeneutical Problem":

> It is not so much our judgements as it is our prejudices that constitute our being. This is a provocative formulation, for I am using it to restore to its rightful place a positive concept of prejudice that was driven out of our linguistic usage by the French and the English Enlightenment. It can be shown that the concept of prejudice did not originally have the meaning we have attached to it. Prejudices are not necessarily unjustified and erroneous, so that they inevitably distort the truth. In fact, the historicity of our existence entails that prejudices, in the literal sense of

the word, constitute the initial directedness of our whole ability to experience. Prejudices are biases of our openness to the world. They are simply conditions whereby we experience something—whereby what we encounter says something to us. This formulation certainly does not mean that we are enclosed within a wall of prejudices and only let through the narrow portals those things that can produce a pass saying, "Nothing new will be said here." Instead we welcome just that guest who promises something new to our curiosity. But how do we know the guest whom we admit is one who has something *new* to say to us? Is not our expectation and our readiness to hear the new also necessarily determined by the old that has already taken possession of us? The concept of prejudice is closely connected to the concept of authority, and the above image makes it clear that it is in need of hermeneutical rehabilitation. Like every image, however, this one too is misleading. The nature of the hermeneutical experience is not that something is outside and desires admission. Rather, we are possessed by something and precisely by means of it we are opened up for the new, the different, the true.[41]

There is a central point to note about this formulation of prejudice or prejudgment. Prejudices are not merely "biases of our openness to the world"; rather, we are opened to the world as truth seekers and knowers. Prejudices do not "inevitably distort the truth," but rather through them "we are opened up for the new, the different, the true." Gadamer makes this clear in the introduction to *Truth and Method*, stating that the book does not stop with a justification of the "truth of art" but instead "tries to develop from this starting-point a concept of knowledge and of truth which corresponds to the whole of our hermeneutic experience."[42] Gadamer is concerned with truths that "go essentially beyond the range of methodical knowledge," but he is nonetheless concerned with truth.

When we understand, we understand the actual or possible truth of something; as conditions of such understanding, prejudices, unlike habits, are, to use Dewey's words, "objects of a cognitive regard, themes of an intellectual gesture."[43] A closer examination of Gadamer's conception of prejudice, knowledge, and experience will reveal a strikingly different view than Dewey's of "the conditions in which understanding takes place,"[44] precisely because it restricts these conditions to the ability of prejudice to know the truth. The meaningfulness of habit, the sense of habit for Dewey, is not limited to meanings known and known as true. Thus, Gadamer accepts what Dewey explicitly rejects, "that all experiencing is a mode of knowing."[45]

Whether translated as prejudice, prejudgment, or preconception, there is little doubt that the history carried or embodied in *Vorurteile* is an epistemological history. Early in the section "Prejudices as Conditions of Understanding," Gadamer notes that "justified prejudices" are "productive of knowledge." Later, Gadamer states that when attempting to understand an author's text, "we try to accept the objective validity of what he is saying." The value of temporal distance is that it "lets the true meaning of the object emerge fully." The truth of one's prejudices and the claim to truth of a text form a kind of epistemological embrace, one founded on the principle that "the discovery of the true meaning of a text or a work of art is never finished; it is in fact an infinite process." Through temporal distance the "really critical question of hermeneutics" can be solved, "distinguishing the true prejudices, by which we understand, from the false ones, by which we misunderstand."[46] Our past, our history, is not embodied in us simply as determinate or indeterminate capacities, or as a determinate or indeterminate horizon. Our history is composed of "true prejudices" and "false ones."

Since prejudices are "conditions whereby we experience something," and since we are constantly called upon to "test" our prejudices—to determine their truth or falsity—it is not surprising that Gadamer's theory of experience emphasizes its openness, that is, its openness to new confirmations and rejections of prejudices. He states that "the fact that experience is valid, so long as it is not contradicted by new experience (*ubi non reperitur instantia contradictoria*), is clearly characteristic of the general nature of experience, no matter whether we are dealing with its scientific form, in the modern experiment, or with the experience of daily life that men have always had."[47] The entire section titled "The Concept of Experience and the Essence of the Hermeneutical Experience" leaves little doubt that Gadamer does not object to science's quest for truth, but rather its forgetfulness that truth and history are not antagonistic but rather complementary:

> Modern science thus simply carries through in its methodology what experience has always striven after. Experience is valid only if it is confirmed; hence its dignity depends on its fundamental repeatability. But this means that experience, by its very nature, abolishes its history. This is true even of everyday experience, and how much more for any scientific version of it. Thus it is not just a chance one-sided emphasis of modern scientific theory, but has a foundation in fact, that the theory of experience is related teleologically to the truth that is derived from it.[48]

Gadamer's theory of experience is a theory of knowing experience, and though he objects to the "epistemological schematization" of experience which "diminishes its original meaning,"[49] for him it is clear that truth and falsity are inherent properties of our experience of things; that is, the "inner historicality of experience" is mediated by "true" and "false" prejudices. This is why Gadamer believes that validity—what is "not contradicted by new experience"—is "characteristic of the general nature of experience."[50] Through the negative, through what "runs counter to our expectation," we can continue to find the truth, to search for it. So it is not a "higher form of knowledge" reached by the experienced man, but instead an aversion to dogmatism. Our prejudices must be tested; they must answer to reality. This is why Gadamer says: "Experience teaches us to recognize reality. What is properly gained from all experience, then is to know what is. But 'what is,' here, is not this or that thing, but 'what cannot be done away with' (*was nicht mehr umzustossen ist*—Ranke)."[51] Knowledge of "what cannot be done away with" is the fulfillment of experience; knowledge is what is gained from all experience.

Gadamer is entirely consistent in his belief that understanding is knowing, that "reaching the truth" is "always our goal."[52] *Vorurteile* are instruments of truth-seeking and truth-making. Experience, it follows, is a sort of battleground upon which our "readiness to recognize the other as potentially right and to let him or it prevail against me" arises out of, and must struggle against, the tradition embodied in my prejudices:

> Every experience is a confrontation. Because every experience sets something new against something old and in every case it remains open in principle whether the new will prevail—that is, will truly become experience—or whether the old, accustomed, predictable will be confirmed in the end.... So it is basically with all experience. It must either overcome tradition or fail because of tradition. The new would be nothing new if it did not have to assert itself anew against something.[53]

Vorurteile are the persisting, continuity-making structures of experience, the epistemological braces without which past, present, future could not present themselves as historicity. The entire life of these braces is devoted to acting as a kind of frontier—an epistemological frontier—along which the new and the old confront each other, each seeking dominion and with one or the other being "confirmed." This is Gadamerian experience.

To think of *Vorurteile* as epistemological frontier underscores two very important points regarding their nature and function in experience. The task of *Vorurteile* is to invest the object not simply with meaning, but meaning that seeks validation as its perfection. *Vorurteile*-based understanding necessarily involves the use of criteria of truth. Meanings may be projected falsely; they may not be true to the *Sache Selbst*. One must thus be on guard that one's experience is not guided by "inappropriate foremeanings," that is, meanings that "come to nothing in the working-out."⁵⁴ Which meanings are to be allowed passage through the epistemological frontier? Those that are legitimate, whose nature permits experience to affirm their truth and correctness.⁵⁵ The aim of understanding—and experience—is truth, not definitive truth but truth nonetheless. The truth function of understanding is so central to Gadamer that he accords it a transcendent status: "Every textual understanding presupposes that it is guided by transcendent expectations, expectations whose origins must be looked for in the relation between the intentional object of the text and the truth."⁵⁶ Experience perfects itself when it has been confirmed, when it has uncovered what is true.

The second point has already been mentioned. *Vorurteile* as the braces of experience are constantly confronted with challenges to their validity; hence, openness to experience is a necessary feature of all experience:

> Experience is always actually present only in the individual observation. It is not known in a previous universality. Here lies the fundamental openness of experience to new experience, not only in the general sense that errors are corrected, but that it is, in its essence, dependent on constant confirmation and necessarily becomes a different kind of experience where there is no confirmation (*ubi reperitur instantia contradictoria*).⁵⁷

New experience may contradict our *Vorurteile* and require their revision. This negative or negating aspect of experience requires that the epistemological frontier provided by *Vorurteile* be kept open and be prized for its openness. The *Vorurteile* that have proved to be true in past experience may become too settled, too satisfied with their successes, thus making the past unavailable for modification by the present and new. What our *Vorurteile* lead us to expect and what they actually encounter should occasion a reexamination of their merits, their truth.

Experience is thus a series of minor and major epistemological crises. The epistemological frontier of *Vorurteile* is the scene of an endless battle between truth claims. As we mature, as we gain more experience and become more experienced, we come to be less surprised by the failures of our past to truly grasp the present. Rather, I develop a positive readiness for such epistemological dislocation and rebuilding precisely because I know that my history may be proved wrong. This is why Gadamer believes that it is with Hegel that "the element of historicality comes into its own. He conceives experience as scepticism in action."⁵⁸ The experienced person is precisely one who is able to learn from experience and who has learned from experience:

> The experienced person proves to be ... someone who is radically undogmatic; who, because of the many experiences he has had and the knowledge he has drawn from them is particularly well equipped to have new experiences and to learn from them. The dialectic of experience has its own fulfillment not in definitive knowledge, but in that openness to experience that is encouraged by experience itself.[59]

The epistemological frontier must be an open frontier, it can have no borders other than the provisional ones established by *Vorurteile* that are "borne out by the things themselves." The epistemological frontier constructed by *Vorurteile* requires the experienced person to keep alert to his prejudices: "A person who does not accept that he is dominated by prejudices will fail to see what is shown by their light."[60] The experienced person "knows the limitedness of all prediction and the uncertainty of all plans. In him is realised the truth-value of experience."[61] The value of experience is measured and realized by its truth; openness is one of the necessary conditions and consequences for the fulfillment of the transcendent expectation of understanding—knowledge and truth.

Because *Vorurteile* are so insistent, because the truths they embody appear so natural and beyond doubt, what Gadamer calls temporal distance is needed in order to let "the true meaning of the object emerge fully."[62] Temporal distance is the filter enabling the interpreter to separate the "productive prejudices that make understanding possible from the prejudices that hinder understanding and lead to misunderstanding."[63] Temporal distance might be conceived of as the temporalization of the epistemological frontier of *Vorurteile*.

The immediate results of the confrontation between old and new cannot be counted on to determine whether the "true meaning" of an object has emerged. Truth must be assessed in time—"in time you will understand." Temporal distance reminds us that "we miss the whole truth of the phenomenon when we take its immediate appearance as the whole truth."[64] What is immediately given does not exhaust what is or may be true. Temporal distance instructs us in the art of questioning our prejudices, of risking them in the play of the epistemological frontier. Through the question—the essence of which "is the opening up, and keeping open, of possibilities"[65]—we can suspend the validity of a prejudice in order to establish whether it comes closer to, or moves further away from, the "true meaning" of the object.

Experience for Gadamer means we must talk about the truth of experience, and the truth of experience requires us to talk about the openness of experience and a preparedness for revision: "The hermeneutical consciousness has its fulfillment, not in its methodological sureness of itself, but in the same readiness for experience that distinguishes the experienced man by comparison with the man captivated by dogma."[66] In the section titled "The Hermeneutical Priority of the Question," Gadamer seeks to deepen his reflection on openness; he wishes to "examine the logical structure of openness." He commences his analysis with the proposition that "we cannot have experience without asking questions." Through questioning, we see the openness of experience, the "openness of being this or that." Questioning finds its fulfillment "in a radical negativity: the knowledge of not knowing." Experience has the structure of a question, and "the deciding of the question is the way to knowledge."[67] The objects we seek to understand, their very presence in our experience, are answers to questions; to understand these objects, we must understand the question to which the object is an answer.

In Gadamer's discussion of questioning, we find one of the central passages where the epistemological frontier of competing truth claims is contrasted with meaning:

> The close relation that exists between question and understanding is what gives the hermeneutic experience its true dimension. However much a person seeking understanding may leave open the truth of what is said, however much he may turn away from the immediate meaning of the object and consider, rather, its deeper significance, and take the latter not as true, but merely as meaningful, so that the possibility of its truth remains unsettled, this is the real and basic nature of a question, namely to make things indeterminate. Questions always bring out the undetermined possibilities of a thing.[68]

Questioning bids us to "leave open the truth," to leave it "unsettled," by treating competing truth claims "merely as meaningful." Meaning is a prelude to truth. Meaning is truth composing itself, unsettled and indeterminate. Meaning is an intermediary, neither chaos nor truth. Meaning waits to be, aims to be, true meaning, destined to be eternally questioned in the epistemological frontier of truth-establishing *Vorurteile*. While there certainly are places where Gadamer seems to allow *Vorurteile* to function as vehicles for a sort of existential comprehension of the world, they are far fewer than those where *Vorurteile* assert their need to have a meaning's truth determined before that meaning can claim any other kind of merit or importance. In this sense, Dreyfus was right to say of Gadamer that "at times he seems to side with cognitivists like Quine." My own analysis suggests that these times constitute a much larger proportion than Dreyfus seems to think. For Gadamer, truth aids, benefits, and ultimately reveals existence more profoundly than the "merely" meaningful.

At the risk of overextending this metaphor of *Vorurteile* as epistemological frontier, it is important to mention one other aspect of this frontier. Besides being the field upon which true and false prejudices vie for dominion, and besides the necessity that the frontier be open, the frontier is also unifying. If parts of the frontier did not have some connection to each other, if there were a significant lack of coherence among its parts, the legitimacy of the parts and the integrity of the whole would be in doubt. The "hermeneutic circle" is understanding's system of checks and balances: Part and whole must be fitted to each other so as to establish their harmony:

> The movement of understanding is constantly from the whole to the part and back to the whole. Our task is to extend in concentric circles the unity of the understood meaning. The harmony of all the details with the whole is the criterion of correct understanding. The failure to achieve this harmony means that understanding has failed.[69]

Understanding is not simply circular, nor does it merely seek unity. It anticipates a unity of meaning as a formal condition of understanding:

> The anticipation of completion that guides all our understanding is, then, always specific in content. Not only is an immanent unity of meaning guiding the reader assumed, but this understanding is likewise guided by the constant transcendent expectations of meaning which proceed from the relation to the truth of what is being said.[70]

The *Vorgriff der Vollkommenheit* permits us to expect a text to present a unity of meaning and to expect what it says to be true. If we could not expect unity and truth, the epistemological frontier would dissolve or disintegrate, leaving us defenseless in our effort to winnow out true from false *Vorurteile*. If *Vorurteile* are the epistemic braces of experience, not only is the *Vorgriff der Vollkommenheit* a necessary condition for their effective functioning, it also defines their purpose: "The anticipation of perfect coherence presupposes not only that the text is an adequate expression of a thought, but also that it really transmits to us the *truth*."[71] Only a coherent unity or completion of meaning is understandable, but of even greater importance to Gadamer is the conviction that in presupposing the unity of understood meanings, we have a basis for questioning the truth of our *Vorurteile*. Unity is truth's ally, and though the epistemological frontier of *Vorurteile* must be open and permeable, it cannot be fragmented and uncoordinated.

Before proceeding to a consideration of how habit and *Vorurteil* understand a letter, the main point of Gadamer's position should be summarized. Rising above all other considerations, *Vorurteile* are servants of truth. Prejudices "constitute the initial directedness of our whole ability to experience."[72] This "initial directedness" is an epistemological direction. In understanding a text "what we always expect is that it will *inform* us of something."[73] *Vorurteile* are a living record of what we know and what we can know. *Vorurteile* see the world as validities and confirmations, agreements and disagreements, questions decided and questions left open. The historicity of understanding is inseparable from the epistemic subject, for our "initial directedness" always involves criteria of truth.

All understanding is a claim to understand, and as a claim it demands an examining response to determine if its claim is true or false. A prejudice is not simply a taken-for-granted meaning, a useful meaning, a reliable meaning. A prejudice reaches out to the world to be tested and either verified or overthrown. Its place in the world is not secured until it has been tested and its validity established. Understanding is haunted by misunderstanding: that is not what that book, statement, wallpaper, glance means. You have misunderstood. What we gain from experience is knowledge; prejudice-grounded experience aims at agreement and confirmation, and though it constantly questions itself and its achievements, "the deciding of the question is the way to knowledge."[74] *Vorurteile* are the bases of a world well or poorly known, and to experience the world is to know it well or poorly; it is to be "open to the claim to truth."

III

To contrast habit and prejudice as sharply as possible, I will use an example offered by Gadamer: reading a letter. How do we understand a letter? Which concept—habit or prejudice—gives us a better basis for determining, in Gadamer's words, "what is common to all modes of understanding?" Does one or the other concept too narrowly restrict what understanding a letter consists of? What kind of being is it who understands a letter?

Gadamer's example of letter-reading occurs in his treatment of the foreconception of completion and truth:

> The anticipation of completion that guides all our understanding is, then, always specific in content. Not only is an immanent unity of meaning guiding the reader assumed, but his understanding is likewise guided by the constant transcendent expectations of meaning which proceed

> from the relation to the truth of what is being said. Just as the recipient of a letter understands the news that it contains and first sees things with the eyes of the person who wrote the letter, i.e., considers what he writes as true, and is not trying to understand the alien meanings of the letter writer, so we understand texts that have been handed down to us on the basis of expectations of meaning which are drawn from our own anterior relation to the subject. And just as we believe the news reported by a correspondent because he was present or is better informed, we are fundamentally open to the possibility that the writer of a transmitted text is better informed than we are, with our previously formed meaning. It is only when the attempt to accept what he has said as true fails that we try to "understand" the text, psychologically or historically, as another's meaning. The anticipation of completion, then, contains not only this formal element that a text should fully express its meaning, but also that what it says should be the whole truth.[75]

A letter (1) offers news (2) which we take to be true, that is, a true account of some event.

Gadamer uses the same example of reading a letter in "The Problem of Historical Consciousness," and it is part of the same discussion of what the translator here calls the "anticipation of 'perfect coherence'" and the transcendent expectation of truth:

> When we receive a letter, we see what is communicated through the eyes of our correspondent, but while seeing things through his eyes, it is not his personal opinions, but, rather, the event itself that we believe we ought to know by this letter. In reading a letter, to aim at the personal *thoughts* of our correspondent and not at the matters *about which* he reports is to contradict what is meant by a letter. Likewise, the anticipations implied by our understanding of a historical document emanate from our relations to "things" and not the way these "things" are transmitted to us. Just as we give credence to the news in a letter, because we assume that our correspondent personally witnessed the event or has validly learned of it, in the same way we are open to the possibility that the transmitted text may offer a more authentic picture of the "thing itself" than our own speculations. Only the disappointment of having let the text speak for itself and having then arrived at a bad result could prompt us to attempt "understanding" it by recourse to a supplementary psychological or historical point of view.[76]

Again a letter (1) offers news about an event (2) which we "ought to know." A letter for Gadamer transmits a truth; it is a truth claim. Although considerable attention has been devoted to the question of precisely what Gadamer means by truth, it does not appear to be such an esoteric matter when the letter example is carefully considered. This example seems to me to seriously weaken the effectiveness of any Heideggerian shield that might be raised to protect Gadamer from the sort of criticism I am making of his position. A letter informs us about an event and we permit ourselves to be compelled by that information because "the correspondent personally witnessed the event or has validly learned of it." A letter is an assertion about what is or was, of what truly is or was, about the "matters" reported on, not the "personal *thoughts*" of the reporter. Our response to a letter, like our response to any understandable object, is governed by the norm of truth, a norm of truth that does not appear to be grounded in any sort of existential comprehension that might be expected from a Heideggerian hermeneutics.

Following is a portion of a letter from Robert Frost to Louis Untermeyer, written in 1924:

> The boys had been made uncommonly interesting to themselves by Meiklejohn. They fancied themselves as thinkers. At Amherst you *thought*, while at other colleges you merely *learned*. (Wherefore if you love him, send your only son and child to Amherst.) I found that by thinking they meant stocking up with radical ideas, by learning they meant stocking up with conservative ideas—a harmless distinction, bless their simple hearts. I really liked them. It got so I called them young intelligences—without offense. We got on like a set of cogwheels in a clock. They had picked up the idea somewhere that the time was past for the teacher to teach the pupil. From now on it was the thing for the pupil to teach himself using, as he saw fit, the teacher as an instrument. The understanding was that my leg was always on the table for anyone to seize me by that thought he could swing me as an instrument to teach himself with. So we had an amusing year. I should have had my picture taken just as I sat there patiently waiting, waiting for the youth to take education into their own hands and start the new world. Sometimes I laughed and sometimes I cried a little internally. I gave one course in reading and one course in philosophy, but they both came to the same thing. I was determined to have it out with my youngers and betters as to what thinking really was. We reached an agreement that most of what they had regarded as thinking, their own and other peoples, was nothing but voting—taking sides on an issue they had nothing to do with laying down. But not on that account did we despair. We went bravely to work to discover, not only if we couldn't have ideas, but if we hadn't had them, a few

of them, at least, without knowing it. Many were ready to give up beaten and own themselves no thinkers in my sense of the word. They never set up to be original. They never pretended to put this and that together for themselves, never had a metaphor, never made an analogy. But they had, I knew. So I put them on the operating table and proceeded to take ideas they didn't know they had out of them as a prestidigitator takes rabbits and pigeons you have declared yourself innocent of out of your pockets trouserslegs and even mouth. Only a few resented being thus shown up and caught with the goods on them.[77]

It is possible to confirm what Frost says. Each sentence can be taken to be a truth claim. The boys could be polled to determine if they in fact believed what Frost imputed to them; members of the faculty could be queried; perhaps Frost's relatives could be contacted. Naturally, this is not how we understand Frost's letter, or at least it is not the principal way in which we understand the letter. We do not read Frost's letter as a confirmable or falsifiable report on education at Amherst. Gadamer steadfastly maintains that the text "really transmits to us the *truth*."[78] But what truths is Frost transmitting to us? What the attitudes of his "youngers" were? That he called them "young intelligences"?

Gadamer makes the remarkable claim that "in reading a letter to aim at the personal *thoughts* of our correspondent and not at the matters *about which* he reports is to contradict what is meant by a letter." This is true if the primary intent of all letter-writing is the promotion of knowledge. Our interest, however, in Frost and his teaching is not his knowledge of pedagogy or Amherst traditions. It is not principally the tenability of his beliefs about "the boys" that commands our attention. The ways in which Frost's wit and invention work upon us are not reducible to what he knew and did not know. Frost is not presenting a thesis about education at Amherst, and we do not understand it as such. In Dreyfus's language, we do not need to believe it to understand it.

Gadamer's letter example is critically important since it provides one of the clearest examples in *Truth and Method* of what he means by "truth." Truth may be disclosure, self-knowledge, dialogue, "fusion of horizons," *Vollkommenheit*, and so on. The letter example makes clear that although truth may also be these sorts of things for Gadamer, it is at least knowledge in the rather straightforward sense of asking someone, How do you know that? Is that really true? In other words, Is what you say knowledge of the *Sache Selbst* or just "personal thoughts"? In understanding a letter, I understand "the event itself that we believe we ought to know by this letter." This view of letter-writing and letter-reading as a vehicle for knowledge claims supports Gadamer's central contention: "The primordial significance of the idea of understanding is that of 'knowing about something.'"[79] As the bases of understanding and our "initial directedness," *Vorurteile* are dedicated to "knowing about something."

Dewey would not, I think, read Frost's letter as an instance of "knowing about something," since his idea of habit leads to the conclusion that "objects are found and dealt with in many other ways than those of knowledge."[80] Both Dewey and Gadamer agree that to grasp the universality and historicality of understanding requires, in Dewey's words, "beginning back of any science."[81] For Dewey this means beginning back of knowledge. To understand Frost's letter, it is not necessary to read it as a report providing information about an event "we ought to know." The experience prompted by Frost's letter exemplifies and confirms Dewey's belief that "things present themselves in characteristic context, with different savors, colors, weights, tempos and directions."[82] The "savors" and "colors" motivated by a phrase like "young intelligences" are not equivalent to "knowing about something." Knowledge is simply not the relevant standard or measure in our experience of "young intelligences." What is in my experience of "young intelligences," of thinking as "voting," and my general experience of Frost's gentle, playful provocations confirms Dewey's central contention that "what is really 'in' experience extends much further than that which at any time is *known*."[83] This is not a condition that can be overcome, simply because habit gives us an affinity to the world in ways not governed, in the first instance, by questions of doubt, belief, and verification. Not all our habits are prejudgments or preconceptions waiting for justification or rejection.

Let us take as another example a letter from James Agee to Father Flye, written in 1938:

> At the same time, I feel more shaken, confused, and ignorant, through my own actions, than I can remember having felt before. Yet my sense of confusion, ignorance, guilt and disintegrity is not to be cured by reversing and betraying such few things as in all faith and vigilance and scepticism not only of authority but of myself, still seem to me to be so. Quite plainly I know that in the most important things, or many of them, in my existence, I cannot know for sure what I am doing, or why, or at all surely the difference between right and wrong, which latter very often appear to be identical or so interlocked that the destruction of one entails the destruction of the other, like separating Siamese twins who use the same heart and bloodstream. This may simply mean that he who

moves beyond the safety of rules finds himself inevitably in the "tragedy" of the "human condition," which rules have been built to avoid or anaesthetize, and which must be undertaken without anaesthetic: but I am suspicious of laying pity and grief and sadness to such a general, fatal source rather than to a source for which I am personally responsible.[84]

From Gadamer's perspective, this letter is not really a letter but a "treatise":

> Letters ... are an interesting transitional phenomenon: a kind of written conversation that, as it were, stretches out the movement of talking at cross purposes before seeing each other's point. The art of writing letters consists in not letting what one says become a treatise on the subject, but making it acceptable to the correspondent. But it also consists, on the other hand, in preserving and fulfilling the measure of finality possessed by everything stated in writing.[85]

Is Agee attempting to get Father Flye to see his point? Is he attempting to make his doubts and confusions "acceptable" to Father Flye? What knowledge claims is Agee making? What shall we resolve or decide having read Agee's letter? That he was depressed? That he was insincere? Shallow? Self-destructive? When *Vorurteile* engage this letter they begin a movement of understanding wherein my projected meanings either are or "are not borne out by the things themselves." Are my prejudices "productive of knowledge"?[86] Is, however, the cognitive significance of Agee's letter reducible to what knowledge it affords?

I do not ask whether there is warrant for Agee's remark that right and wrong are "so interlocked that the destruction of one entails the destruction of the other," simply because I do not take it as a claim. Gadamer insists that "understanding means, primarily, to understand the content of what is said, and only secondarily to isolate and understand another's meaning as such."[87] How is this possible? Is Agee's "content" distinguishable from his "meaning"? For Gadamer it must be and is. In understanding the "content" of the letter, in being open to the experience it may provide us, Gadamer believes we shall be "knowing about something."

Dewey would understand Agee's letter differently. The meanings solicited by Agee's letter and those solicited by my habits form a pact, the dramatic nature of which is not simply an anticipation of a "truly valid understanding."[88] My first hold on Agee's meanings is not necessarily inspired by a desire to "conform to what the thing is."[89] That is, my experience of Agee's is not controlled by a desire to make true statements about it. Dewey undoubtedly would criticize Gadamer's philosophy of experience as a not-so-well-disguised intellectualism:

> By "intellectualism" as an indictment is meant the theory that all experiencing is a mode of knowing, and that all subject-matter, all nature, is, in principle, to be reduced and transformed till it is defined in terms identical with the characteristics presented by refined objects of science as such. The assumption of "intellectualism" goes contrary to the facts of what is primarily experienced. For things are objects to be treated, used, acted upon and with, enjoyed and endured, even more than things to be known. They are things *had* before they are things cognized.[90]

My experience of Agee experiencing himself, including my enjoyment and endurance of his experience, is not a "mode of knowing," is not a Gadamerian "knowing about something." It is not simply the methodic knowledge of science—"the refined objects of science"—which Dewey indicts in his criticism of intellectualism, but all systems which forget that "*being* and *having* things in ways other than knowing them, in ways never identical with knowing them, exist, and are preconditions of reflection and knowledge."[91] "Being" and "having" are not deficient modes of experience or understanding. The meanings brought into existence through them are not appropriately gauged or measured by the intellectualist's standards of cognitive importance, for though they are not irrelevant to the achievements of "being" and "having," what these forms of intentionality may reveal is not governed by an anticipation of truth and knowledge. The being and having of meaning, and the world understood through such meaning, do not presuppose a will to knowledge and truth.

The point is strikingly made in some of Emily Dickinson's letters. First, one to Louise Norcross, written in 1865:

> I am glad my little girl is at peace. Peace is a deep place. Some, too faint to push, are assisted by angels.
>
> I have more to say to you all than March has to maples, but then I cannot write in bed. I read a few words since I came home—John Talbot's parting with his son, and Margaret's with Suffolk. I read them in the garret, and the rafters wept.
>
> Remember me to your company, their Bedouin guest.
>
> Every day in the desert, Ishmael counts his tents. New heart makes new health, dear.
>
> Happiness is haleness. I dreamed last night I heard bees fight for pond-lily stamens, and waked with a fly in my room.
>
> Shall you be strong enough to lift me by the first of April? I won't be half as heavy as I was before. I will be good and chase my spools.
>
> I shall think of my little Eve going away from Eden. Bring me a jacinth for every finger, and an onyx shoe.[92]

My experience of this letter may be odd, eccentric, not sensitive or responsive to its solicitations, but is my experience of it a "bold venture that awaits its reward in confirmation by the object"?[93] Are the meanings solicited by "Some, too faint to push, are assisted by angels," the beginning of knowledge, knowledge for which we could—or would—provide evidence and arguments? Are *Vorurteile* being "tested" here to distinguish the true from the false, or are habitual meanings participating in and inventing "savors, colors, weights, tempos and directions"? How shall I proceed to determine whether my *Vorurteile* conflict with what is "true" concerning the object? Is my reward here "confirmation by the object" or what D. H. Lawrence called a "new effort of attention," that is, a reconstruction of the meanings through which the world is familiar to me?

Here is another letter of Emily Dickinson, this one to Susan Gilbert Dickinson, written in 1871: "Has All—a codicil?"[94] The "savors" and "colors" of meaning in Dickinson's letter do not require a structuring principle as excluding and constraining as knowledge conditions, precisely because the meanings set in motion by Dickinson's four words overflow the constraints and concerns of truth and knowledge. Justification and validation simply are not essential features of my experience and understanding of Dickinson's words, not unless one has decided that being and being known—being true—are indistinguishable. Gadamer has made this decision; this no doubt is partly why he sees his effort as one of formulating "an entirely different notion of knowledge and truth," one which he believes grows out of experience itself. This "different notion of knowledge and truth," however, does not do justice to Emily Dickinson's letter. Dewey would not be surprised, for in his view all those philosophical systems must fail—including in this case Gadamer's hermeneutics—which rest on the assumption that, in Dewey's words, "everything in its reality . . . is what a knower would find it to be."[95] As Dewey recognized, this is contrary to our experience of a habit-made world.

IV

In contrasting habit and prejudice, I have tried to show that truth-anticipating prejudice foreshortens and renders monochromatic the colors and intensities of experience. My comparison of Dewey and Gadamer has not disclosed any strong grounds upon which Gadamer's hermeneutics could be called "universal." On the contrary, meaning that seeks validation as its perfection is, in Dewey's view, a rather specialized sort of meaning and certainly cannot be the basis of a universal hermeneutics that purports to illumine "what is common to all modes of understanding."[96] Qualities and properties are specified and grasped—sensed—prior to testing, confirming, argumentation. Gadamer's theory of *Vorurteil* requires us to say that experience is not experience unless it is "continually confirmed," unless it is "an encounter with something that asserts itself as truth."[97] There is little of interest or importance in the mind unless it is before the mind as a belief or argument, as "an event of truth."

Perhaps, though, I still do not do justice to the radical transformation of truth in Gadamer along Heideggerian lines. Although it seems clear that experience for Gadamer is always an occasion for testing our "claim to truth," perhaps truth is a far more subtle concept in Gadamer than I have made it out to be. That it is elusive there seems to be general agreement. Richard Bernstein's remark that Gadamer "is employing a concept of truth that he never fully makes explicit," is fairly representative on the issue of truth in Gadamer.[98] If, however, close attention is paid to the letter-writing example in Gadamer, not as something incidental to his whole project but rather as a consummation of it, it is apparent that the "ideal of truth" is—at least—that of being validly informed, of receiving an "authentic picture" of the "thing itself," of giving assent to someone who has "validly learned" of an event. A letter transmits a truth and is a truth claim. The letter writer should be prepared to defend his statements because they are "not his personal opinions" but rather confirmable reports about the "event itself." I understand a letter, according to Gadamer, not through an appreciation of the "personal thoughts" of the writer, but through "knowing about something." Letter writer and letter reader are united by truth-telling. This example accords with Bernstein's characterization of Gadamer's general position on truth: "I am suggesting that what Gadamer himself is appealing to is a concept of truth that comes down to what can be argumentatively validated by the community of interpreters."[99] I think this is a perceptive and fair account of Gadamer's position. Bernstein's worry about Gadamer is that he locates the basis of critical judgments and standards, despite numerous qualifications, in tradition. This is not sufficient justification; Bernstein believes "what is required is a form of argumentation that seeks to *warrant* what is valid in this tradition."[100]

Thus, whereas Bernstein sees Gadamer as being insufficiently robust in his validations, warrants, justifications, and arguments, I do not see where Gadamer has transfigured truth in such a way that "reaching the truth"—which is "always our goal"—does not in the end represent an unacceptable deformation of experience and understanding. Dreyfus, who criticizes Gadamer for siding with the "cognitivists," is going in the right direction; not Bernstein, who wants Gadamer to be more cognitive, more argumentative. But Bernstein's analysis of Gadamer does succeed in showing that regardless of whatever Heideggerian extensions may occur in Gadamer's hermeneutics, the idea of truth as what can be "argumentatively validated" is a fair description of how truth functions in Gadamer.

Gadamer's hermeneutics succeeds in this respect: He establishes how the workings of *Vorurteile* should be conceived so that they immanently structure a world for me. In this respect they govern me (and others, through tradition), yet permit a degree of transcendence that entitles me to say I am the author of my understanding and thus cannot be rendered invisible by objectivity or method; so, in this respect, I govern my *Vorurteile*. Yet Gadamer's theory ultimately fails because it rests upon an indefensible premise—that understanding requires the use of truth criteria, reaching its perfection in "knowing about something." Gadamer wishes to construct "a concept of knowledge and of truth which corresponds to the whole of our hermeneutic experience."[101] Gadamer wants a *better* theory of knowledge, and the way to achieve this is to show that experience *is* knowledge, *is* a series of confirmations and revisions, and is thus necessarily open. Dewey also wants a better theory of knowledge, but his way of accomplishing this end is to distinguish knowledge and experience, not to identify them as Gadamer does.

Because Dewey does not require his theory of experience or understanding to serve epistemological definitions of truth and validity, his theory of experience does not take as its measure meanings actually or potentially verified: "The whole wide universe of fact and dream, of event, act, desire, fancy and meanings, valid or invalid, can be set in contrast to nothing. And if what has been said is taken literally, 'experience' denotes just this wide universe."[102] Thus, Gadamer wishes to construct a theory of knowledge faithful to experience, and accomplishes this by making all experience a knowing experience, and then affirms the necessary incompleteness and openness of experience since our knowledge is forever incomplete. Dewey, however, is both more accurate and more profound in his theory of experience, and what it requires us to be "open" to is far more demanding than Gadamer's openness to "constant confirmation":

> When the varied constituents of the wide universe, the unfavorable, the precarious, uncertain, irrational, hateful, receive the same attention that is accorded the noble, honorable and true, then philosophy may conceivably dispense with the conception of experience. But till that day arrives, we need a cautionary and directive word, like experience, to remind us that the world which is lived, suffered and enjoyed as well as logically thought of, has the last word in all human inquiries and surmises. This is a doctrine of humility; but it is also a doctrine of direction. For it

tells us to open the eyes and ears of the mind, to be sensitive to all the varied phases of life and history. Nothing is more ironical than that philosophers who have so professed universality have so often been one-sided specialists, confined to that which is authentically and surely known, ignoring ignorance, error, folly and the common enjoyments and adornments of life; disposing of these by regarding them as due to our "finite" natures—a blest word that does for moderns what "non-being" was made to do for the Greeks.[103]

The sensitivity Dewey urges upon us is not an epistemological sensitivity, for an adequate theory of experience reveals that our sensitivities are not governed solely by "that which is authentically and surely *known*." Gadamer's universal hermeneutics appeals to our finitude to account for the necessary openness of understanding, that is, the openness of knowledge. Dewey affirms finitude as a fact of experience, one urged upon us by the recognition that being and being known are not equivalent.

I have tried to show in this analysis that when something is brought to mind and invites understanding, *Vorurteil* and habit respond differently. *Vorurteil* enables me to understand because it enables me to know. For Gadamer, there is no understanding that is not a knowing; to understand is to know. I can understand something because through my *Vorurteile*, I have knowledge of that something or knowledge relevant to it. For Dewey, there is understanding that is not a knowing: "*Being* and *having* things in ways other than knowing them, in ways never identical with knowing them, exist, and are preconditions of reflection and knowledge. *Being* angry, stupid, wise, inquiring; *having* sugar, the light of day, money, houses and lands, friends, laws, masters, subjects, pain and joy, occur in dimensions incommensurable to knowing these things which we are and have and use, and which have and use us."[104] My understanding of a rose, a poem, an adolescent's moods, an old ironing board, the tone of the dean's memo, the melancholy of a John Updike short story, the water-stained wallpaper in my bedroom, may occur in "dimensions incommensurable" to knowing these sorts of things. In understanding them, in "being" and "having" them, I am not solving a problem, reaching a decision, giving an answer, settling doubt, or verifying a claim.

This suggests why it is a serious misunderstanding of Dewey's pragmatism to see it as essentially a theory of practical knowledge and practical reasoning. Dewey's metaphysics of "being" and "having" based upon habit must reserve an important place for the practical modes of "being" and "having" and of course it does. "Being" and "having," though, are not limited to the practical. This also suggests why it is beside the point to argue that Gadamer's notions of "application" and phronesis link up with Dewey's thinking on "interest" or the practical character of ideas. Meaning's genesis from prereflective "being" and "having"—what Dewey generally refers to as having a "sense of"—through predicative knowledge and truth, and its return to "being" and "having," is not simply a fluid anticipation of a secure, known meaning, a meaning "grown-up" enough to truthfully mediate past and present and to be action orienting.

Meaning does not wait to become knowledge, practical or otherwise, before becoming a real possession of our intentional life. Habit shows how meanings are incorporated into our intentional life, becoming vehicles of understanding in ways other than "knowing about something," indeed, in ways "incommensurable" with such knowing. "What is really 'in' experience extends much further than that which at any time is *known*."[105] Dewey's standpoint is not merely a limiting condition for Gadamer's "universal hermeneutics" which claims to elucidate "the general relationship of man to the world."[106] It suggests that it would be a radical misconception of the relationship of human beings to the world to see being "informed," reaching "agreement," and seeking "confirmation" as the essential conditions or aims of all understanding.

The central issue at stake between Dewey and Gadamer and their conceptions of habit and *Vorurteil* concerns how the past is present. Prejudice preserves the past as an achievement of reason; Gadamer believes "preservation is an act of reason, though an inconspicuous one."[107] In Gadamer, reason is inspired by the quest for truth. In Dewey, reason is inspired by the quest for meaning. For Dewey, the persistence or preservation of the past accomplished through habit is not solely nor even principally the work of an inconspicuous "act of reason" which can be, in Bernstein's words, "argumentatively validated." What was once experienced as wonderful, interesting, degrading, instructive, caring, or transcendent, is not necessarily (and probably not even most likely) preserved by such a truth-seeking "act of reason" with its interest in knowing and the knowable.

Whether the preserved is an incalculably moving experience of a Beethoven symphony, or the gentle, quiet experience of lying on warm grass on a late Sunday afternoon, these experiences become abiding influences upon me not through the testing of *Vorurteile*, but through emphatic or barely detectable resonances and reverberations of my habits. What is understood in experiences like these has little to do with an expectation that we will be better "informed" about something or that an "agreement" will have been reached. Dewey does not see being "informed" about something or reaching "agreement" as the fulfillment of the historicality of experience, principally because the historicality of experience is achieved through habit, which does not reach its perfection in knowledge.

Dewey says: "Seeing and handling the flower, enjoying the full meaning of the smell as the odor of just this beautiful thing, is not knowledge because it is more than knowledge."[108] Dewey's theory of experience and habit permits us to grasp the ways we may be said to understand a flower, an understanding that we do not expect to "inform" us about anything or "decide" a question. If, as Dewey says, a flower is "more than knowledge," how shall Gadamer understand a flower, when, for him, "the primordial significance of the idea of understanding is that of 'knowing about something'"?[109] Habit reveals, and *Vorurteil* obscures, how a rose and roselike experiences are understandable prior to acts of knowing and other acts of truth-determining consciousness, and why it is a mistake to believe that a meaning or sense has sufficient solidity to become a valuable part of my history only after or until it appears as a judgment, knowledge claim, or candidate for truth. Experienced meaning need not be true in order for it to possess other kinds of merit or importance. In this way, Dewey's theory of habit enables us to see clearly why it is a fallacy, as Arendt says, "to interpret meaning on the model of truth," an interpretation demanded by Gadamer's conception of *Vorurteil* and decisively rejected by Dewey's theory of habit.

· CHAPTER 8 ·

Faith and the Unseen

A *Common Faith* may be viewed as Dewey's weak attempt to speak a language of first and last things, which, given *his* first and last things, can never envision an experience of transcendence. The book is, it has been said, an invitation to piety, reverence, and ideality but without the promise of, or need for, transcendence. Specifically, God is naturalistically recast as the union of the actual and the ideal. I wish to reflect on the first chapter of the book, "Religion versus the Religious," not as a rejection of the supernatural but rather as a defense of the supersensible. I consider it an example of Dewey's attraction to the intangible, the invisible, the transcendent. To put the matter in terms seemingly rather foreign to Dewey, I should like to propose that in this widely discussed chapter, Dewey makes what George Steiner calls "a wager on transcendence":

> This wager—it is that of Descartes, of Kant and of every poet, artist, composer of whom we have explicit record—predicates the presence of a realness, of a "substantiation" (the theological reach of this word is obvious) within language and form. It supposes a passage, beyond the fictive or the purely pragmatic, from meaning to meaningfulness.[1]

Dewey, I shall suggest, does go "beyond the fictive or the purely pragmatic," and the variety and importance of his beyonds are indeed upsetting to a determined naturalist reading of *A Common Faith*. However, his wager on transcendence does not, at least does not clearly, fulfill itself in Steiner's second wager, the wager on the supernatural God. My discussion is restricted to the wager Dewey does make, the wager on supersensible transcendence.

If the reading I offer is sound, then the struggle I describe is of a quite different nature than that described by John E. Smith. Characterizing Dewey's thought, Smith says:

> If life is essentially a struggle, it is a struggle against *present* problems in the environment. When human energy is directed either to the contemplation of the past for its own sake or to reveling in the attractions of mere ideals and visions of other worlds, it is energy misplaced. The precarious nature of life hedges us in from birth to death; we can survive and improve our lot only insofar as we succeed in focusing our energies on the actual problems before us.[2]

In Smith's view, the struggle for Dewey is carried on against actual and present problems which are decisively "before us," that is, sensible to anyone who properly realizes that "ideal goals are not 'starry-eyed' projections of human desire but rather visions of improvement rooted in the actual possibilities of situations." For Dewey, the struggle occurs this side of transcendence. Smith concludes: "Unlike James, Dewey did not have an intimate sense of the transcendent ideal from which religion draws its life, although his *Common Faith* proved to be a most provocative book on the subject."[3] No. Dewey had a quite "intimate sense of the transcendent ideal." If indeed life is a struggle, and particularly if goodness is a struggle, it is not principally because there are so many problems and so little time. It is because, as Dewey tries to show in the first chapter of *A Common Faith*, the authority of an ideal requires us to be "starry-eyed" in the "actually existent world." To set our bodies to work on the sensibly here and now, we must set our mind on ideals which are not sensible or visible. We must wager on transcendence.

Dewey takes his bearings from a definition of religion found in the *Oxford English Dictionary*: "Recognition on the part of man of some unseen higher power as having control of his destiny and as being entitled to obedience, reverence and worship."[4] Dewey is doing two things at once. He immediately worries that the definition is "surcharged with implications" of a supernatural character, but he says nothing about its appeal to the supersensible. Two paragraphs after citing the definition, he notes, in an unremarkable way, that "unseen powers" have been conceived in quite different ways. Again, though, he raises no objection to the "unseen."

Soon it becomes apparent that Dewey is not withholding or delaying an objection to either the notion or the experience of the "unseen." The reason is simple and profound: he has none. Indeed, he wishes to continue to search for a more adequate conception of the "unseen." Given the enormous historical variety of conceptions and actions associated with the "unseen," his approach is direct, almost spare:

> It compels us to ask what conception of unseen powers and our relations to them would be consonant with the best achievements and aspirations of the present. It demands that in imagination we wipe the slate clean and start afresh by asking what would be the idea of the unseen, of the manner of its control over us and the ways in which reverence and obedience would be manifested, if whatever is basically religious in experience had the opportunity to express itself free from all historic encumbrances.[5]

What "conception of unseen powers," in other words, suits the pragmatist? How does the unseen, the invisible, function in the pragmatic world of seeing and doing, of ceaselessly winning determinate meaning from indeterminate situations? The force of these questions falls well outside the scope of a specifically religious consideration. In other words, the openness to the unseen and the invisible in "Religion versus the Religious" decisively takes Dewey's idealism in the direction of the transcendentally ideal. To see the chapter simply as his good-natured, good naturalist attempt to fuse the ideal and the actual is to miss how deeply he undercuts the authority of the visibles present in experience. In this chapter, faith's opening to the supersensible ideal shows rather clearly that, contra Smith (and many other Dewey interpreters), Dewey's attention was not absorbed by present and actual problems. His "beyond" was firm, his transcendence not particularly shy.

Nor was it new. In 1885, at the end of his article "The Revival of the Soul," Dewey lists some of the traits of a "true religion." Boldly, indeed triumphantly, he says: "She would rise to her divine prerogative of life in things unseen, and faith in things yet unrevealed to sense."[6] The "life in things unseen" is our main entry point, our main invitation to a life of faith. Such a life may afford a significant measure of tranquility and serenity. It also may be unfathomably *trying*: "It is in this setting of the whole soul; upon this staking of the whole being; though this utterance of entire devotion be amid things not yet known, that the religious life exits."[7] Six years later, in the section of *Outlines of a Critical Theory of Ethics* which I considered in chapter 3, Dewey again puts the self at stake, this time in the service of the moral life: "We have to surrender the enjoyed good, and stake ourselves upon that of which we cannot say: We *know* it is good."[8] We stake ourselves—morally and religiously—on what is beyond ourselves, on "life in things unseen." With our very selves at stake, it is not surprising that Dewey is intent to work out a detailed "conception of unseen powers."

Dewey's first step in thinking the unseen or invisible is to place theoretical and historical interpretations of the unseen in phenomenological brackets. He looks to the experience rather than the "doctrinal apparatus" used by a particular religion to interpret the experience. In most important respects he is simply following Peter L. Berger's advice — start with the experience: "The inductive option is to turn to experience as the ground of all religious affirmations — one's own experience, to whatever extent this is possible, and the experience embodied in a particular range of traditions."[9] Berger refers to this option as a "deliberately empirical attitude," one clearly in accord with Dewey's intentions. The inductive option is not, however, simply empirical. Berger says: "The inductive option entails the taking of a deliberately naive attitude before the accounts of human experiences in this area, trying as far as possible, and without dogmatic prejudices, to grasp the core contents of these experiences. The inductive option is, in this sense, phenomenological."[10] The first half of "Religion and the Religious" is a proposal to view from the standpoint of phenomenology some of the "core contents" of religious experience: imagination, the experience of "unseen powers," and faith. Dewey of course does not refer to this endeavor as phenomenology; rather, he wishes to inquire into what he calls "the quality of experience" designated by the adjective "religious."

There are four points to notice about this phenomenology. The first is that its focus is not the antagonism between the natural and the supernatural, or more precisely, Dewey's presumed effort (presumed by sympathetic and critical interpreters) to turn the discussion of the religious in a naturalistic direction. Further, the focus is not a negative one, specifically, to demonstrate that the religious is not a "certain kind of experience." The center of the chapter, a mere six paragraphs actually, is Dewey's turn toward transcendence, his realization that not only is there more to the actual than meets the eye, but also that there is more to the actual than meets, or can meet, the idea.

The second point is that his phenomenology of the religious is not only brief; it is not very good. To put it more generously, it is not as fully realized, or imagined, as it might be. Compared to some of the finest paragraphs in *Art as Experience*, the paragraphs I wish to consider are not phenomenologically nuanced, revelatory, compelling. There is no equivalent, say, of Dewey's discussion of the intentionality of "having" an experience or the act of expression. Rather than affording the reader the sense of having returned "to the things themselves," these passages convey a peculiar sense of abstraction and detachment. For one seeking an "idea of the unseen" derived from experience rather than from doctrines, Dewey's account seems more metaphysical than phenomenological.

The reason, I think, for this apparent phenomenological disappointment is the third point I wish to note. Dewey has reached the furthest distance from the viewable and sensible and hence falters when he tries to think, concretely, the unseen. He wants to speak of ends which cannot be viewed, ends which are given to consciousness only as intimations of meaning rather than as sources of action. In short, his pragmatism has found it necessary to bracket existence and to imagine regulative ideals which cannot be traced back to an individual's, society's, or culture's practices and the evidence they afford.[11]

The final point is that Dewey does not attempt to keep his account of the unseen distinct from faith, and indeed they quickly become absorbed into each other. How is the unseen experienced, not just once in a soul-turning experience, but enduringly, lastingly? The answer of course is through faith. The depth at which Dewey has staked his wager on transcendence is suggested by a remark from Robert C. Neville: "Faith involves the belief or trust in something the authority for which is not wholly present."[12] Dewey's pragmatism is moved not by what is, in John E. Smith's language, "before us," but rather by what is, in Neville's language, "not wholly present." But Dewey's wager on transcendence still has not reached its greatest depth. The object of faith is the ideal. What is actual and sensibly before us opens to possibility, to ideal meanings or senses which can be only obscurely glimpsed from our local and finite habitations.

It is with perfect cunning (and one senses, respect) that Dewey begins his compact phenomenology of the unseen with George Santayana, the philosopher who thought Dewey, and pragmatism generally, was dominated by the foreground. Santayana says: "Pragmatism may be regarded as a synthesis of all these ways of making the foreground dominant: the most close-reefed of philosophical craft, most tightly hugging appearance, use, and relevance to practice today and here, least drawn by the lure of speculative distances."[13] It has rarely been noted, if at all, that Dewey's wager on transcendence takes its point of departure from the preface to Santayana's *Interpretations of Poetry and Religion*. Dewey approvingly cites Santayana's description of the "single idea" represented by the papers collected in the work: "This idea is that religion and poetry are identical in essence, and differ merely in the way in which they are attached to practical affairs. Poetry is called religion when it intervenes in life, and religion, when it merely supervenes upon life, is seen to be nothing but poetry."[14] Dewey regards this as a "penetrating insight." The first part of Dewey's comment on this idea is itself not particularly penetrating. Imagination which intervenes rather than merely supervenes "interpenetrates," according to Dewey, "all the elements of our being." His move is predictable: intervening imagination harmonizes, unifies the self as well as harmonizing and unifying the self's relationship with the Universe. But Dewey's commentary on Santayana does begin to agitate and then wholly unsettle his own naturalism in a surprising way.

Dewey says that "the *whole* self is an ideal, an imaginative projection."[15] This has a good, familiar ring to it. It sounds like something which could be found in many of his writings, from 1890 to 1930. The message is almost constant: unification as an activity guided by intelligent purpose. However, what Dewey says immediately before this sentence is not familiar:

> The connection between imagination and the harmonizing of the self is closer than is usually thought. The idea of a whole, whether of the whole personal being or of the world, is an imaginative, not a literal, idea. The limited world of our observation and reflection becomes the Universe only through imaginative extension. It cannot be apprehended in knowledge nor realized in reflection. Neither observation, thought, nor practical activity can attain that complete unification of the self which is called a whole.[16]

It does no injustice to Dewey's position to propose that "harmonizing of the self" is a good for him, perhaps even *the* good, though one of only approximate and temporary realization. The harmonious self is the better self, the unified self, the more nearly perfect self. The good at which we aim—the "idea of a whole"—is not, however, a "literal" idea but rather an "imaginative" one. Something is wrong here. First, the distinction between "literal" and "imaginative" is coarse to the point of being confusing. What is a "literal" idea? An idea that refers to an existent? An imaginable existent? Second, where is the familiar antidualist Dewey? Whatever "literal" may mean for him, how did "imaginative" get so starkly distinguished from it? Two realms of being appear to be predicated. Can this be Dewey's intention?

The answer to this question is not clear but the consequence of the ambiguity is quite clear. As imagination works more and more aggressively on behalf of the self's transcendent ideal, the central presuppositions of Dewey's naturalism are being ignored, forgotten, set aside. Phenomenologically, perhaps we can say that they are being put "out of play," bracketed, suspended. The "natural attitude" is of almost no help in orienting us to the ideal or good of the whole self. "Observation and reflection" are a "limited world." The self imaginatively extended to—as well as into—the Universe "cannot be apprehended in knowledge nor realized in reflection."

Still not satisfied that he has closed the distance between imagination and the harmonizing self, Dewey adds: "Neither observation, thought, nor practical activity can attain that complete unification of the self which is called a whole." This last sentence from Dewey is almost a self-parody. Subtract observation, thought, and practical activity from Dewey and do you still have Dewey?[17] Can one even simply bracket or temporarily suspend them and still have Dewey?

The answer I have been advancing in this work is that one doesn't "still" have Dewey (as if he is barely able to survive such a subtraction or suspension procedure), but rather one has the Dewey whose wager on transcendence required such procedures. Dewey did not consistently meet the requirements of that wager, with the result that often at his most transcendentally ambitious, he can appear to be naturalistically relaxed.[18] However, for the attentive reader, it is evident that as Dewey makes his way into the unseen of ideality, enormously large ranges of his thinking cannot be taken in a relaxed naturalistic manner. For example, in "The Good of Activity" in *Human Nature and Conduct*, Dewey says: "Instruction in what to do next can never come from an infinite goal, which for us is bound to be empty. It can be derived only from study of the deficiencies, irregularities and possibilities of the actual situation."[19] Dewey certainly wants us to take this as good, naturalistic advice, and it is precisely the kind of outlook which might justify Santayana's criticism of the dominance of the foreground in Dewey. Dewey advises that the self with a moral aspiration, one trying to figure out "what to do next," should study the "actual situation." When, however, Dewey takes his longest perspective on the self's aspiration, he turns neither to "study" nor to the "actual situation" for guidance but rather to the imaginative ideal of the "whole self." This ideal can be presented to consciousness in "neither observation, thought, nor practical activity." As we shall see, this assertion begins to challenge Santayana.

In the terms I use in chapter 9, on Dewey and Wallace Stevens, the actual has been subordinated to the possibilities of imagination. It will not do to argue in dualism-condemning ways that Dewey never really meant to put imagination in such a position of exclusive authority with respect to the "actual situation." What, though, is left of cognitive significance or authority in the "actual situation" after observation, thought, and practical activity are suspended? Will? Dewey notes that "this composing of the self is not voluntary in the sense of an act of special volition or resolution. An 'adjustment' possesses the will rather than is its express product."[20] No, will too is suspended. What remains, then, other than imagination as the cognitive center of gravity, the ground of religious consciousness? It is not likely that the meaning of "adjustment" will be found in the foreground, and it certainly is not evident how it would be identified in a background which is nothing less than the Universe. In one of Dewey's transcendentally ambitious statements which cannot possibly be mistaken for naturalistic overconfidence, he says: "Religionists have been right in thinking of it as an influx from sources beyond conscious deliberation and purpose — a fact that helps explain, psychologically, why it has so generally been attributed to a supernatural source and that, perhaps, throws some light upon the reference of it by William James to unconscious factors."[21] This is good, old-fashioned "beyond" talk, and rather than rejecting it, Dewey is getting ready to make a plea for faith in the invisible ideal which Santayana himself might have admired.

Dewey's faith in the unseen and unseeable ideal takes him deeper and deeper into the background, the offstage, the transcendent. Even at this early stage in his exploration of the unseen, it is fairly clear that Dewey is rejecting much less than is usually claimed. For example, we have this from Steven C. Rockefeller:

> The supernatural and transcendental, in Dewey's view, are inherently dualistic notions which by definition involve the idea of something that exists beyond nature and the reach of experience and which involve the setting up, over against experience, of other authorities and methods in matters of belief such as special historical revelations, dogmas, and pure reason.[22]

But through what authority has Dewey retained the whole, the Universe, Jaspers' Encompassing? It is not any authority to be found in observation, knowledge, reflection, will, thought, practical activity, conscious deliberation, or purpose. His answer is imagination. Dewey is not unclear about this: "The idea of a thoroughgoing and deep-seated harmonizing of the self with the Universe (as a name for the totality of conditions with which the self is connected) operates only through imagination." "Only" marks the spot for Dewey: it is this and nothing else. When he is very confident regarding what is essential for the experience of something, Dewey can be remarkably tolerant of categorical exclusions. In other words, what is Dewey being other than "dualistic" when he puts everything on the opposite side of imagination?

Perhaps, though, even if Dewey is taxing imagination almost to the transcendental breaking point, he still loops its energies back to everything that can be seen, thought, and done in nature. This avoids the central question: does imagination exist "beyond nature and the reach of experience"? Let us allow that the experience of imagination may reside this side of the natural, a concession which Dewey usually, but not always, makes. This concession provides, however, little naturalistic reassurance, since more often than not imagination's intentional objects outrun "the reach of experience," at least the reach of those experiences ranging from observation to thought. The reach of imagination extends beyond "the limited world of our observation and reflection." Having completed his rapid, even cursory, remarks on the unseen and imagination, he is ready for faith and the ideal.

Dewey decisively rejects the naturalistic hope or expectation that by "unseen powers" he simply means what has yet to be made visible, seeable, sensible. No. We address the unseen and invisible through faith, and faith is not the anticipation of an eventual visibility. He says that faith "has been regarded as a substitute for knowledge, for sight. It is defined, in the Christian religion, as *evidence* of things not seen. The implication is that faith is a kind of anticipatory vision of things that are now invisible because of the limitations of our finite and erring nature."[23] First, note the equivalence of knowledge and sight. To have knowledge is to see, to attend to the world in such a manner that experience is taken as evidence (evident to our perceptual and intellectual seeing). But this phenomenology will not do for Dewey. The ideal is not sighted or seen. That we can do something in light of an ideal does not mean that experience thereby functions as evidence for the worth of the ideal. Put differently, moral faith, that is, faith in the ideal, is not an anticipation of a set of possibilities simply waiting to be seen and evaluated in a determinate context. In this respect, it is mistaken to argue that Dewey wished to "idealize" the world by converting ideals into "ends-in-view." Such a view leaves unexamined how the ideal makes its claim upon us before it has become an end-in-view, before it has been approved by demonstrative reason. Is it possible that the valued and the valuable, the prized and the appraised, are not as clearly or explicitly continuous as the standard view of Dewey would have it?

Consider again Rockefeller. In his view of Dewey "there is no gulf separating the ideal and the real, nature and human values." He continues:

> [Dewey] emphasizes that ideals exist in nature as possibilities rather than as actualities. Ideals are possibilities resident in natural events. Such possibilities become ideals when they are apprehended by human intelligence and projected by the human imagination as desired objectives and guides to action.[24]

Possibilities become ideals "when they are apprehended by human intelligence." Dewey, however, does not say this but rather its exact opposite. The ideal of the whole — of personal being or the world's — "cannot be apprehended in knowledge nor realized in reflection." The religious composing of the self is a matter of faith, and because faith is not "intellectual in quality," it ought not to be treated as a "substitute for knowledge."[25] Faith, in other words, is not an anticipation of the visible or sensible. Faith, like ideality, cannot provide evidence or justification for the meanings it intends. Dewey has made it clear that religious faith and religious experience intend meanings which cannot be naturalized by the usual processes of naturalistic certification: knowledge, reflection, observation, thought, practical activity. What he fails to make clear is how his opening to the supersensible, to "sources beyond conscious deliberation and purpose," does not lead to the supernatural. Thus, even though the overwhelming consensus of Dewey commentary places him, approvingly or disapprovingly, decidedly on the anti-supernaturalist side of things, there is almost no attention to this supersensible side of Dewey. What is the naturalistic — or supernaturalistic — status of meanings which, in fact and in principle, cannot be viewed? How much ought a person, particularly the naturalist, live in the light of faith when faith is not "regarded as a substitute for knowledge, for sight"?

It is important to note that Dewey's next step is intended to place his discussion in an intellectual and philosophical context not limited to matters theological: "Apart from any theological context, there is a difference between belief that is a conviction that some end should be supreme over conduct, and belief that some object or being exists as a truth for the intellect."[26] Imagination, meaning, truth, thought — these philosophical "issues" or "problems" range beyond theology and "God talk." Whatever trouble Dewey stirs up here in the province of religious faith will be felt in regions seemingly rather remote from the holy, the sacred, the transcendent, God. Dewey's widening of the context of his discussion of moral faith is nothing less than a widening of the place of transcendence and faith in every area of his philosophy.

A brief comparison of religious faith and aesthetic experience helps to illuminate the remarkable step Dewey is taking here: call it a "beyond" step. The physical object of an aesthetic experience is determinable (but not always without difficulty): a painting, a musical performance, a sunset, a conversation, a new or vintage watch, a face, a memory, an image. We can attend to these objects in such ways as to determine a fair amount regarding the nature of their existence in the world (for example, the saying and telling of traits, characteristics, and to some extent, qualitative immediacies). As intentional objects, however, these physical objects typically occasion or solicit responses which go beyond these determinations. In other words, the intentional object, the object-as-meant, is less readily determined to be this or that, "like" this or that. Analytic accounts of the properties of an aesthetically considered object, say the colors in Caravaggio's *The Taking of Christ* or the colors of a sunny, winter Sunday settling over a deserted playground, these must have a "beyond"; the colors must be "had" or "lived." In other words, they must be appreciated, but such an appreciative meaning-bestowing, while not in opposition to intellect, does not take the form of "a truth for the intellect." Speaking of the aesthetic experiences of W. H. Hudson and Emerson, Dewey says:

> I do not see any way of accounting for the multiplicity of experiences of this kind (something of the same quality being found in every spontaneous and uncoerced esthetic response), except on the basis that there are stirred into activity resonances of dispositions acquired in primitive relationships of the living being to its surroundings, and irrecoverable in distinct or intellectual consciousness.[27]

When we are aesthetically "stirred," we are beyond "distinct or intellectual consciousness."

Similarly, when through religious faith we invite a religious ideal "to stir and hold us,"[28] we are beyond "a truth for the intellect." The intentional objects of faith experience are not presentable to knowing, thinking, observing. The faith experience is meaningful, meaning bestowing, but its meanings are not "a truth for the intellect." In short, what Dewey is about to say regarding the "authority of an ideal" has an importance and consequence which extends far beyond the issues and problems customarily associated with theology, religion, God. It goes to the very center of what, in *The Quest for Certainty*, he calls the "conflict of authorities." It goes to the center not simply of pragmatic epistemology but also pragmatic metaphysics as found in *Experience and Nature*. Having served notice that what he is now saying is "apart from any theological context," Dewey raises considerable difficulty for what he so confidently asserted in *The Quest for Certainty*, that "standards and tests of validity are found in the consequences of overt activity."[29] This is not simply a matter of how we are to properly know and inquire. At stake is "intellectual regard for the values which are to have authority over our desires and purposes and thus over our entire conduct."[30] What Dewey is now about to authorize does not necessarily establish that he "really" was a supernaturalist or had supernatural longings. It does suggest that for him some of the sources of guidance and regulation for experience may transcend what is evident to the senses or evidentially compelling to the intellect.

First, consider this statement, which comes immediately after Dewey's initial effort at distinguishing what he calls "justifying faith" and some object or being which "exists as a truth for the intellect":

> Conviction in the moral sense signifies being conquered, vanquished, in our active nature by an ideal end; it signifies acknowledgment of its rightful claim over our desires and purposes. Such acknowledgment is practical, not primarily intellectual. It goes beyond evidence that can be presented to *any* possible observer.[31]

Faith, conviction, the ideal, practical action, what is "beyond evidence," these elements have always been at the center of Dewey's attention, but where? If the central contention of this study has merit, then one should be able to answer that these elements are to be found in numerous places throughout Dewey's works. This certainly is the case. But it is nothing less than stunning to realize that Dewey said nearly the exact same thing in 1891, in the passage I examined in some detail in chapter 2. In *Outlines of a Critical Theory of Ethics*, in the section titled "Goodness as a Struggle," Dewey says that we press on beyond the old good. The pressure we apply—to ourselves and the situation—is the measure of our moral aspiration. Such aspiration is based on faith, and for Dewey faith is not fed by what can be seen: "Only the old good is of sight, has verified itself to sense. The new ideal, the end which meets the situation, is felt as good only in so far as the character has formed the conviction that to meet obligation is itself a good, whether bringing sensible satisfaction or not."[32] Desire and purpose (and interest) are regulative of what we do and how we act. Proponents and critics of pragmatism agree on this. But its proponents tend to neglect as often as its critics what regulates desire and purpose—the ideal. In 1891, Dewey argues that the ideal end which "meets the situation" is good "only in so far" as it embodies our *conviction* "to meet obligation." In 1934, he argues that the ideal end conquers or vanquishes our active nature (our desires and purposes) and that acknowledgment of the ideal's "rightful claim" over us is precisely what we mean by "*conviction* in the moral sense" (emphasis added). The bracket Dewey places around faith is pretty complete: neither sensory experience nor reflection will succeed in providing "evidence that can justify intellectual assent."[33] It is a remarkable light indeed authorizing what we do in light of the ideal.

If Dewey frustrates the most dedicated reader, it is partly owing to his occasionally eccentric sense of proportion. Having just made the most remarkable claims about claims—theological and nontheological—Dewey closes the paragraph with one sentence: "The authority of an ideal over choice and conduct is the authority of an ideal, not of a fact, of a truth guaranteed to intellect, not of the status of the one who propounds the truth."[34] We have in this sentence a view of the authority of the ideal which does not cohere very well with most conceptions of "pragmatic," including much of what Dewey has said about his pragmatism. The ideal has authority "over choice and conduct," and it is an authority which is at work as a "rightful claim" prior to action, prior to, as he calls it in *The Quest for Certainty*, "operations to be performed," "acts to be performed."[35] In Dewey's words, we are "vanquished" or "conquered" in a very particular way by the ideal end: our "active nature" is slowed down, put on hold, suspended. And by what? By an ideal which is not visible and which "goes beyond evidence that can be presented to *any* possible observer." The circularity of the sentence under consideration is real, not apparent: "The authority of an ideal over choice and conduct is the authority of an ideal." What *is* the authority of the ideal? Dewey relies upon what he has said to this point: the "rightful claim" of an ideal, of a possible good, places me in the position of obligation, obligation to act in accordance with it, regardless of whether it brings "sensible satisfaction or not." The last phrase is the kind typically associated with, and restricted to, the "early" Dewey. Nonetheless it is perfectly consistent with everything that Dewey said in "Religion versus the Religious" in 1934. It is through faith, not evidence-dependent inquiry, that we experience intimations of a good which not only is invisible, but is not existent.

The existence and inexistence of ideal meanings is the topic of Dewey's next paragraph. There is an almost inverse relationship between its supreme importance and the little commentary and criticism it has received since *A Common Faith* was published. One likely reason for this neglect is that Dewey's remarks do not appear to be very different from his previous discussions of the actual and the ideal, particularly his discussion in *The Quest for Certainty* in the chapter "The Copernican Revolution." The first interpretive pass through it seems to yield something relatively straightforward: ideals are already existent in the world even if the human observer fails to see, grasp, and assent to them. Compact this just a little more and we have something perhaps more sticky: ideals are real and they are "already in existence." This position Dewey indeed opposes. Why, though, does he oppose it? To provide what I think is a more compelling answer than is usually offered, I shall make my way through the paragraph with the help of John N. Findlay's article "Intentional Inexistence."[36] Why do this? Because although the paragraph is not unique in Dewey, it does take him to the limits of his naturalism and, perhaps, a little beyond.

First, though, a brief look back. There are few American philosophers more reluctant than Dewey to go beyond what he calls the "possibilities of nature."[37] We have seen, though, that nature's possibilities have been considerably abbreviated by the time we reach the present point in "Religion versus the Religious." Recall Dewey's assertion: "The authority of an ideal over choice and conduct is the authority of an ideal, not of a fact, of a truth guaranteed to intellect, not of the status of the one who propounds the truth." The authority of the ideal is not equivalent to fact (facts of nature), or truth (truths determined or determinable regarding nature), or the status of the propounder of truths (let us say the expert or the professional on nature). In short, the "rightful claim" of an ideal end requires us to attend to what transcends "evidence that can be presented to *any* possible observer." We will not find in nature the evidence or justification for "conviction in the moral sense." Conviction has a basis which goes beyond what experience warrants. At its furthest reaches, conviction is faith, and as Dewey has reminded us, faith is not a "substitute for knowledge, for sight." Faith intends an object which is not visible or perceptually available and which cannot be known like hotels, paintings of Monet, arguments of Kant. To take something "on faith," to have faith despite contrary evidence or no evidence at all, would appear to be at its best a kind of cognitive comfort station. At its worst, it is the easy way out of (and around) the actualities and possibilities of this world.

So Dewey begins where he must: "Such moral faith is not easy." Why isn't it "easy"? Because the ideal does not exist: "Moral faith has been bolstered by all sorts of arguments intended to prove that its object is not ideal and that its claim upon us is not primarily moral or practical, since the ideal in question is already embedded in the existent frame of things."[38] On first examination, this sounds like Dewey's standard "already" argument against idealism. In *The Quest for Certainty* he says: "In this basic problem of the relation of the actual and ideal, classic philosophies have always attempted to prove that the ideal is already and eternally a property of the real."[39] The ideal is not actual, or more precisely, it is not, Dewey says in *The Quest for Certainty*, "an antecedent possession of actuality." The ideal is not "already" here, existing, and this is not because we are, as the idealists believe, so imperfect: "It is argued that the ideal is already the final reality at the heart of things that exist, and that only our senses or the corruption of our natures prevent us from apprehending its prior existential being."[40] It would appear as if Dewey wishes to put some distance between the ideal and the antecedent, the actual, the existent. The ideal is not "already and eternally a property of the real."

Dewey is not, however, consistent or reliable with respect to the kind and magnitude of distance he wishes to put into play regarding the ideal and the actual. In *The Quest for Certainty* he says: "'The actual' consists of given conditions; 'the possible' denotes ends or consequences not now existing but which the actual may through its use bring into existence."[41] Remember that Dewey rejects the view that the ideal "is already embedded in the existent frame of things." There is a tension here which, though not quite adding up to an incoherence in his philosophy, is still nonetheless a clear sign that Dewey is at the limits of naturalism and instrumentalism.

On one hand, he wishes to reject the view that the ideal is "an antecedent possession of actuality," and on the other he wishes to affirm that the actual may be used to "bring into existence" ideal possibilities. Idea (and ideal) is a "projection of what something existing may come to be."[42] The problem is that it is very far from clear how one is to use the actual to "bring into existence" ideal possibilities when, by Dewey's stipulation, use has loosened its ties to evidence, fact, and truth. What is to guide use? Ground it? One might argue that this question is exactly the one which Dewey does not want asked, at least not in *A Common Faith*, regarding the authority of the ideal. The "rightful claim" of the ideal is practical, "not primarily intellectual." Period. It is quite important to remember that Dewey's aim in this chapter is to "ask what conception of unseen powers and our relationship to them would be consonant with the best achievements and aspirations of the present." How, precisely, is the unseen to be "used" to bring anything into existence? The question presumes another more fundamental question: how is it possible for ideal meanings to exist and not to exist? With this question, we turn to Findlay's "Intentional Inexistence."[43]

The aim of Findlay's essay is stated in admirably clear and bold terms:

> This paper is an attempt to deal, with determined non-technicality and awareness of the shimmering mirages of the question, with the old issue of what Descartes and Spinoza called "objective being," and what Brentano and the Schoolmen he derived from called "intentional inexistence," and what might less perplexingly simply be called "being for thought."[44]

The facts and states of affairs of the world, in order to be accorded objective status, require us to postulate "the existence of personal splinters of consciousness, or patterned wholes of such splinters, in which the objective matter in question is specifically 'constituted' for the mind, is set up in an appropriate category *for* it, is in some manner present *to* it."[45] In certain respects, this is an alternate formulation of Dewey's "The Postulate of Immediate Empiricism."[46] Both Findlay and Dewey are interested in how the experienced object, the intentional object, is present to the mind, person, experiencer. Findlay offers a helpful example.

There is a man with the name "James." This name, says Findlay,

> not only serves to pick out a man in the world and perhaps credit him with certain characters and relations: it also serves to express a highly personal, only partially definite pattern of personal expectations, terminating in sensuous or imagined fulfillments which may or may not be carried out, which pattern is *not only* a far-flung readiness to do or say or imagine or perceive this or that, but which is also, at least on some pregnant occasions, a single concentrated point of lived experience, my sense of who or what the man is, what he altogether amounts to, at least as far as I am concerned.[47]

When James is "set before consciousness," when James is the intentional object of my regard or attention, I am not only reporting a fact that James is in the world. James is also "a concentrated point of lived experience, my sense of who or what the man is." Dewey, of course, was consistently concerned with the phenomenology of sensing and having a sense of.[48] This sensing, based on prereflective habit, is outward-turning and inward-turning. James is not James for just anyone, that is, everyone. James as present to me, my sense of James, my sense of (the fact of) James, is "highly personal."

The matter is made even richer if we consider the utterance, "James is a teacher." As Findlay notes, this utterance "not only purports to state a fact in the world, but it also points to my possible inward grasp of this fact." This idea is eventually of great importance to Dewey's account of our "inward grasp" of an ideal which, in his language, "goes beyond evidence." Fortunately, Findlay provides a quite helpful elaboration of "inward grasp": "The same linguistic expressions which, seen in one light, voice a commonplace fact, can be used also to bring out the far from familiar way in which that fact is registered in our life of understanding, in which it is made one with that inward grasp which is one of the deep layers, if not the deepest layer, of ourselves."[49] This does not immediately sound like Dewey. It is too subjective, too interior, even despite the fact that Findlay is referring to how a fact is registered in our consciousness. Nonetheless, I do not see how any real importance could attach to Dewey's theory of qualitative immediacy unless it is regarded as an account of "inward grasp," an account, say, of how an interview (to use one of the examples in *Art as Experience*) is experienced, had, or lived by the applicant and the interviewer. Whether one can give a naturalistic account of "inward grasp" is certainly not Findlay's worry or concern: "The positions I am taking are strong, and I have no doubt that many will refuse to understand my key-phrases of being-there-for-me, etc., and will interpret them in some naturalistic sense that quite by-passes or blindly presupposes their essential sense."[50] The brilliance of so much of Dewey's thought is that he wanted to have it both ways: he wanted to understand the constitution of the "being-there-for-me" dimension of lived experience and he wanted to understand what is objectively there for all of us.

For Findlay, an account of the intentionality of consciousness, or from Dewey's standpoint, the habit-based, prereflective intentionality of qualitative immediacy, does not entail a compromise of objectivity. Findlay says:

> There may be much which seems unanalysably qualitative, merely sensational, merely affective, a mere colouring of our interior selfhood, but we adhere to the principle, by no means obvious in its statement, but clear in what we do and say, that each such seeming nuance of quality permits of a use, in a unique and peculiar sense of "use," to add some shade of difference to the objective tapestry spread out before us and around us, and then also, by a sort of secondary indirection, to attract attention and direct difficult descriptive effort to its more mysterious self.[51]

My sense of James, my "inward grasp" of James as teacher, is "highly personal." This "personal interiority," this "being-there-for-me" grasp of James the teacher, is not solely interior and for me; my sense of James may be used to "add some shade of difference to the objective tapestry." What I say or do with respect to James expresses, and thus installs into the world, a "shade of difference." Through Twain's Huck Finn or Updike's Mark Prosser, the objective tapestry has been expanded as has the field of language and experience inviting us to the most subtle and inventive "inward grasps." In short, an intentionalist standpoint such as Dewey's or Findlay's, lands me inside myself and projects me outside myself.

Left like this, Findlay's account of intentionality is suggestive as a vehicle for the explication of Dewey on ideality and transcendence, but not luminously or compellingly so. Fortunately, Findlay presses on with his analysis of intentionality, and offers much more for an understanding of how the ideal functions in Dewey (and perhaps in himself). There are three aspects of intentionality which Findlay wishes to discuss. The first "is that intention is so little a mere reflection of what it intends or is 'of,' that it may completely fail of its precise target, or indeed of any target, without thereby ceasing to be the peculiar sort of intention that it is, aimed and directed at the precise sort of object and situation at which it is directed."[52] This is the heart of what Findlay means by intentional inexistence, so it is worthwhile to quote him in full:

> It is of the essence of the correlativity of conscious intentions with their objects, that, while it must be possible to conceive of something as being that of which they are, it is not necessary to conceive of anything *actual* which fits them, nor even of anything actual that *could* fit them. We must, in other words, always *be able* to specify the sort of thing or situation our mental grasp is of, without necessarily being able to take this sort of thing out of its object-position, its "intentional brackets" and thereby make it a logical subject of predications. Intentional possibility, is, if we may so phrase it, not the same as possibility tout court, the possibility of being or being the case.[53]

It might be thought that such a conception of intentionality is not consistent with Dewey's usual desire to keep things steady, concrete, present. This, however, is simply one aspect of Dewey's view of the intentionality of habitual meaning. The fundamental presupposition of Dewey's theory of mind and consciousness is that what is present to mind may not be present to the body or the senses. Thus, in *Experience and Education,* he says:

> An experience is always what it is because of a transaction taking place between an individual and what, at the time, constitutes his environment, whether the latter consists of persons with whom he is talking about some topic or event, the subject talked about being also a part of the situation; or the toys with which he is playing; the book he is reading (in which his environing conditions at the time may be England or ancient Greece or an imaginary region); or the materials of an experiment he is performing. The environment, in other words, is whatever conditions interact with personal needs, desires, purposes, and capacities to create the experience which is had. Even when a person builds a castle in the air he is interacting with objects which he constructs in fancy.[54]

Toys, books, and materials exist in a manner in which the objects of fancy and the imaginary do not exist. The intentional inexistence of these objects does not rob them of educational or existential importance, of being, in Findlay's terms, occasions for "mental grasp." That we cannot conceive of anything "actual" which fits these mental grasps and that we cannot make true and false predications based on intentional possibility, does not mean that we cannot see the actual in light of what does not exist.

And the ideal? How are ideal meanings present to consciousness for Dewey and Findlay? Dewey would have liked Findlay's formulation: "It is the privilege of mind, we may say, that it can raise, *as it were* or 'in brackets,' a novel creation, that it can intend what cannot be taken out of such intentional brackets, what in fact is not or what perhaps cannot be."⁵⁵ Whether an ideal meaning can be taken out of "intentional brackets" is for Dewey an empirical and experimental question . . . up to a point. He has been arguing in "Religion versus the Religious" that the authority of the ideal may *not* be experimentally established, but rather that its authority derives from our moral faith and conviction—Findlay's "privilege of mind." Dewey's consistent standpoint, from the turn of the century to the end of his life, was that ideals are not "already embedded in the existent frame of things," not "already the final reality at the heart of things that exist," in short, that ideals are not "antecedently existing actualities." What was not consistent was his willingness to leave ideal meanings in brackets, to permit them to exercise their force or authority as meanings which conquer or vanquish us, rather than ones to which we assent as a result of evidence, as a "truth for the intellect." Findlay's analysis of intentional inexistence (which he acknowledges "received the classical notice of Brentano") is indispensable if any sense is to be made of what appears dangerously close in Dewey to a tautology: "the authority of an ideal is the authority of an ideal." However, it is no tautology Dewey is proposing, but rather the authority of intentional possibility, the authority exhibited by our "privilege of mind" in "intending the nonexistent or the impossible." Intentional inexistence requires faith for any realization or fulfillment of what we see in its light. By definition, "it goes beyond evidence." Dewey utters no platitude, then, when he says, "Such moral faith is not easy." As we saw in chapter 2, moral faith is inseparable from moral struggle.

The second aspect of intentionality which Findlay wishes to address is, one might say, cautionary: "One's excitement over the possibility of intending the nonexistent or the impossible, must not . . . be allowed to seduce one into the notion that it is impossible to intend anything else." We can, and do, direct our thought at an object with the aim of hitting it. In other words, "it is part of what we understand by the thinking upon objects that such thinking may progressively be corrected in a manner which suits the objects thought of, until in the end it is only by a confusion that we draw a sceptical distinction between the object as it is given to us and the object as it truly or in itself is."⁵⁶ As I discuss in chapter 4, thinking moves closer to doing justice to the phenomenon but in a manner which "suits the objects thought of." To this point, Dewey and Findlay are in surprising accord. The difference between them is more subtle than one might anticipate. The cognitive confidence, perhaps even certitude, which characterizes this knowledge should not, Findlay says, be "thought of in terms of some external certification which would require further certification without end: it lies rather in the steady vanishing of all grounds of doubt, until one really has the thing itself given as it itself is."[57] From Dewey's point of view, the progressive correction of thought is inspired not only by the "steady vanishing of all grounds of doubt," but by the requirements of practice which may not be able to eliminate "all grounds of doubt." Dewey is thus more demanding and more lenient than Findlay. Progressive correction which "suits the objects thought of" may not only have to settle for something less certain than "the object as it truly or in itself is," it may only do justice to that object when it allows the intentional object a horizon of indeterminacy suited to it. What has yet to be determined may not be determinable, either in fact or in principle.

Finally, "not only may there be intentions which hit their target or which fail to hit their target, but there may also be targets which intentions do not hit, and do not even perhaps try to hit." Where the intersection between Dewey and Findlay narrows momentarily with respect to the removal of "all grounds of doubt," it broadens again with regard to the central place accorded the self as participant in understanding and not spectator to its unfolding: "intentions will differ according to the degree and content of their ignorance, or, what is the same thing otherwise put, the completeness and definiteness with which they envisage their object, and the precise angles or respects from which they envisage it."[58] Here is the Deweyan agent: trying, trying out, working to get a better perspective, a better idea, a better grasp. In seeking to do justice to the phenomenon, the Deweyan agent tries to see things in different lights. The notion of "conscious light" is a brilliant aspect of Findlay's philosophy, specifically, his phenomenology. It also happens to clarify why Dewey rejects the "vast intellectual schemes, philosophies, and theologies" which attempt to "prove that ideals are real not as ideals but as antecedently existing actualities."[59] Findlay says:

> We see or think of our object or objects, or our situation, in this or that "light," and the "light" in which we see it floats ambiguously between ourselves and the thing or situation seen or thought of, so that it is as much a part of our individual personal life as of the parcelled, divided world of things around us, while at other times it seems to be broken by what it connects into two wholly diverse, if correlated aspects: the seeing or conceiving of something *as*, e.g., a rather washed out red cushion, on the one hand, and its simply *being* such a washed out red cushion, on the other.[60]

When we see something in the light of an ideal, we see it in a light "which floats ambiguously between ourselves and the thing or situation." We have an intimation of an ideal object and end which inspires us, corrects us, stops us. But the authority of that idealizing light is not to be found in evidence, fact, truth. Its authority is a matter of faith, faith in a good, a possible good.

The pragmatic question, as well as the religiously significant one, is what are we to make of the intentional experience of the other, particularly one who professes faith in an unseen power. In Findlay's language, we can see things from the inside: "We can enter, as it were, into the brackets of a man's intentional cage, and see what there is to see from its vantage-point, without thinking of it *as* an intentional cage endowed with anything like a special, perhaps delusive point of view." Or, we can view intentionality "from the outside." The third alternative is perhaps the most interesting, difficult, and deeply pragmatic. In this case, we "stand hesitantly in the doorway of the intentional cage, seeing the world as it appears from its vantage-point and yet continuing to evaluate that vision from an outside critical standpoint." At first glance, this third alternative may not appear to shed much light on Dewey, other than perhaps offering an alternative formulation of what he calls interaction or transaction. However, Findlay's account of "intentional cages" reminds us of a fundamental point in Dewey: experience is there for, is had by, a person. As Findlay says: "This world has to be there *for him* and not merely *simpliciter*." Findlay was not afraid to venture inside intentional cages and brackets, for "to remain resolutely outside of all intentional brackets, as counselled in certain forms of objective naturalism or metaphysics is in the end to liquidate the world and its contents."[61] I have been proposing throughout the present study that Dewey's is not one of the forms of naturalism which loses the world by making the objective, actual world all that there is.

Findlay is aware that his third alternative is logically and phenomenologically in need of clarification. Fortunately, he provides such clarification, and through it he almost perfectly describes the person of faith in Dewey who stands at the gateway between what is made visible and evident through observation and reflection and what is entertained and intimated by imagination:

> What then is the remaining stance we may take which alone casts a difficult illumination on the scene before us? It is the alternative of constantly confounding and mixing categories, as they are in reality and experience livingly mixed; it is the alternative of constantly entering intentional cages and seeing things as they appear within them and yet constantly going outside of those cages and *comparing* what one has seen with a totally different outside vision, a comparison of things as indistinguishably like in one regard as they are categorically unlike in another.[62]

Interpretations of pragmatism (certainly James's and Dewey's) which neglect or regret the "livingly mixed," almost invariably overemphasize or underemphasize the inner or outer intentional cage. The actual, material, natural world is promoted by some interpretations. The created, invented, imagined world is promoted by others. In both instances, the transcendent, the ideal, and the intangible are rendered harmless, dogmatic, or both.

A little more of Findlay's (very) long paragraph serves to bring home just how far Dewey has taken his search for an adequate "idea of the unseen," which, it is to be remembered, was the ambition of the chapter under consideration, "Religion versus the Religious." Findlay says:

> Antinomies and absurdities are ready to jump out at every step, and can only be coped with by very subtle formulae, yet it is only by continuing to face and cope with such antinomies that one can master the shimmering, ever reduplicated and multiply refracted structure of the world. Intentional objects must be in fact treated rather as phantoms are treated in ghost-stories, as things which are and are not, which have some but not all the defining features of fully real objects, which appear solidly where they should not be and vanish into thin air or simply lose themselves in ordinary objects when the occasion warrants, which have not merely to be dealt with but even talked of in a very propitiatory manner.[63]

Dewey wishes to have it both ways: affirm that ideal meanings are "resident in the actualities discovered" and deny that ideal meanings are "an antecedent possession of actuality."[64] He can succeed only if ideal meanings are construed as intentional objects. Findlay's advice to Dewey is simple and profound: treat ideal meanings "as things which are and are not." To "have some but not all the defining features of fully real objects" is not a state of deficiency for Findlay. It might appear to be a quite lamentable state for Dewey, but it is not. I look at this matter more closely in chapter 9, but it is important to note here that Dewey does not require make-believe (reality denying or transfiguring) or reverie or dream to be excluded from aesthetic experience. In fact, if the aesthetic is to "set us on fire" it must have these elements in it. The shortcoming of what Dewey calls the "make-believe" theory of aesthetic experience is not found in what it contains but in what it leaves out—purpose. He says that "the error of the make-believe or illusion theory of art does not, then, proceed from the fact that esthetic experience lacks the elements upon which the theory builds."[65] Dewey understood as well as Findlay the nature of "things which are and are not," whether they are phantoms, memories, intimations, possibilities—the entire "ideal realm."

So Dewey can have it both ways: the ideal is immanent and transcendent. What Dewey achieves in "Religion versus the Religious" is of fundamental importance to his entire philosophy. Ideals are not wholly absent from reality, nor are they, as he calls them in "Changed Conceptions of the Ideal and the Real," "ready-made."[66] But neither are "reals" ready-made. Noting how the experimental sciences have changed our conceptions of the real and the ideal, Dewey says:

> [The real] ceases to be something ready-made and final; it becomes that which has to be accepted as the material of change, as the obstructions and the means of certain specific desired changes. The ideal and rational also ceased to be a separate ready-made world incapable of being used as a lever to transform the actual empirical world, a mere asylum from empirical deficiencies. They represent intelligently thought-out possibilities *of* the existent world which may be used as methods for making over and improving it.[67]

Neither "ready-made" suits Dewey: the ready-made of a closed, absolute reality or the "ready-made" of the perfect Ideal, the Absolute. Dewey's confidence in rejecting the "ready-made" should not disguise the fact that the above quotation contains two inconsistencies which he does not appear to resolve, does not appear to *seek* to resolve.

First, the real "has to be accepted as the material of change." But Dewey just two pages prior to this assertion notes how the carpenter engages reality: "If he forgoes his own purpose and in the name of a meek and humble subscription to things as they 'really are' refuses to bend things as they 'are' to his own purpose, he not only never achieves his purpose but he never learns what the things themselves are." It can be argued that Dewey is simply saying that the real has to be accepted as the basis, the material basis, of any subsequent bending, making, or building. But it is precisely the authority of the "really are" which is at stake for the carpenter and for Dewey, even on the level of the material. The carpenter does not simply or fully accept real properties as the "material of change." Such properties are given to consciousness as both actual objects and intentional objects. Dewey is careful that he does not go too far here and thus notes in a somewhat restrained way that "what makes the carpenter a *builder* is the fact that he notes things not just as objects in themselves, but with reference to what he wants to do to them and with them; to the end he has in mind."[68] But the end is itself not a "ready-made" but rather a sensed meaning, an intimation, a possible good. The carpenter, or artist, or moral agent, has already partially refused "subscription to things as they 'really are'" in the interest of a possible good.

Findlay's phenomenology of intentional inexistence points to the second strain in Dewey's attempt to (usually) remain on the immanentist side of possibility ("possibilities *of* the existent world"). Intentional possibility for Findlay is not a real or "true" possibility, that is, one based on the actual or real; nor is it a hypothetical possibility which places a more glancing, but still determinable, blow on the actual. He says: "Intentional possibility is, if we may so phrase it, not the same as possibility *tout court,* the possibility of being or of being the case." Contrast that with this from Dewey: "Nature and society include within themselves projection of ideal possibilities and contain the operations by which they are actualized."[69] When Dewey is stirred (a favorite word of his) by a possibility which lies "beyond evidence that can be presented to *any* possible observer," he clearly has turned his attention from natural possibility to intentional possibility.[70]

This happens throughout the chapter we are considering and reaches its conclusion as Dewey places the religious attitude in the wider natural and social context of "art, science and good citizenship." One expects to find natural and social "projection of ideal possibilities." Invisible and intangible ideals are intelligently and deliberately transformed into visibilities and tangibilities. Instead, Dewey preserves the intentional character of ideal possibilities, and the first step in this preservation program is to remind us what he has been doing the whole chapter: attending to the unseen. So he says: "An unseen power controlling our destiny becomes the power of an ideal."[71] Is nature the "unseen power"? Society? In what sense are they unseen? The unseen with the natural/social does not appear to be a convincing fit.

Dewey agrees, but the agreement is merely stated, not announced. He does not draw conclusions from his "beyonds," his "beyond evidence," "beyond conscious deliberation and purpose." Because he hesitates to conclude, it is not apparent how deeply he has committed himself and his philosophy to the control and authorization of the "unseen," to what does not appear to the senses. Still, an objection to his "unseen" is readily apparent. What controls does not necessarily authorize, and possibilities must prove themselves in visible and tangible workings out. The working out—the working—authorizes. To see how well things work out is the pragmatic test. When things aren't working out, when there is conflict, we must be more determined, more resolute in seeking resolution.[72] But to what precisely are we attending all the while that "an unseen power" controls destiny? Do we attend to the unseen? How? Dewey makes the authority of the unseen, or more, precisely, faith in the unseen, even more controlling: "The artist, scientist, citizen, parent, as far as they are actuated by the spirit of their callings, are controlled by the unseen." Remember that just a few pages earlier Dewey has rejected the view of faith as a "kind of anticipatory vision of things that are now invisible because of the limitations of our finite and erring nature." Faith is not a developmental lag in knowledge, sight, evidence. Faith does not blind us to projections of possibilities originating from actuals and visibles, but neither does it affirm them as the limit of possibility. In fact, faith in ideal possibility requires a certain kind of loving insubordination, a recognition that "all endeavor for the better is moved by faith in what is possible, not by adherence to the actual."[73] If we are moved by the better and its better, then the actually seen—seen in nature and in society—cannot be the ultimate ground or auspices for the movement toward the better. Faith moves and grounds.

Let us think of faith as at least one source of intentional possibilities, "as things which are and are not, which have some but not all the defining features of fully real objects." Faith-held possibilities raise our eyes not only to what cannot be determined by the senses, but also to what does not "depend for its moving power upon intellectual assurance or belief that the things worked for must surely prevail and come into embodied existence." Experimental intelligence is a little less confident, impressive, even reliable, if "intellectual assurance" is not the determining authority in our "endeavor for the better." What, then, does—or ought to—determine our outlook, our effort, our measure for success? Dewey says: "The authority of the object to determine our attitude and conduct, the right that is given it to claim our allegiance and devotion is based on the *intrinsic nature of the ideal.*"[74] Does the ideal have a nature so complex that it warrants the aporetic and yet peculiarly proleptic resonance of "the intrinsic nature of the ideal"? Yes, it does, contrary to Smith's view noted at the start of this chapter that Dewey lacks an "intimate sense of the transcendent ideal." It is only in the chiaroscuro light of the transcendent ideal that one can appreciate the actual, "master," as Findlay says, "the shimmering, ever reduplicated and multiply refracted structure of the world."[75] Such mastery, for Findlay and Dewey, requires acts of faithful attention to what is sensible and present, and transcending acts of faith in what is unseen and absent.

CHAPTER 9

Dewey, Wallace Stevens, and the "Difficult Inch"

In "Wallace Stevens: The False and True Sublime," Helen Vendler remarks that "in his American environment—pragmatical, inventive, derisive—there seemed no room for a poetic sublime, either in experience or in language."[1] Underlying this statement is an assumption of considerable interest and importance, namely, that the "pragmatical" and the sublime are, if not mutually exclusive, then at least not easily reconciled. It is not difficult to sympathize with Stevens's reservations (or more precisely, Vendler's reading of these reservations) concerning the possibility of an American sublime. Pragmatism, viewed either as a philosophical position or more generally as a mood or sensibility defining the "American environment," would appear to be uncongenial to otherworldly talk about the sublime, the transcendent, the mysterious. Pragmatism even would like to give imagination a practical bent or slant. "Use your imagination" to the pragmatist means use imagination's power to present absent realities to consciousness. Imaginative presentations help to solve problems, or in aesthetic and religious experiences, they deepen our appreciation of the real, not fanciful, possibilities interwoven in and through ordinary experience. Pragmatism cannot permit imaginings to depart too far from the environment, from the data of concrete experience and reality, because its center in the determinate and the finite would be decentered by indeterminacies and infinitudes. Thus, Stevens's absorption with the question of an American sublime asks both a culture and a philosophy to reflect on what is, in Kant's words, the "absolutely great."

That a "pragmatical" environment might not be sufficiently generous in its interpretation of what is most magnificent, splendid, and excellent is at least one implication of Tocqueville's remark in *Democracy in America* that Americans have "a taste for the tangible and the real." What can nobility and grandeur, what Vendler calls "a sizable awe and a posture of ecstatic reverence," mean for a culture—and a philosophy—so inclined toward "the tangible and the real"? In Vendler's view, the question was not merely a technical or craft question for Stevens: "The preeminent question life asked of Stevens was whether the sublime was livable." This question was not a general one directed to anyone's life. The question was quite specific to Stevens's life and "whether in it he could find any sublimity or any human grandeur."

The purpose of this chapter is to suggest that the basic question life asked of Wallace Stevens regarding "whether the sublime was livable" is essentially the same one asked of John Dewey, or at least the same one asked by Dewey in his philosophy. What can sublimity, imagination, or transcendence mean in Dewey's pragmatism? In "The American Sublime" Stevens says:

> How does one stand
> To behold the sublime,
> To confront the mockers
> The mickey mockers
> And plated pairs?[2]

It seems to me that Dewey had a profoundly difficult time determining how one stands to behold the sublime. There are, I shall argue, equivocations early to late in Dewey on the matter of any sort of imaginative beholding which, however briefly, loosens our adherence to the external world. That Dewey was deeply uncertain about the status of imaginative acts and objects is rather strongly suggested by the fact that one does not need to inspect years or even decades of his philosophical development to see the tensions and struggles take shape. Often, from one page to the next in an article or chapter, Dewey moves back and forth between the projection of possibilities founded on and continuous with the actual and the projection of possibilities which do not inhere in the actual and which mark a break with the ordinary. Usually Dewey insists that the situation or context imposes requirements on imagination which keep it from losing its anchor in the actual.[3] Other times, Dewey extends to imagination a freedom which allows it to suspend the actual, to put it out of play, by creating an order internal to its own workings.

I shall not be looking for problems in Stevens but rather looking for a phrase, a thought, an idea which helps to provoke a closer view of Dewey's problems with imagination. The "more"—the imaginative and occasionally sublime more—was the center of Stevens's poetry and philosophy of poetry.[4] The nature of this transcendent more was, I believe, the philosophical center of what Stevens called "my reality-imagination complex." This transcending more posed a profound challenge to Dewey's empiricism/naturalism/pragmatism. The empirical self built up through experience cannot be crowded out by a transcendental more. Just as "the waters of metaphysical criticism leak at every joint" into James's psychology, so experience soaks all the larger projections of the mind and spirit in Dewey, leading him with Emerson to disavow "the reputed transcendental worth of an overweening Beyond and Away."[5] We drag our ordinary selves with us as we approach something resembling a "Beyond and Away," for without such ordinariness and finitude, against what would the extraordinary and infinite be braced? Indeed, Stevens and Dewey might be called a poet and philosopher of the ordinary, both agreeing that reality has much to offer imagination. Yet neither was wholly steady in his vision that reality is the principal occasion and measure for imaginative acts. A reality-bound imagination is not more agreeable than an imagination-bound (deconstructed) reality. Where does one stand, pragmatist or not, to behold the sublime?

The view of Dewey as a clearheaded, earthbound thinker who preferred to stay close to the world-assurances provided by science, reflection, method, and social intelligence, has started to give way as a result of the appearance of books such as those by Thomas M. Alexander, Russell B. Goodman, and Steven C. Rockefeller.[6] Each of these works contributes to a finer understanding of why it might be said that the deepest part of Dewey's entire philosophy is to be found in an investigation of the meaning and ramification of the second chapter of *Art as Experience*. "The Live Creature and 'Etherial Things'" is indeed one of Dewey's most extended answers to the question of how pragmatism stands to behold the sublime, the "absolutely great." Nonetheless, I shall rather cautiously suggest that the works of Alexander, Goodman, and Rockefeller do not give an adequate account of the aporia to be found in Dewey's repeated attempts to establish a standpoint from which to behold the sublimity of "etherial things" without indulging in what Stevens called "heavenly psychology." Despite the bravado evident in most of Dewey's naturalistic pronouncements, these pronouncements often are accompanied by remarks which slightly decenter his attempt to naturalize imagination, to bring the sublime down to earth. While the above-mentioned studies attend to certain of the ways in which Dewey's project does not fully achieve his purposes, they tend to take unification as the goal which defined Dewey's purposes. Inner and outer, spiritual and secular, ideal and actual, transcendent and immanent, imagination and reality, sublime and ordinary were to be unified or integrated. To see Dewey through some of the colors and moods of Stevens's "reality-imagination complex" will, I think, suggest why unification did not completely solve all of Dewey's problems regarding imagination, transcendence, and the ideal.

My procedure is simple. I shall look at one chapter of *Psychology* (1887) and some chapters of *Art as Experience* (1934) to observe Dewey trying to find a standpoint from which to behold the sublime and its elevations.

I

An initial orientation to Dewey's chapter on imagination in his 1887 *Psychology* is provided by Stevens in "The Sail of Ulysses":

> The living man in the present place,
> Always, the particular thought
> Among Plantagenet abstractions,
> Always and always, the difficult inch,
> On which the vast arches of space
> Repose, always, the credible thought
> From which the incredible systems spring,
> The little confine soon unconfined
> In stellar largenesses — these
> Are the manifestations of a law
> That bends the particulars to the abstract,
> Makes them a pack on a giant's back,
> A majestic mother's flocking brood,
> As if abstractions were, themselves
> Particulars of a relative sublime.[7]

An exaggeration to be sure to call Dewey the philosopher of the "difficult inch," but it is a necessary exaggeration. It keeps before us the centrality in Dewey's philosophy of "the living man in the present place." Stevens's "living man" and Dewey's "live creature" can never be unmindful of the "particular thought" and the "credible thought," for these are the bases of "Plantagenet abstractions" and "incredible systems." Yet basis, foundation, ground will not quite do to describe the indebtedness of "vast arches of space" to the "difficult inch." Is an inch, in all its difficultly, the cause of space, in all its vastness? No. The "particular thought" is not a "Plantagenet" abstraction in lower case.

"The little confine soon unconfined / In stellar largenesses" perfectly suggests our awe or wonder at the releasement of the particular, of the "little confine." And "stellar largenesses" will do as well as anything to remind us that we are concerned with a "more" which is not simply a magnification of an antecedently existing reality or ideal. All these reposings of a greater magnitude on a more modest magnitude "Are the manifestations of a law / That bends the particulars to the abstract." The abstract does not bend to the particulars; the particulars bend to the abstract. We have been reposing on the credible as it bends toward the incredible. Abstractions, compressed by the "difficult inch" and "stellar largenesses," are "particulars of a relative sublime."

It is the nature of the unconfining of the "little confine" which Dewey attends to in his chapter on imagination in *Psychology*. The first section is titled "Nature of Imagination," and in it Dewey notes that imagination is like perception and memory "in that its product is always *particular*; it is an idea of this or that object, person, event." He then distinguishes imagination from perception and memory by noting that "this particular mental existence is not necessarily referred to some one place or time as existing there. It is, in short, an idea; not an object or event. It is, however, an idea of some object or event.[8]" Imagination is definitely once removed from existence and perhaps even twice. What is imagined does not exist, yet what is imagined is "an idea of some object or event," something which had or could have a place in existence. Is Dewey saying that the inexistence of imagined objects is temporary ("some one place or time as existing there") and that we can only imagine the existent and possibles born of existence? Or is he saying that we can imagine the nonexistent and the impossible and that the only restriction on such imagining is that it must have an intentional object, must possess "an idea of this or that object, person, event"?[9] It would seem that Dewey inclines toward the latter view: "Othello is, indeed, given a local and temporal habitation, but it is recognized that this is done purely from motives of the mind itself, and not from constraint of external fact."[10] In imagination the "motives of the mind itself" liberate idea from the "difficult inch" of fact. Dewey is well on the way to bending particulars to the mind's—and imagination's—abstractions.

After considering briefly how imagination is involved in perception and memory, Dewey identifies three stages of imagination. Mechanical imagination is the lowest: "It deals with real material—things and events previously experienced—and confines its activity to forming abstractions, and producing combinations not experienced." The next stage is fancy or fantasy, and "its home is romance." Dewey cites *A Midsummer Night's Dream* as an example of fancy and notes that such fancy "is not revealing in its nature; it is only stimulating. It affords keen delight rather than serves as an organ of penetration." The highest form of imagination, creative imagination, is, Dewey says, "an organ of penetration into the hidden meaning of things—meaning not visible to perception or memory, nor reflectively attained by the processes of thinking."[11] Although different in some respects, this passage brings to mind Dewey's discussion of "negative capability" forty-seven years later in "The Live Creature and 'Etherial Things.'" Creative imagination is not restricted to the combination of experiences already had: "It is virtually creative." The projections of imagination do not receive their auspices from the past, from "experiences already had"; neither do the exertions of imagination have to do principally with the visible. When we are, to use D. H. Lawrence's phrase, "heaving into uncreated space," the past and the visible are blurred particulars of a yet indeterminate abstraction.

Dewey lacks no vigor in setting imagination free, in reducing its indebtedness to, and even memory of, the "difficult inch":

> Imagination takes the idealized element by itself, and treats it with reference to its own value, without regard to the actual existence of the things symbolized. There is an ideal element in both perception and memory, but it is tied down to some particular thing. Creative imagination develops this ideal element, and frees it from its connection with petty and contingent circumstance. Perception and memory both have their worth because of the *meaning* of the perceived or remembered thing, but this meaning is subordinate to the existence of the thing. Imagination reverses the process; existence is subordinate to meaning.[12]

Imagination effects a most profound reversal, the subordination of existence to meaning. Freed from "petty and contingent circumstances," imaginative meanings range beyond present, evident, manifest meanings. Through imagination, meaning is drawn toward the transcendent, toward the hidden and invisible. This reversal is not a means to an end; it is an end: "Imagination has no external end, but its end is the free play of the various activities of the self, so as to satisfy its interests."[13] Imagination exceeds use, truth, actual and factual circumstance. It is meaning's freedom.

Where does one stand to behold such a reversal, such "free play"? Clearly, one cannot stand outside—not easily—"stellar largenesses." Such meanings must be had or lived within the horizons they establish. How such meanings are given or presented to consciousness requires a phenomenology which Dewey did not possess in 1887. This partly accounts for his vacillation in the chapter "Aesthetic Feeling" concerning the status of ideal meaning. As we have seen, the reversal achieved by imagination subordinates existence to meaning. Ideal meanings are not restricted to things of "actual existence." They are freed from "petty and contingent circumstances." However, in the section titled "Idealism and Realism in Art," Dewey seems to retreat from this position:

> In strictest sense, a purely realistic, as a purely idealistic, art is impossible—that is to say, pure realism would have no meaning to appeal to the mind, for meaning is a product of idealization, and would have no interest to appeal to the emotions, for interest is a product of putting of self into fact. And pure idealism, if interpreted to mean that sensuous material shall not be used, is impossible, for an ideal unembodied, unmanifested, would have no meaning whatever. Furthermore, all meaning is meaning *of fact*, of reality. It cannot exist in the air. The careful, minute, and faithful study of actual fact is needed, therefore, first, that one may know what the value of an experience really is; and secondly, that one may know the concrete sensuous material which shall be used in presenting it.[14]

Earlier, Dewey points to imagination as an excess of meaning over fact or "actual existence." Now "all meaning is meaning *of fact*, of reality." Why, we ask, is interest "a product of the putting of self into fact"? Does the self not have other interests besides fact? Clearly, Dewey is having trouble sustaining the reversal described in the imagination chapter. There, imagination's play is not restricted to playing with facts: "Its very essence is spontaneous, unfettered play, controlled only by the interests, the emotions and aspirations, of the self."[15] Perhaps something has been missed in the chapter on imagination which might provide a smoother transition between the self put into meaning and the self put into fact.

The link, of course, is the universalizing capacity of imagination, which I have left out of the discussion to this point. I have separated the idealizing and universalizing activities of imagination in order to better identify the tensions in Dewey's thought. In the section titled "Universalizing Activity of Imagination," Dewey says that "the function of the creative imagination everywhere is to seize upon the permanent meaning of facts, and embody them in such congruous, sensuous forms as shall enkindle feeling, and awaken a like organ of penetration in whoever may come upon the embodiment."[16] Idealizing imagination overshoots fact and reality. Universalizing imagination overshoots fact and reality in order to return to them the "permanent meaning of facts." In the latter, unlike in the former, existence is *not* "subordinate to meaning" because natural existence is construed by Dewey to be a condition for the possibility of meaning.

Idealizing imagination is, in some respects, an intermediary. It withdraws our attention from the real, the actual, the factual. In this form it has, Dewey says, "no external end," and its essence is "unfettered play." This is where the "difficult inch" is "unconfined." But this essence expresses the interests of the individual, the solitary person. When the interests controlling the idealizing imagination are "general in their nature," they may come to "express the universal aspect of mankind."[17] The meanings of idealizing imagination range beyond existence. The universalizing imagination bends these meanings back to existence, back to natural existence. Dewey says:

> We find joy in any scene of nature just in the degree in which we find ourselves therein, and are able to identify the workings of our spirit with those of nature. The art which deals with nature is perfect and enduring just in the degree in which it reveals the fundamental unities which exist between man and nature. In Wordsworth's poetry of nature, for example, we do not find ourselves in a strange, unfamiliar land; we find Wordsworth penetrating into those revelations of spirit, of meaning in nature, of which we ourselves had already some dumb feeling, and this the poetry makes articulate. All products of the creative imagination are unconscious testimonies to the unity of spirit which binds man to man and man to nature in one organic whole.[18]

Idealizing imagination draws us away from reality and toward the unreal. The universalizing moment of imagination draws us through and then away from the unreal and fantastic so as to transform the real. Thus does the "difficult inch" become the sublime inch.

Dewey is not very far from Stevens, or at least one part of Dewey's position is not very far from one part of Stevens's position. Stevens says in "The Noble Rider and the Sound of Words": "The imagination loses vitality as it ceases to adhere to what is real. When it adheres to the unreal and intensifies what is unreal, while its first effect may be extraordinary, that effect is the maximum effect that it will ever have."[19] Dewey undoubtedly would agree with Stevens that in order for imagination to possess vitality, the ability to "sustain us," then it must be the case that "it has the strength of reality or none at all."[20] But Stevens's equivocations are not any less noticeable than those of Dewey. In "Holiday in Reality," Stevens says:

> Intangible arrows quiver and stick in the skin
> And I taste at the root of the tongue the unreal of what
>   is real.[21]

Dewey too could "taste at the root of the tongue the unreal of what is real." His universalization could elaborate what he found "at the root of the tongue" in a way that seemingly contributed to what Stevens called the "strength of reality," but neither the philosopher nor the poet could put aside "the unreal of what is real."

Left like this, the picture I have sketched of Dewey's position in *Psychology* is not entirely convincing. It might be argued that the idealizing and universalizing imaginations are not nearly as incompatible as I have portrayed them and that even to think of idealizing imagination as an intermediary between fact and the universalizing imagination is to make all three entirely too external to each other. This is a fair reading and cannot be discounted. On this reading, the idealizing imagination is simply an immature universalizing imagination. When, in connection with the idealizing action of the imagination, Dewey says that it functions "without regard to the actual existence of the things symbolized," he has ceded control not to meaning but to "permanent meaning of facts," that is, universal meaning. Yes, idealizing imagination frees or unconfines its meanings from "connection with petty and contingent circumstances," but this is merely an initial and imperfect approximation to the permanent meaning discoverable in the facts of nature. The subordination of existence to meaning is the principal condition for, not a refutation of, imagination's fascination with the "difficult inch." This would justify Dewey's conviction that "creative imagination is not to be considered as the production of unreal or fantastic forms, nor as the idle play of capricious mind working in an arbitrary way."[22] The workings of the "creative imagination" should not result in a fantasy (reality as a pretext), nor should it yield a duplicate (reality as the original). If its product is the former, then we have merely "idle play." If it produces the latter, then the particular is *simply* a particular. The universal is what prevents imagination's alienation from reality from degenerating into narcissistic self-deception and self-dispersion.

The universal thus is what makes the "hidden meaning of things" humanly relevant, humanly meaningful. The universal redeems imagination's excesses, but also, and more important, it gives the imaginer a place to stand to behold the sublime:

> To say more than human things with human voice,
> That cannot be; to say human things with more
> Than human voice, that, also, cannot be;
> To speak humanly from the height or from the depth
> Of human things, that is acutest speech.[23]

For Dewey "to speak humanly from the height or from the depth of human things" is to place the imaginer not simply in nature, but in universal nature. Thus he says: "The poem of Homer, the art of Michael Angelo, and the drama of Shakespeare are true to the universal side of humanity, not to the individual and peculiar tastes and experiences of their authors."[24] To behold the sublime we do not stand in the visible, human particular only to watch it disappear into the inhuman invisible. We stand in the particular, and lifted up by imagination's desire for universality and wholeness, we see what was hidden in the particular. In short, there can be no experience of transcendence for human beings which involves "more than human things" or "more than human voice." As William James said in "Pragmatism and Humanism": "You can't weed out the human contribution," including "the human contribution" to "stellar largenesses."

Let us call the poles that define his early equivocations insubordinate imagination and natural imagination. The former resists the authority of the real, the factual, the actual, the universal, the natural. Excursions and excesses of the insubordinate imagination are not controlled by adherence to the real or mindfulness of the natural. Insubordinate imagination resists naturalization. In contrast to this groundless play, natural imagination enables the mind to find its true grandeur. The natural escorts us to whatever is, or can be, ultimate for human beings. Insubordinate imagination offers alternatives to reality. Natural imagination completes reality. Dewey's unification of these two expressions of imagination must, we might say, stay one step ahead of imagination's desire to express its freedom by surpassing any ground or home in nature. Having given life to imagination as an insubordinate ranging of mind beyond existence, how shall Dewey incorporate the "unconfined" into his philosophy of experience?

II

In "Imagination as Value" Stevens says:

> Nietzsche walked in the Alps in the caresses of reality. We ourselves crawl out of our offices and classrooms and become alert at the opera. Or we sit listening to music as in an imagination in which we believe. If the imagination is the faculty by which we import the unreal into what is real, its value is the value of the way of thinking by which we project the idea of God into the idea of man. It creates images that are independent of their originals since nothing is more certain than that the imagination is agreeable to the imagination.[25]

There is something unmistakably Deweyan in the image of us crawling out of our offices and classrooms and coming alive at the opera. Ordinary experience often is dull, mechanical, and lacking aesthetic quality. We turn to enclaves of meaning and experience which refresh us by suspending the everyday and ordinary, the all-too-real. Dewey of course begins *Art as*

Experience with an objection to this sort of separation of art from ordinary experience. In the first page, he says that a primary responsibility of one writing on the philosophy of the fine arts "is to restore continuity between the refined and intensified forms of experience that are works of art and the everyday events, doings, and sufferings that are universally recognized to constitute experience."[26] The height and depth of concern to poetry and art are "of human things," things of the everyday, the mundane, the ordinary. When art takes us to the extraordinary, it does so by virtue of the debt paid, no matter how indirectly, to what Dewey called "normal experience."

The first chapter of *Art as Experience*, "The Live Creature," advances two propositions, only one of which is explicitly stated. Dewey says: "The first great consideration is that life goes on in an environment: not merely *in* it but because of it, through interaction with it."[27] The somewhat disguised or at least covert premise of the chapter is that meaning does not originate in itself, but like life itself it is an accommodation to, and transformation of, what is other than itself. For the same reason that "no creature lives merely under its skin," no meaning lives merely under its skin. Meaning's origin, its original, is the environment of the empirical world with which we are in constant interaction. We may be in step with the environment, in accord with it, or we may be out of step. Life—and meaning—is a matter of contrasts:

> Contrast of lack and fullness, of struggle and achievement, of adjustment after consummated irregularity, form the drama in which action, feeling, and meaning are one. The outcome is balance and counterbalance. These are not static nor mechanical. They express power that is intense because measured through overcoming resistance. Environing objects avail and counteravail.[28]

Coming to terms with the environment requires meaning to find an accord with the environment. Such accord is the basis of "inner harmony" but Dewey cautions that "when it occurs on any other than an 'objective' basis, it is illusory—in extreme cases to the point of insanity." Thus, Dewey locates the root or origin of art in the contrast between lack and fullness and their reconciliation in a fulfillment "that reaches to the depths of our being—one that is an adjustment of our whole being with the conditions of existence."[29] Dewey is echoing Stevens: "To speak humanly from the height or from the depth / Of human things, that is acutest speech." Harmonies of meaning that so completely overshoot reality, that have no hint of an objective basis, cannot "speak humanly."

We clearly find no trace of imagination's reversal in "The Live Creature." There is no subordination of meaning to existence but rather the "adjustment" of meaning to existence. Having established the primacy of environing objects in the first chapter, Dewey wishes to take the needed next step in "The Live Creature and 'Etherial Things'": he wants to make the objects of nature the material for imagination. He has begun *Art as Experience* on good naturalistic grounds. Live creature, environment, interaction all proclaim that art's origin, its original, is to be found in natural existence. The imaginings of art cannot be independent of natural existence, for that is what the imaginings are about, that is the material of art. Dewey quotes Keats in a footnote: "The Sun, the Moon, the Earth and its contents, are material to form greater things, that is, etherial things—greater things than the Creator himself made."[30] Nature provides the originals from which art produces images of "greater things." These art-created "etherial" and greater things cannot be independent of nature's originals since they are nature's perfections.

Suppose, though, imagination has no original. Suppose not even nature subordinates imagination's energies. Suppose, with Stevens, that imagination "creates images that are independent of their original since nothing is more certain than that the imagination is agreeable to the imagination." How are "etherial things" to be regarded when they no longer are ultimate expressions of the harmony of nature and imagined meaning (what I have called natural imagination) but rather evidences of imagination's agreeableness to itself (what I have called insubordinate imagination)? Can Dewey tolerate an imagination so agreeable to imagination that reality and fact withdraw and leave imagination to do what it will with nature? Yes and no.

Dewey begins "The Live Creature and 'Etherial Things'" with the central question: "Why is the attempt to connect the higher and ideal things of experience with basic vital roots so often regarded as betrayal of their nature and denial of their value?" Why, in other words, is spirit cut off from sense? His answer is brief: "We undergo sensations as mechanical stimuli or as irritated stimulations, without having a sense of the reality that is in them and behind them: in much of our experience our different senses do not unite to tell a common and enlarged story."[31] With such diminishment and impoverishment of their powers, "sense and flesh get a bad name." Most of "The Live Creature and 'Etherial Things'" is devoted to giving sense a good name.

The basic strategy is to make sense equal to whatever the mind and spirit can accomplish, that is, to make sense the point of intersection between the finite and the infinite. The first step in accomplishing this is to make sense a full-fledged point of meaning-producing contact with the world: "Sense, as meaning so directly embodied in experience as to be its own illuminated meaning, is the only signification that expresses the function of sense organs when they are carried to full realization."[32] Under these circumstances, interaction with the environment approaches the highest and deepest realization of its possibilities and becomes fully human participation and communication. Art is a refinement of this sense:

> It is proof that man uses the materials and energies of nature with intent to expand his own life, and that he does so in accord with the structure of his organism—brain, sense-organs, and muscular system. Art is the living and concrete proof that man is capable of restoring consciously, and thus on the plane of meaning, the union of sense, need, impulse and action characteristic of the live creature.[33]

In short, art offers evidence that the natural and the ideal are continuous. Indeed, so sure is Dewey that art is the expression of the ideal meanings of nature that in a footnote he refers his readers to a passage in *Experience and Nature* where he says that art "is the complete culmination of nature."

Having given a full vote of confidence to the meaning-bestowing power of sense, Dewey takes his second step in giving sense a good name. He cites some well-known accounts from Hudson and Emerson of what he calls experiences of "acute aesthetic surrender." Based on these kinds of experiences he concludes:

> I do not see any way of accounting for the multiplicity of experiences of this kind (something of the same quality being found in every spontaneous and uncoerced esthetic response), except on the basis that there are stirred into activity resonances of dispositions acquired in primitive relationships of the living being to its surroundings, and irrecoverable in distinct or intellectual consciousness. . . . There is no limit to the capacity of immediate sensuous experience to absorb into itself meanings and values that in and of themselves—that is in the abstract—would be designated "ideal" and "spiritual."[34]

Nature allows, is agreeable to, idealization. However, idealizing activities such as those of the imagination can never fully silence the "resonances of dispositions acquired in primitive relationships of the living being to its surroundings." Poetry, all art, deepens rather than cancels out the indebtedness of reality-defying projections of the mind to the reality-affirming resonances of the "difficult inch."

At this point, Dewey's rehabilitation of sense reaches its most assertive expression. At the same time, tensions internal to this rehabilitation begin to manifest themselves. In a clearly triumphant tone Dewey proclaims: "Nothing that a man has ever reached by the highest flight of thought or penetrated by any probing insight is inherently such that it may not become the heart and core of sense."³⁵ What, though, of imagination? Can the highest and deepest things reached by imagination "become the heart and core of sense"? Can, and must, the flights of imagination be bodied forth in a sense always bearing traces of, resonances of, its natural environment? To the natural imagination the answer is yes. To the insubordinate imagination the answer is no.

Unlike in *Psychology*, where Dewey himself proposes a subordination of existence to meaning, here it is his appeal to Keats which occasions an unobtrusive, almost imperceptible abridgement of the sanctions afforded by fact. Dewey initially appeals to Keats to show that since "etherial" things are available to sense they cannot be divorced from nature. Sense is the *via media* through which higher and lower pass into each other. Dewey then notes that he appealed to Keats because "he identified the attitude of the artist with that of the live creature."³⁶ In both appeals, imagination works within the bounds of nature and with no suggestion of transgressing or negating these limits.

Dewey then appeals to Keats's description of Shakespeare as a man possessed of enormous "negative capability," one who was "capable of being in uncertainties, mysteries, doubts, without any irritable reaching after fact and reason." Dewey enthusiastically endorses Keats's view that the meanings summoned by imagination need not reach after "consecutive reasoning." He is silent as to whether imaginative meanings must reach after fact. Dewey in effect accepts only one half of Keats's "negative capability." This is further suggested by his remark that for Keats "'reasonings' have an origin like that of the movements of a wild creature toward its goal, and they may become spontaneous, 'instinctive,' and when they become instinctive are sensuous and immediate, poetic."³⁷ Reasoning's origins are to be found in the interaction of live creature and environment and while imagination may overshoot reason, it cannot overshoot their common stem—originating and original nature.

One must wonder, though, whether Dewey was not at least minimally aware that he was turning his attention away from one half of the force of "negative capability." Do not reason, knowledge, and reflection in some nontrivial way take account of the environment, incorporating it into their determinations? If so, does not the "putting aside" of reason's objections mean that the objections of fact, of actual existence, also have been put aside? Perhaps Dewey was not minimally but deeply aware that for one possessing "negative capability" meaning cannot be anchored in fact any more than it can be anchored in reason. We "trust" in our intuitions, our "imaginative sentiments" and "imaginative intuitions." What is contained in our trust is both more and less than the provisions of fact and reason. Perhaps, after all, Dewey did recognize that the capacity for being in "mysteries" (he does not capitalize it, as it is in Keats's letter) necessarily means that reason's longings cannot be fulfilled, even when abetted by nature.

The limited evidence, though, works against this interpretation. Dewey really gives no clue that he sees the extent to which "negative capability" throws into question his "first great consideration," the belief that "life goes on in an environment; not merely *in* it but because of it, through interaction with it." "Negative capability" gives the poet, the artist, the ordinary person, freedom from earthly materials. The environment is held off, resisted, subordinated to the sanctionless meanings imagination can invent for itself. The interactions or crossings so common in Dewey between self and nature are not nearly so stable or stabilizing as "the Sun, the Moon, the Earth and its contents." The self may not be proportioned to nature. Keats says:

> Now it appears to me that almost any Man may like the spider spin from his own inwards his own airy Citadel — the points of leaves and twigs on which the Spider begins her work are few and she fills the Air with a beautiful circuiting: man should be content with as few points to tip with the fine Webb of his Soul and weave a tapestry empyrean — full of Symbols for his spiritual eye, of softness for his spiritual touch, of space for his wandering of distinctness for his Luxury —[38]

Dewey could not, I think, happily embrace a view which closed down the interaction of self and world to such a trickle that things are created from one's "own inwards." Neither could he reject that view if, as Keats suggests, "etherial things" are symbols of the capacity of the "spiritual eye" to reduce to a vanishing point its indebtedness to "points" of reality.

III

Dewey's longest treatment of imagination in *Art as Experience* is spread out in two chapters. It begins toward the end of "The Human Contribution" and concludes in the beginning of "The Challenge to Philosophy." If the meanings of these titles are slightly extended, they provide an astonishingly apt description of imagination's place in Dewey's philosophy. Imagination is the highest human contribution to experience and as such its role in Dewey's philosophy of experience hardly can be exaggerated. Thus, he says, "esthetic experience is pure experience," and "imaginative experience exemplifies more fully than any other kind of experience what experience itself is in its very movement and structure."[39] In other words, aesthetic experience discloses more fully than any other kind of experience the logic of any actual and possible experience. The center of this logos is imagination.

The challenge posed to Dewey's philosophy by imagination is, I have been arguing, profound, since he was not of one mind regarding the nature of its contribution. What he has to say about imagination in "The Human Contribution" is not fully consistent with what he says about "negative capability," if the latter means that the claims of environment may be resisted rather than supported by imagination. The central argument of Dewey is that imagination achieves a reconciliation of inner and outer:

> There is a conflict artists themselves undergo that is instructive as to the nature of imaginative experience. The conflict has been set forth in many ways. One way of stating it concerns the opposition between inner and outer vision. There is a stage in which the inner vision seems much richer and finer than any outer manifestation. It has a vast and enticing aura of implications that are lacking in the object of external vision. It seems to grasp much more than the latter conveys. Then there comes a reaction; the matter of the inner vision seems wraith-like compared with the solidity and energy of the presented scene. The object is felt to say something succinctly and forcibly that the inner vision reports vaguely, in diffuse feeling rather than organically. The artist is driven to submit himself in humility to the discipline of the objective vision. But the inner vision is not cast out. It remains as the organ by which outer vision is controlled, and it takes on structure as the latter is absorbed within it. The interaction of the two modes of vision is imagination; as imagination takes form the work of art is born.[40]

The inner, imaginative vision must "submit" to the "objective vision." This objective reality is, to borrow from James, "reality to which defeat can't happen." Imagination cannot ultimately defeat reality, cannot detach itself from it and subordinate it to invented meanings. When "mind stays aloof" from reality, when mind and reality do not form a union, we have not imagination but fancy and, ultimately, insanity. And yet "inner vision is not cast out." It is through the inner vision that the outer vision is "controlled." Dewey must have his reciprocity of influence, and hence what starts out as a "conflict" or "opposition" of two modes of vision ends up a much friendlier "interaction" of these formerly conflicting modes of vision. Perhaps Dewey wanted to say something like this: inner and outer vision are in conflict, but the character of this conflict is heavily influenced by reality's willingness, even invitation, to be imagined. He in fact says something quite different: outer, objective vision is "controlled" by inner, imaginative vision. What, precisely, has the objective contributed if imagination controls, directs, the objective? How does the "object of external vision" offer much resistance to the inner vision when the latter controls external vision?

We have, I think, a variation on the "airy Citadel" built by "a beautiful circuiting" which has become detached from the resistances—"points"—provided by reality. "The material is too slight to call forth the full energy of the dispositions in which values and meanings are embodied; it does not offer enough resistance, and so mind plays with it capriciously."[41] But suppose the objecting and objective material is substantial and offers "enough resistance." Whether controlling imagination "plays with it capriciously" or magnificently is a question which Dewey cannot answer very well on the basis of his standard interaction equation. Dewey is less than sure that an "airy Citadel" might be an imaginative achievement of considerable worth precisely because it minimizes reality's resistance. To say, as Dewey does, that the "interaction" of inner and outer vision is imagination simply affirms the reciprocal, egalitarian character of the activities of natural imagination. It also, however, tends to gloss all those assertions of the insubordinate imagination which do not measure themselves according to whether mind and material "squarely meet and interpenetrate."[42] Joining with nature, becoming one with it, is not imagination's sole aim. Often, imagination would like to control—in all the transforming and transfiguring senses of "control"—the objective, the outer, the natural.

Dewey cannot long suppress his own "negative capability" and concludes "The Human Contribution" in a slightly less naturalistically confident way than his talk about interaction promises: "Philosophy is said to begin in wonder and end in understanding. Art departs from what has been understood and ends in wonder. In this end, the human contribution in art is also the quickened work of nature in man."[43] Dewey is again attempting a reversal, but whereas forty-seven years earlier the terms of the reversal—meaning and existence—were reasonably clear, now one of the terms is rather obscure. What does "wonder" mean to Dewey? Is it a more ultimate word than his usual "consummation"? Are all consummations experiences of wonder? What contrasts are implied in this reversal of beginnings and endings, specifically, what differentiates understanding from wonder? Does wonder take possession of an environment of objects and materials in the same way that Dewey wishes imagination to come to terms with the environment? Does wonder perhaps take Dewey as close as he can come to a transcendence not possessed by a self because the self has dissolved? Having given rise to such troubling questions, imagination's contribution to aesthetic experience inevitably evolves into a challenge to philosophy itself, Dewey's in particular. What happens to pragmatism when "the real world" it wishes to handle, the reality with which it wishes to interact and penetrate, is unconfined by wonder and imagination?

Dewey seems to know that his pragmatism, as well as his aesthetics, has something important at stake in his account of imagination. Hence, he begins "The Challenge to Philosophy" with a sentence that concedes that the work of the previous chapter is unfinished: "Esthetic experience is imaginative." Dewey cannot let go of the problem of imagination. He does not directly identify imagination as one of the challenges to philosophy which he intends to take up in the chapter, yet his treatment of make-believe theory and play theory is formulated in terms of imagination. Make-believe theory depends on the "contrast between the work of art as an experience and experience of the 'real.'" The environment created by the work of art is not an imitation of the environment provided by the "real." Dewey initially finds much of make-believe theory quite congenial, and indeed his chief objection to it derives "from the fact that in isolating one constituent, it denies explicitly or implicitly other elements equally essential." In short, Dewey readily concedes that the essential element of make-believe theory, namely reverie, is a component in the creation of art and in the experience of an artwork. This is why he does not hesitate to say that "because of the domination of esthetic experience by imaginative quality, it exists in a medium of light that never was on land or sea."[44] Never having been "on land or sea," such light is a contribution or addition to reality. Its original, though, is not in nature, nor is this light's aspiration to be an interrogation of reality, nature, environment, or fact. It is *unlike* the environment, underived and underivable from it. For a moment, Dewey agrees with Stevens that imagination "creates images that are independent of their originals."

This detachment and independence of existence and meaning, the *unlikelihood* of meanings encountered in dreams and reveries, provides for a work of art but is not in itself the matter or material of a work of art. What is missing is selection and development of material by purpose:

> The characteristic of dream and reverie is absence of control by purpose. Images and ideas succeed one another according to their own sweet will, and the sweetness of the succession to feeling is the only control that is exercised. In philosophical terminology, the material is subjective. An esthetic product results only when ideas cease to float and are embodied in an object and the one who experiences the work of art loses himself

in irrelevant reverie unless his images and emotions are also tied to the object, and tied to it in the sense of being fused with the matter of the *object*.⁴⁵

Is the "state of reverie" which had been simply "material *for* a work of art" prior to its organization by purpose into "matter *of* a work of art," now something different than reverie or dream, something more objective? In its uncontrolled state, Dewey seems willing to allow that there is not "anything in existence" with which reverie has interacted or could interact, nothing that is, discoverable by "outer vision." Dewey says reverie is subjective, and clearly he wants to contrast this reverie to the reverie controlled by purpose. What sort of reverie, though, is purpose-controlled reverie? Objective reverie? Has purpose found or constructed an "outer vision" for the "inner vision" of reverie? Do the ideas "floating" in reverie float less when purpose builds them into a work of art? Dewey apparently thinks so: "Even if we were to suppose that the image first presented itself in an actual dream, it would still be true that its material had to be organized in terms of objective materials and operations that moved consistently and without a break to consummation in the picture as a public object in a common world."⁴⁶ The dream finds its way into aesthetic experience "in terms of objective materials." Even should the original and its image become detached—in reverie, dream, or illusion—the image is never wholly orphaned, for there are other originals, other "objective materials" which give it a purpose-defined home in a "common world."

Reverie, dream, illusion, and insubordinate imagination are elisions. They displace or at least disrupt reality by making and marking a break with the environment. In their grip, I become detached from "objective materials." Objects float. I float. Natural objects are unconfined, but so too is the self. Having a place to stand to behold the elision of the real is unimportant, since the self as standpoint has been elided. Simply put, both environment and self are transcended in moments of sublimity. How do we get back to reality?

Dewey is at a critical point not only in his discussion of make-believe but also in his more general effort to make aesthetic experience a standard for all experience. Dewey's vision of the consummations afforded by aesthetic experience, his concept of what the "absolutely great" is, shows us what to look—and hope—for when the pragmatist gets around to telling us what is most wonderful, splendid, and sublime. But the real world is relentless. An aesthetic experience that transcended ordinary experience and the ordinary self with finality could never be worked back into experience. The self would have no standpoint from which to behold the sublime and certainly no control over it. In such a circumstance, there would be little doubt how to answer Richard Poirier's question: "Is there an I for an Eye"?[47] No, there is not an "I," or at least there may not be. Such a dispersed self simply is not acceptable to Dewey. He can allow a reversing subordination of existence to meaning early in the aesthetic experience; indeed he must have such a reversal in order for an aesthetic experience, say, one involving Cezanne's apples or Vermeer's windows, to realize possibilities not realized in ordinary experience. But the reversals cannot continue so far into the aesthetic experience that "inner vision" becomes autonomous, for then the self would have no way out of itself. Self-consumption and self-dispersal, not self-transcendence, wait for those who lose their hold on reality. Thus, "negative capability" gives Dewey the opportunity to be large-minded about reality-deferring acts of imagination, including the make-believe, but it also requires him to find a path, a thread of continuity, from make-believe to material objects. In short, on what basis does the self survive an explosive burst of "negative capability"?

Dewey's answer is framed in terms of purpose. His paragraph on purpose is critically important not because it is one of his most profound (which it is not), nor because its argument blatantly fails. The argument holds together, just barely, but in holding together we see what price Dewey has paid to maintain continuity between "etherial things" and "objective materials." Immediately after saying that the material provided by "an actual dream" had to be organized through the use of "objective materials and operations," and that this organizing process moved "without a break" to "a public object in a common world," Dewey begins a new paragraph and says:

> At the same time, purpose implicates in the most organic way an individual self. It is in the purposes he entertains and acts upon that an individual most completely exhibits and realizes his intimate selfhood. Control of material by a self is control by more than just "mind"; it is control by the personality that has mind incorporate within it. All interest is an identification of a self with some material aspect of the objective world, of the nature that includes man. Purpose is this identification in action. Its operation in and through objective conditions is a test of its genuineness; the capacity of the purpose to overcome and utilize resistance, to administer materials, is a disclosure of the structure and quality of the purpose. For, as I have already said, the object finally created *is* the purpose both as conscious objective and as accomplished actuality. The thoroughgoing integration of what philosophy discriminates as "subject" and "object" (in more direct language, organism and environment) is the characteristic of every work of art. The completeness of

the integration is the measure of its esthetic status. For defect in a work is always traceable ultimately to an excess on one side or the other, injuring the integration of matter and form. Detailed criticism of the make-believe theory is unnecessary because it is based upon violation of the integrity of the work of art. It expressly denies or virtually ignores that identification with objective materials and constructive operation that is the very essence of art.[48]

Something immediately strikes one as being askew here. If purpose represents the self's capacity to be in control and if "negative capability" represents the self's capacity to set at least the controls of fact and reason aside, on what grounds has Dewey determined that it is the former whereby the individual self "most completely exhibits and realizes his intimate selfhood"? Is not our experience of "etherial things" the most complete realization of our selfhood? How are these related? Are not "etherial things" something more than simply extensions, higher-level manifestations, of human purposes? Is it not precisely the excess of dream and reverie, of insubordinate imagination, which enables "etherial things" to come into view in the first place and which enables them to be objects of aesthetic consummations? Is this not why we ultimately must, as Dewey says, "trust" the deliverances of imagination, since indeed they are in excess of the resistances provided by fact and reason and the purposes provided by fact and reason?

There is yet a further problem. Dewey says that "all interest is an identification of a self with some material aspect of the objective world, of the nature that includes man." This is a peculiarly nonempirical claim for an empiricist to make. What "material aspect of the objective world" is the counterpart to our daydreams, fantasies, pretendings, musings, reveries? Are these not empirically bone fide ways in which we take an interest in ourselves and the world? What sort of world-regarding interest does Keats have in mind when he affirms that "almost any Man may like the spider spin from his own inwards his own airy Citadel"? For Dewey, the self's thorough "identification" with "some material aspect of the objective world" safeguards it from shrinking or enlarging to the point where its expressions are "subjective and hallucinatory."[49] Braced against nothing but itself, proportionate to nothing but itself, the self can behold neither the ridiculous nor the sublime. It vanishes or goes insane. In short, the self should become more, not less, in moments of aesthetic consummation.

This, however, is not how Keats and Emerson see the matter. For Keats, the imagining self is annihilated. For Emerson, the imagining self loses track of itself and is nothing. First, Keats:

> It is a wretched thing to confess; but is a very fact that not one word I ever utter can be taken for granted as an opinion growing out of my identical nature—how can it when I have no nature? When I am in a room with People if I ever am free from speculating on creations of my own brain, then not myself goes home to myself: but the identity of every one in the room begins to [*for* so?] to press upon me that, I am in a very little time an[ni]hilated—not only among Men; it would be the same in a Nursery of children.[50]

Can the self become ethereal? *Must* the self become ethereal in order to catch a glimpse of what transcends it? Dewey passionately endorses the Keats who finds "etherial things" in the sun, the moon, the earth, but he falls silent on Keats' annihilated self, the self without a nature.

Similarly, Dewey does not ask too much of Emerson. The very same Emersonian self that was "glad to the brink of fear" and which was so inspiring to Dewey, is the eradicated self: "Standing on the bare ground,—my head bathed by the blithe air, and uplifted into infinite space,—all mean egotism vanishes. I become a transparent eyeball; I am nothing; I see all; the currents of the Universal Being circulate through me; I am part or parcel of God."[51] Dewey is not prepared to let go of the self in this way, neither in his discussion of "levels of selfhood" in "The Act of Expression" nor in his account of the human contribution later in the book. Undoubtedly, Dewey would not consider the sort of control or regulation he is advocating as an instance of "mean egotism." What controlling purposes, though, characterize a "transparent eyeball"?

Can imagination survive reality? Can reality survive imagination? Both questions can be answered affirmatively if reality and imagination resist each other. If imagination is not to destroy the self, it must give the self a place to stand, to behold the real world. But such a standpoint cannot be too beholden to the real world. If imagination is to loosen reality's grip, it must offer resistance to the real, stand up to it, penetrate it. Imagination cannot simply turn away from reality. In short, it must be more of a force or center than what is suggested by Emerson's "transparent eyeball." We imagine reality's resistances.

IV

In "The Noble Rider and the Sound of Words," Stevens says:

> Don Quixote will make it imperative for him to make a choice, to come to a decision regarding the imagination and reality; and he will find that it is not a choice of one over the other and not a decision that divides

them, but something subtler, a recognition that here, too, as between these poles, the universal interdependence exists, and hence his choice and his decision must be that they are equal and inseparable.[52]

This sounds very Deweyan: inseparability, interdependence. Yet Dewey could not have written this, and for the same reason that Stevens could not have written the following from Dewey:

> In art as an experience, actuality and possibility or ideality, the new and the old, objective material and personal sense and meaning, are integrated in an experience in which they are all transfigured from the significance that belongs to them when isolated in reflection.[53]

The answer to why Stevens's interdependence is not equivalent to Dewey's integration is found in a remark made by Stevens in a letter to Bernard Heringman: "Sometimes I believe most in the imagination for a long time and then, without reasoning about it, turn to reality and believe in that and that alone. But both of these things project themselves endlessly and I want them to do just that."[54] Imagination and reality are interdependent for Stevens, but this interdependence takes advantage of their independent natures. Stevens believes in one then the other: imagination *then* reality and "that alone." Each can sustain Stevens for a long time. Both project themselves "endlessly." In other words, imagination for Stevens is not a completion of reality or way of filling it out. Facts are not fragmentary, incomplete meanings which are guided to their natural conclusion through the intervention of imagination. Imagination projects a horizon of meanings which can intersect reality narrowly or broadly — or perhaps not at all. Imagination and reality need not be integrated in order to be interdependent. Dewey, however, tends to prefer an intersection of imagination and reality so broad and deep that it is a fusion or integration. He wants reality to feel the full weight of imagination, and he wants imagination to feel the full weight of reality. He wants to bring imagination down to earth in order to uncover the sublimity of the earthly.

The contrast between Dewey and Stevens is dramatically reflected in their different understandings of how reality and imagination pressure each other. Dewey says:

> Imaginative experience exemplifies more fully than any other kind of experience what experience itself is in its very movement and structure. But we also want the tang of overt conflict and the impact of harsh conditions. Moreover, without the latter art has no material; and this fact is more important to aesthetic theory than is any contrast supposed to

exist between play and work, spontaneity and necessity, freedom and law. For art is the fusion in one experience of the pressure upon the self of necessary conditions and the spontaneity and novelty of individuality.[55]

It is not clear whether Dewey here is allowing "spontaneity and novelty of individuality" to stand for "negative capability" or insubordinate imagination. Even were this the case, it is apparent that Dewey is not content to permit the "pressure upon the self" and the pressure afforded by spontaneity to evade each other. The pressures must be "fused." Thus, Dewey would respond sympathetically to Stevens's remarks about the "pressure of reality" only up to that point when Stevens says "the resistance to this pressure or its evasion in the case of individuals of extraordinary imagination cancels the pressure so far as those individuals are concerned."[56] Why, from Dewey's perspective, should resistance cancel the pressure of reality rather than make it more complex? And how can the pressure of reality possibly be evaded?

I return, then, to my starting point. Can imagination depart from reality in a way that would be understandable and acceptable to a pragmatist? What must—or can—imagination promise? Must the sublime moment have its fulfillment in the real world, the natural world? Such questions generalize into one: is there a pragmatic "negative capability"? The phrase is unappealing and the concept strange, but perhaps it is preferable to something even worse: the "pragmatic sublime." Is it not, though, precisely the pragmatic which is displaced or surpassed in sublime experiences? Dewey's equivocal responses to this question suggest that his thinking on imagination is an attempt to reconcile the two most obvious ways of answering this question. If the place of immanence in Dewey is emphasized, that is, the integration of reality and imagination, we have a position like that of Roger Shattuck. In "The Innocent Eye and the Armed Vision," Shattuck likens a work of art or literature to the "loop roads" found in Texas. The side roads of literature divert us into a "partly imaginary domain where we can encounter thoughts and feelings that would not have occurred to us on the highway." The essential philosophical point is well stated by Shattuck:

> This loop analogy presents a work of art as a form of delay or relay along the path of living. Its processes are only temporarily autonomous; they turn off from and return to the realities of human existence.... Art is free to try all the genres and modes it can imagine; some of them travel a long way from reality. Its responsibility is to return us to reality better prepared to continue our journey.[57]

Imagination is compressed by reality, turning off from and returning to it. This is very Deweyan and very pragmatic. Literature's loops are not self-contained and endlessly self-referencing, for they delay, not displace, their eventual rejoining with—immanence within—reality.

If the transcendent in Dewey is emphasized, namely, imagination's subordination of existence to meaning in "negative capability," then we have a position more like Geoffrey H. Hartman's:

> As a guiding concept, indeterminacy does not merely *delay* the determination of meaning, that is, suspend premature judgments and allow greater thoughtfulness. The delay is not heuristic alone, a device to slow the act of reading till we appreciate (I think here of Stanley Fish) its complexity. The delay is intrinsic: from a certain point of view, it is thoughtfulness itself, Keats's "negative capability," a labor that aims not to overcome the negative or indeterminate but to stay within it as long as is necessary.[58]

The delays in Shattuck occur along the side roads and thus are external or extrinsic; that is, they have to return to reality and connect with it. The delays in Hartman are intrinsic to thought and reality; they do not have to "return" to reality since they have already transcended the givens of reality. They helped constitute it by applying imaginative pressure from within. This position is very pragmatic, very Deweyan, and especially pragmatic is Hartman's answer to the question of how long it is necessary to stay within the negative or indeterminate: "That cannot be abstractly answered."[59]

Perhaps, after all, a pragmatic "negative capability" or pragmatic sublime only sounds strange. The "pressure of reality" does not require one to become a pragmatist, but it does require a deep respect for "the living man in the present place." It is tempting to think of Stevens's localities—the "particular thought," the "difficult inch," the "credible thought," the "little confine"—as the natural standpoint from which we behold the "stellar largenesses" of the sublime. For Stevens the "pressure of reality," for example, "twenty men crossing a bridge," may call out an imaginative response whose resisting pressure far exceeds the "pressure of reality." Stevens grants that this may be the case far more willingly than does Dewey. Stevens can live in a world where imagination "creates images that are independent of their originals since nothing is more certain than that the imagination is agreeable to the imagination." But Stevens also lives in a world where nature's originals have earned the right to very serious consideration, and who better represents nature's originals than Dewey? Commenting on an issue of the *Partisan Review*, Stevens says that "there is an article by John Dewey on Philosophic Naturalism which strikes me as being valuable."[60] Why? All we can say based on this one sentence is that possibly Stevens did not regard Dewey's naturalism as contributory to an American environment wholly inimical to the poetic sublime.

And Dewey? It is even more tempting to think of Dewey's localities—his love of the ordinary and concrete, his respect for what in *Experience and Nature* he calls "the recalcitrant particular"—as the natural standpoint for beholding the sublime. Nevertheless there is good reason, I think, to take his endorsement of "negative capability" in the thirties as a continuation of his endorsement of idealizing imagination in 1887. In *Psychology*, he says that "imagination takes the idealized element by itself, and treats it with reference to its own value, without regard to the actual existence of the things symbolized." Both the later "negative capability" and the earlier reversal of imagination leave large tracts of "actual existence" suspended or displaced. Without "the recalcitrant particular" to orient us through the resistances of "actual existence," we live, in Roger Shattuck's phrase, "beyond our immediate means or experience."[61] After having subordinated existence to meaning, reinserting ourselves back into reality—living within our means—may not be quite as easy as getting back onto the main highway after a detour on a Texas loop. It is as much an act of faith as it is a discovery of fact that we behold the sublime at the intersection of imagination and reality, or indeed at any intersection at all.

When Dewey's pragmatism comes face to face with its deepest assumptions, one senses that he might have more than an incidental recognition that, as Stevens says:

> It must be visible or invisible,
> Invisible or visible or both:
> A seeing and unseeing in the eye.[62]

The more—the "absolutely great"—unconfined by imagination and experienced in moments of sublimity, is not fully presentable, not fully visible. Neither Dewey nor Stevens, however, complacently accepts a more which exceeds "human things" or "human voice." Fortunately, the "human contribution" is capable of "a seeing and unseeing in the eye." This capacity, at once both practical and sublime, enables Stevens and Dewey to live in an abstraction only dimly prefigured in the particular, if at all. And so, often in Dewey's philosophy, and just as often in Stevens's poetry, it is "as if abstractions were, themselves / Particulars of a relative sublime."

· NOTES ·

Chapter One
1. I observe a rather straightforward, though not unproblematic, distinction between "transcendent" and "transcendental." The former I take to be whatever is significantly discontinuous with the ordinary, the everyday, the taken-for-granted and which eludes reflective verification. "Transcendental" I take to refer to certain conditions of consciousness which are necessary for the structure of the ordinary and its occasional annulments.
2. John Dewey, "Philosophy and Civilization," in *Philosophy and Civilization* (New York: Capricorn Books, 1931), 4; *LW* 3:4. Although where possible I cite the early editions of Dewey's work, I also provide throughout the volume and page references to the critical edition edited by Jo Ann Boydston: *The Collected Works of John Dewey, 1882–1953* (Carbondale: Southern Illinois University Press, 1969–91), published as *The Early Works, 1882–1898* (*EW*), *The Middle Works, 1899–1924* (*MW*), and *The Later Works, 1925–1953*) (*LW*).
3. For a penetrating analysis of some of the issues associated with meaning, truth, and practice, see the section titled "Heidegger's Pragmatism," in Daniel O. Dahlstrom, *Heidegger's Concept of Truth* (New York: Cambridge University Press, 2001).
4. J. Glenn Gray, *The Promise of Wisdom: An Introduction to Philosophy of Education* (New York: J. B. Lippincott, 1968), 84.
5. Victor Kestenbaum, *The Phenomenological Sense of John Dewey: Habit and Meaning* (New Jersey: Humanities Press, 1977).
6. I was not, however, fully convinced that aesthetic experience as the intensification of the prereflective intentionality of habit was as unifying as Dewey believed it to be.
7. Neal Coughlan, *Young John Dewey: An Essay in American Intellectual History* (Chicago: University of Chicago Press, 1975), 154.
8. Herbert W. Schneider, "Introduction to Dewey's Psychology," *EW* 2:viii.
9. John Dewey, *Human Nature and Conduct: An Introduction to Social Psychology* (New York: Modern Library, 1922), 75; *MW* 14:53.
10. John Dewey, *Outlines of a Critical Theory of Ethics, EW* 3:318.
11. Edgar S. Brightman, *A Philosophy of Ideals* (New York: Henry Holt, 1928), 157, 158.
12. R. F. Alfred Hoernle, "The Revival of Idealism in the United States," in *Contemporary Idealism in American* (New York: Macmillan, 1932), 314.

13. Ibid., 313.
14. Maurice Cornforth, *Science versus Idealism: In Defence of Philosophy against Positivism and Pragmatism* (New York International Publishers, 1955), 383.
15. H. S. Thayer, *Meaning and Action: A Critical History of Pragmatism* (Indianapolis: Hackett Publishing, 1981), 174.
16. Thomas M. Alexander, *John Dewey's Theory of Art, Experience, and Nature: The Horizons of Feeling* (New York: State University of New York Press, 1987), 42.
17. Ibid., 36, 37, 39.
18. Ibid., 258. Another instance of the "experience as ground" tradition of Dewey interpretation is found in John J. Stuhr's article "Consciousness of Doom: Criticism, Art, and Pragmatic Transcendence," *Journal of Speculative Philosophy* 12, no. 4 (1998). See note 55.
19. Russell B. Goodman, *American Philosophy and the Romantic Tradition* (New York: Cambridge University Press, 1990), 91.
20. Ibid., 93, 97, 103.
21. Max Otto, *The Human Enterprise: An Attempt to Relate Philosophy to Daily Life* (New York: F. S. Crofts, 1940), 121.
22. William James, *Psychology* (New York: World Publishing, 1948), 467–68.
23. Richard E. Palmer, *Hermeneutics: Interpretation Theory in Schleiermacher, Dilthey, Heidegger, and Gadamer* (Evanston: Northwestern University Press, 1969), 234.
24. Heinrich Wölfflin, *Principles of Art History: The Problem of the Development of Style in Later Art* (New York: Dover Publications, 1929), 19.
25. "From Absolutism to Experimentalism," in *John Dewey on Experience, Nature, and Freedom*, ed. Richard J. Bernstein (New York: Liberal Arts Press, 1960); *LW* 5.
26. James Collins, *Interpreting Modern Philosophy* (Princeton: Princeton University Press, 1972), 228. "Porous in principle" is not a license for interpretive chaos. The governing intent for Collins is "to do historical justice." His thoughts on this matter are particularly pertinent to the present work: "There can be a deadening sort of fidelity or accuracy concerning the thought of modern philosophers. It consists in that sort of formalist precision which transcribes past lines of argument, but which recognizes no interpretive obligations toward living minds today. It can make statements about source thinkers, but is unable to achieve their historical actuality and presence for us. At the other extreme lies that converse approach which seeks contemporary significance for the modern sources, but does so at the cost of a historically grounded presentation of their thought in its own context and mode of philosophizing. In the former case, memory is served while present theorizing starves; and in the latter case, our present theorizing is fraudulently stoked with fuel, which does not come from the mines which are claimed to be supplying it" (403–4).
27. Dewey, "From Absolutism to Experimentalism," 13; *LW* 5:155.
28. John R. Shook, *Dewey's Empirical Theory of Knowledge and Reality* (Nashville: Vanderbilt University Press, 2000), 4.
29. Ibid., 210, 211, 266.
30. Louis Menand, *The Metaphysical Club* (New York: Farrar, Straus and Giroux, 2001), xii.
31. Ibid., xi, xii.
32. Randolph S. Bourne, "Twilight of Idols," in *War and the Intellectuals: Collected Essays, 1915–1919*, ed. Carl Resek (New York: Harper Torchbooks, 1964), 61.
33. Ibid.
34. Stanley Cavell, "What's the Use of Calling Emerson a Pragmatist?" in *The Revival of Pragmatism: New Essays on Social Thought, Law, and Culture*, ed. Morris Dick-

stein (Durham: Duke University Press, 1998), 73. The line from *Experience and Education* quoted by Cavell can be found in *LW* 13:59.

35. Cavell, "Calling Emerson a Pragmatist," 73.
36. Ibid., 74.
37. John Dewey, *Experience and Nature* (La Salle, Ill.: Open Court, 1929), 290; *LW* 1:269.
38. Ibid., 21; *LW* 1:28.
39. Cavell, "Calling Emerson a Pragmatist," 75, 78.
40. Dewey, "Custom and Habit," in *Human Nature and Conduct*, 64; *MW* 14:47.
41. Cavell, "Calling Emerson a Pragmatist," 79–80.
42. Michael Eldridge, *Transforming Experience: John Dewey's Cultural Instrumentalism* (Nashville: Vanderbilt University Press, 1998), 39.
43. Ibid., 102.
44. Ibid., 104.
45. Ibid., 105.
46. John William Miller, *The Paradox of Cause and Other Essays* (New York: W. W. Norton, 1978), 20–21.
47. Iris Murdoch, *The Sovereignty of Good* (New York: Schocken Books, 1970), 74–75.
48. James Gouinlock, *John Dewey's Philosophy of Value* (New York: Humanities Press, 1972), 273.
49. A helpful analysis of theories of transcendence (Nussbaum, Barth, Heidegger, Murdoch, Irigaray, Cavell, and Taylor) is available in Fergus Kerr, *Immortal Longings: Versions of Transcending Humanity* (Notre Dame, Ind.: University of Notre Dame Press, 1997).
50. Murdoch, *The Sovereignty of Good*, 93.
51. Stuart Hampshire, *Innocence and Experience* (Cambridge: Harvard University Press, 1989), 131–32.
52. Peter L. Berger, *A Far Glory: The Quest for Faith in an Age of Credulity* (New York: Anchor Books, 1992), 130, 131.
53. Ibid., 131.
54. Maurice Natanson, *The Journeying Self: A Study in Philosophy and Social Role* (Reading, Mass.: Addison-Wesley, 1970), 117.
55. Ibid., 145. Natanson's phenomenology provides a standpoint from which to note the limitations of Stuhr's treatment of transcendence. Stuhr says: "Our desire for a better world must not lead us to pretend that we can justify particular desires or agendas on the basis of supposedly necessary truths or meanings, supposedly universal notions of rationality, or a supposedly experience-transcendent reality—a reality that transcends all experience as opposed to this or that experience or my or your experience" (259). If there is to be any transcendence, it is a "historicized notion of transcendence," in other words, says Stuhr, "inquiry." Dewey's transcendent "beyond" is not equivalent to inquiry.
56. Thomas Weiskel, *The Romantic Sublime: Studies in the Structure and Psychology of Transcendence* (Baltimore: Johns Hopkins University Press, 1976), 23.
57. Ibid.
58. Ibid., 23–24.
59. Ibid., 24.
60. Charles Tomlinson, *Collected Poems* (New York: Oxford University Press, 1985), 104.
61. Dewey, *Human Nature and Conduct*, 288–89; *MW* 14:199.

62. Ibid., 259; MW 14:178.

63. For the importance of the 1925 version of the first chapter, see my paper "'A Thing of Moods and Tenses'—Experience in John Dewey," in *Phenomenology: Dialogues and Bridges*, ed. Ronald Bruzina and Bruce Wilshire (New York: State University of New York Press, 1982).

64. Dewey, "Knowledge as Idealization," *EW* 1:188. Neil Coughlan's interpretation of Dewey's pre-1900 years has as one of its conclusions the following: "Dewey built into his pragmatism a repugnance for antinomies, imponderables, hesitations, distractions, worries; it was, he said, 'a theory which makes activity the final word.'" Far from having a "repugnance" for such matters, Dewey well understood that activity, moving along the "road of meaning," was not possible without respectful attention to antinomies, and so on, as "possible bearers of an ideal quality." See Neil Coughlan, *Young John Dewey: An Essay in American Intellectual History* (Chicago: University of Chicago Press, 1975), 84.

65. Dewey, *Experience and Nature*, 336; *LW* 1:310.

66. Ibid., 35–36; *LW* 1:41.

67. Hannah Arendt, *The Human Condition*, second edition (Chicago: University of Chicago Press, 1958), 95.

68. Hannah Arendt, "On Hannah Arendt," in *Hannah Arendt: The Recovery of the Public World*, ed. Melvyn A. Hill (New York: St. Martin's Press, 1979), 303.

69. Dewey, "Soul and Body," *EW* 1:101.

70. It is interesting and important to note that Dewey uses this phrase from Wordsworth in three of his decidedly "mature" works. In the penultimate paragraph of *Reconstruction in Philosophy*, he says: "And when the emotional force, the mystic force one might say, of communication, of the miracle of shared life and shared experience is spontaneously felt, the hardness and crudeness of contemporary life will be bathed in the light that never was on land or sea" (enlarged edition [Boston: Beacon Press, 1948], 211; MW 12:201). In the chapter "Experience, Nature, and Art," he says of poetry, of the "magic" of poetry: "It radiates the light that never was on land and sea but that is henceforth an abiding illumination." (in *Experience and Nature*, 292; *LW* 1:270). His other reference is in "The Challenge to Philosophy," where he discusses the "make-believe" theory of art: "Now there is no doubt that because of the domination of esthetic experience by imaginative quality, it exists in a medium of light that never was on land or sea." (in *Art as Experience* [New York: Capricorn Books, 1934], 275). The manner in which Wordsworth uses the phrase suggests just how much, and how subtly, the intangible permeates Dewey's "mature" philosophy. It occurs in "Elegiac Stanzas Suggested by a Picture of Peele Castle, in a Storm, Painted by Sir George Beaumont":

> Ah! then, if mine had been the Painter's hand,
> To express what then I saw; and add the gleam,
> The light that never was, on sea or land,
> The consecration, and the Poet's dream...

The Painter adds the "gleam," the "more than common meaning," to what the painter "saw" (*William Wordsworth: The Poems*, ed. John O. Hayden [New Haven: Yale University Press, 1981], 1:640).

71. John Dewey, "Experience and Objective Idealism," in *The Influence of Darwin on Philosophy* (Bloomington: Indiana University Press, 1910), 225; MW 3:144.

Chapter Two

1. John Dewey, "The Moral Struggle or the Realizing of Ideals," in *Outlines of a Critical Theory of Ethics*, *EW* 3:372.

2. Since the entire section from the early work is just three paragraphs, I reproduce here for the reader's convenience the entire text:

LXVI. Goodness as a Struggle

We have already seen that the bare repetition of identically the same acts does not consist with morality. To aim at securing a satisfaction precisely like the one already experienced, is to fail to realize the altered capacity and environment, and the altered duty. Moral satisfaction prior to an act is ideal; ideal not simply in the sense of being conceived, or present to thought, but ideal in the sense that it has not been already enjoyed. Some satisfaction has been enjoyed in a previous activity, but that very satisfaction has so enlarged and complicated the situation, that its mere repetition would not afford moral or active satisfaction, but only what Kant terms "pathological" satisfaction. Morality thus assumes the form of a struggle. The past satisfaction speaks for itself; it has been verified in experience, it has conveyed its worth to our very senses. We have tried and tasted it, and know that it is good. If morality lay in the repetition of similar satisfactions, it would not be a struggle. We should know experimentally beforehand that the chosen end would bring us satisfaction, and should be at rest in that knowledge. But when morality lies in striving for satisfactions which have not verified themselves to our sense, it always requires an effort. We have to surrender the enjoyed good, and stake ourselves upon that of which we cannot say: We know it is good. To surrender the actual experienced good for a possible ideal good is the struggle.

We arrive, in what is termed the opposition of desire and duty, at the heart of the moral struggle. Of course, taken strictly, there can be no opposition here. The duty which did not awaken any desire would not appeal to the mind even as a duty. But we may distinguish between a desire which is based on past satisfaction actually experienced, and desire based simply upon the idea that the end is desirable — that it ought to be desired. It may seem strange to speak of a desire based simply upon the recognition that an end should be desired, but the possibility of awakening such a desire and the degree of its strength are the test of a moral character. How far does this end awaken response in me because I see that it is the end which is fit and due? How far does it awaken this response although it does not fall into line with past satisfactions, or although it actually thwarts some habitual satisfaction? Here is the opposition of duty and desire. It lies in the contrast of a good which has demonstrated itself as such in experience, and a good whose claim to be good rests only on the fact that it is the act which meets the situation. It is the contrast between a good of possession, and one of action.

From this point of view morality is a life of aspiration, and of faith; there is required constant willingness to give up past goods as the good, and to press on to new ends; not because past achievements are bad, but because, being good, they have created a situation which demands larger and more intricately related achievements. This willingness is aspiration and it implies faith. Only the old good is of sight, has verified itself to sense. The new ideal, the end which meets the situation, is felt as good only in so far as the character has formed the conviction that to meet obligation is itself a good, whether bringing sensible satisfaction or not. You can prove to a man that he ought to act so and so (that is to say, that such an act is the one which fits the present occasion), but you cannot prove to him that the performance of that duty will be good. Only faith in the moral order, in the identity of duty and the good, can assert this. Every time an agent takes as his end (that is, chooses as good) an activity which he has not already tried, he asserts his belief in the goodness of right action as such. This faith is not a mere intellectual thing, but it is practical—the staking of self upon activity as against passive possession. (ibid., *EW* 3:372–73)

3. Indeed, one might wish that more of his later writing possessed the agility, compactness, and resonance of his best early thought.
4. Stanley Cavell, *Conditions Handsome and Unhandsome: The Constitution of Emersonian Perfectionism* (Chicago: University of Chicago Press, 1990), 21. Cavell would find considerable support for his picture of Dewey in Jennifer Welchman, *Dewey's Ethical Thought* (Ithaca: Cornell University Press, 1995).
5. Dewey, "The Moral Struggle," *EW* 3:372.
6. Dewey, *Art as Experience*, 29; *LW* 10:35–36.
7. Dewey, "The Moral Struggle," *EW* 3:372.
8. Ibid.
9. Max Otto, *The Human Enterprise: An Attempt to Relate Philosophy to Daily Life* (New York: F. S. Crofts, 1940), 76.
10. Iris Murdoch, *The Sovereignty of Good* (New York: Schocken Books, 1970), 22.
11. Ibid., 23.
12. Ibid., 70.
13. Compare here Marjorie Grene in her elucidation of how tacit clues enable us to inquire, to search, when we do not have a clear or explicit idea of what we are searching for: "Such clues are also aspects of ourselves: they are points in our own attitude, skills, memories, or crypto-memories, hunches. To put it in existentialist language, they are aspects of our transcendence. So we live in the tension between what we are and what we seek: between the world whose facticity we share and ourselves whose shaping makes the world a world" ("The Legacy of the 'Meno,'" in *The Knower and the Known* [Berkeley: University of California Press, 1974], 24.
14. Dewey, "The Moral Struggle," *EW* 3:372.
15. Ibid., 373.
16. Ibid.
17. Ibid.
18. For an interesting account of the "fitting" which parallels Dewey's in many respects, see Maurice Mandelbaum, *The Phenomenology of Moral Experience* (Glencoe, Ill.: Free Press, 1955), 59–71.His account of ideality (89–93) is also quite similar to Dewey's.
19. Dewey, "The Moral Struggle," *EW* 3:373.
20. For an interpretation of Kant which is quite helpful to my analysis of Dewey, see John R. Silber, "Kant's Conception of the Highest Good as Immanent and Transcendent," *Philosophical Review* 68 (October 1959). Silber states: "Obligation does not express what man has done; it states rather what he ought to do. Consequently, obligation may far exceed actuality; it is constrained only by the limits of possibility. And one cannot determine the limits of his freedom and obligation by reference to actuality any better than he can determine his obligation by this means. Since the will cannot determine the limits of its own power in advance of striving, the will cannot have the slightest confidence of attaining even that part of the highest good that does lie within its powers unless it strives to do that which exceeds its known capacities" (491).
21. Dewey, "The Moral Struggle," *EW* 3:373.
22. For a typical, but unusually dramatic, example of the foreshortening of the place of transcendence in Dewey, see James H. Nichols, Jr., "Pragmatism and the U.S. Constitution," in *Confronting the Constitution: The Challenge to Locke, Montesquieu, Jefferson,*

and the Federalists from Utilitarianism, Historicism, Marxism, Freudianism, Pragmatism, Existentialism, ed. Allan Bloom (Washington, D.C.: AEI Press, 1990). In the last paragraph of the article, Nichols acknowledges some positive aspects of what he takes to be Dewey's position, but the positives are to be weighed carefully: "Dewey's pragmatism rejects the foundational principles of American constitutionalism. It therefore lessens the settled sense of security in the functions, structures, and limits of government. Correlatively, as open-endedly progressive, it is constitutionally incapable of reaping the social and political benefits of habitual veneration for long-established principles" (388). Dewey's theory of habit does not prohibit veneration. The stronger the veneration, though, the greater the need for vigilance. For an equally striking example of how Dewey can be distorted, see James Davison Hunter, *The Death of Character: Moral Education in an Age without Good or Evil* (New York: Basic Books, 2000). Just two examples will suffice to show what will be found and not found in Hunter's work. Dewey is credited with major responsibility for "discrediting the character ideal": "His devaluation of character as a force of nature to a mere set of habits that pattern a person's everyday life was a decisive step in this direction" (69). Given the general laxity of analysis, one is not surprised to find Hunter later appealing to Bourdieu's notion of habitus without even a hint of the possible connection of habitus to habit. Later, he confidently affirms: "Moral goods and moral ends, for him, only existed when something needed to be accomplished; that is, say, in the resolution of a concrete problem in real life" (178). On this view, Dewey has no interest in tradition, what is passed on, and so forth. Lacking any appreciable understanding of the complexity of Dewey's theory of habit, one would not expect Hunter to do much with something even as uncomplicated as this from Dewey: "Our individual habits are links in forming the endless chain of humanity. Their significance depends upon the environment inherited from our forerunners, and it is enhanced as we foresee the fruits of our labors in the world in which our successors survive" (*Human Nature and Conduct: An Introduction to Social Psychology* [New York: Modern Library, 1922], 21; MW 14:19). Hunter fails to see any connection between this and his own lament (itself based on a striking simplification of Bourdieu) that "the habitus out of which our moral vocabulary and aspirations come has disintegrated significantly." (*The Death of Character*, 225).

23. Dewey, "The Moral Struggle," EW 3:373.

24. Ibid.

25. Though I should note that my colleague Charles W. Griswold has insisted since 1991 that I am "some kind" of Platonist. Both of his books are relevant to my argument. *Self-Knowledge in Plato's Phaedrus* (New Haven: Yale University Press, 1986) and *Adam Smith and the Virtues of Enlightenment* (New York: Cambridge University Press, 1999).

26. John Herman Randall, Jr., *Plato: Dramatist of the Life of Reason* (New York: Columbia University Press, 1970), 206.

27. For an interesting account of hypothesis as transcendence in Dewey, see Robert J. Roth, S.J., *Radical Pragmatism: An Alternative* (New York: Fordham University Press, 1998). There are important parallels between Roth's outlook concerning Dewey and my own, and one major difference. The difference comes to this: the ambition of Roth's treatment of Dewey is to consider the "potential of his theory of experience to extend itself beyond naturalism and to find its completion in a transcendent." (92–93). My work proposes that the intangible ideal, the transcendent ideal, is present throughout Dewey's philosophy, not as a "potential" but as incompletely realized actuality.

28. For an example of the view described here, see Israel Scheffler, *Four Pragmatists: A Critical Introduction to Peirce, James, Mead, and Dewey* (New York: Humanities Press,

1974), particularly part 4, chapter 5, "Dewey's Psychological Conceptions: Critical Comments," 221–26.

29. Delmore Schwartz, *The Ego Is Always at the Wheel: Bagatelles*, ed. Robert Phillips (Manchester: Carcanet Press, 1987).)
30. Dewey, "The Nature of Aims," in *Human Nature and Conduct*, 234; MW 14:161.
31. Dewey, "The Moral Struggle," EW 3:373.
32. Ibid., 372.
33. Dewey, "The Nature of Aims," 236; MW 14:162.
34. Dewey, "The Nature of Principles," in *Human Nature and Conduct*, 239; MW 14:165.
35. Ibid., 239–40; MW 14:165.
36. Ibid., 241; MW 14:166.
37. Dewey, "Desire and Intelligence," in *Human Nature and Conduct*, 249; MW 14:172.
38. Ibid., 248; MW 14:171.
39. Ibid., 249; MW 14:172.
40. Dewey, "Custom and Habit," in *Human Nature and Conduct*, 71; MW 14:51.
41. Dewey, "Habits and Will," in *Human Nature and Conduct*, 25; MW 14:21–22.
42. Ibid.
43. Dewey, "Desire and Intelligence," 255; MW 14:175.
44. Ibid.
45. Ibid., 256, 257; MW 14:176, 177.
46. Otto, *The Human Enterprise*, 89.
47. Dewey, "Desire and Intelligence," 259; MW 14:178.
48. Rosenthal's discussion of "anteceptive experience" and the a priori in Dewey helps, indirectly, to illuminate some aspects of transcendental possibility in Dewey. See Sandra B. Rosenthal, *Speculative Pragmatism* (Amherst: University of Massachusetts Press, 1986), particularly chapter 4, "Foundational Experience: Epistemic Unity and Ontological Presence." I think, however, Rosenthal's analysis fails to give sufficient attention to what cannot be anticipated or expected. Gregory F. Pappas builds his interpretation of Dewey's ethics around a central contention, reflected in one of his section titles: "the situation as the end of morality." Context—experienced context—is regulative; nothing beyond it troubles it or questions it: "Each concrete morally problematic situation presents a unique moral task with its own immanent end and meaning, even if its resolution happens to produce wonderful instrumentalities for further experiences" ("Dewey's Ethics: Morality as Experience," in *Reading Dewey: Interpretations for a Postmodern Generation*, edited by Larry A. Hickman [Bloomington: Indiana University Press, 1998], 113). The "situation" is so strictly regulative that such things as "principles, ideals, and habits" are instrumentalities or "tools" "to determine what morality requires here and now" (114). The "now" inspires Dewey to embrace that which "outruns the seen and touched." The "here and now" inspires Pappas, as he says, to "look" to the situation for tools. It is not clear why these are incompatible inspirations for Pappas, since they were not incompatible for Dewey.
49. Dewey, "Desire and Intelligence," 259; MW 14:178.
50. Ibid., 261; MW 14:179.
51. Steven C. Rockefeller, *John Dewey: Religious Faith and Democratic Humanism* (New York: Columbia University Press, 1991), 396.
52. Dewey, "Desire and Intelligence," 261; MW 14:179.
53. Ibid.
54. Ibid., 262; MW 14:180.

55. George Steiner, *Real Presences* (Chicago: University of Chicago Press, 1989), 4. James Wood draws attention to some problems in Steiner's use of this concept. See "George Steiner's Unreal Presence," in *The Broken Estate: Essays on Literature and Belief* (New York: Modern Library, 1999).
56. Dewey, "Desire and Intelligence," 263; MW 14:180.
57. Ibid.
58. Steiner, *Real Presences*, 4.
59. Ibid., 8.
60. Dewey, "Desire and Intelligence," 263; MW 14:180.
61. Ibid., 263–64; MW 14: 180–81.
62. Ibid., 264; MW 14:181.

Chapter Three
1. Jonathan Levin, *The Poetics of Transition: Emerson, Pragmatism, and American Literary Modernism* (Durham: Duke University Press, 1999), 5.
2. Ibid., 6.
3. John Dewey, *Human Nature and Conduct An Introduction to Social Pyschology* (New York: Modern Library, 1922), 32; MW 14:26.
4. Ibid., 54–55; MW 14:40.
5. John Dewey, *Art as Experience* (New York: Capricorn Books, 1934), 297; LW 10:301.
6. Erazim Kohák sees this quite clearly. Dewey, he says, relied to some extent on Aristotelian functionalism, with "ends" becoming "means," "ever justified by new receding means and ends." However, continues Kohák: "In [Dewey's] thought, the transparent weakness of that schema was redeemed not simply by a faith in the intrinsic value of process—characteristically, Dewey preferred the vitalistic term, 'growth'—but by a conception reminiscent of Whitehead, that of enjoyment or, simply, joy." The experience of joy or enjoyment "breaks out of the entire instrumental chain as a moment of encounter between a human and an Other, be it an entity, an act, a person, in cherishing, appreciation, enjoyment. It is precisely the experience of eternal reference" (*The Embers and the Stars: A Philosophical Inquiry into the Moral Sense of Nature* [Chicago: University of Chicago Press, 1984], 200). I am, however, doubtful that the "instrumental chain"—the instrumental/consummatory chain—is broken solely by experiences of "joy or enjoyment." Staking oneself on a transcendent ideal, as I described in chapter 2, may require one to endure what does not, and cannot, bring joy. I also am doubtful whether the sole reference of transcendence is necessarily to an "eternal reference," to what earlier in the paragraph Kohák calls "an absolute reference." Despite these reservations, Kohák's reflections on pragmatism, phenomenology, and transcendental subjectivity are rewarding. See also "'Knowing Good and Evil' (Genesis 3:5b)," *Husserl Studies* 10 (1993): 31–41; "Truth and the Humanities," *Human Studies* 16 (1993): 239–53. Note that Kohák is cautious about the absolute in the latter article: "Absolute knowledge—and absolute truth—would require an absolute standpoint and that is a contradiction in terms" (242).
7. Levin, *Poetics of Transition*, 85.
8. Dewey, *Art as Experience*, 17; LW 10:23.
9. Ibid., 268; LW 10:273.
10. Levin, *Poetics of Transition*, 87.
11. Ibid., 101.
12. For a truly full-scale materialist critique of Dewey, see Paul Jay, *Contingency Blues: The Search for Foundations in American Criticism* (Wisconsin: University of

Wisconsin Press, 1997). According to Jay, *Art as Experience* begins promisingly enough, but eventually "Dewey yields to the temptation to locate an authentic, essential, intrinsic set of qualities in aesthetic objects and experiences, so that art becomes invested with the kind of idealism he rejected in philosophy" (14). Where Levin commends Dewey's pragmatism for resisting "hidden and ideal realities," Jay believes that Dewey's "preoccupation with the authentic and the intrinsic in aesthetic experience reveals a latent idealism in Dewey's thought that works to undermine the materialist and pragmatic orientation of his project" (92). Ultimately, Jay is as much interested in process as Levin, finding concepts such as border, space, frontier acceptably dynamic and permeable and thus congenial to his materialist, historicist tastes. Ethnocriticism is especially pleasing since it "inhabits the interactive space between cultures in order to understand the hybrid processes of cultural formation, deformation, and reformation that take place there." (175).

13. Levin, *Poetics of Transition*, 169.
14. Richard Poirier, *A World Elsewhere: The Place of Style in American Literature* (New York: Oxford University Press, 1966), 4; see also Poirier, "Why Do Pragmatists Want to Be Like Poets?" in *The Revival of Pragmatism: New Essays on Social Thought, Law, and Culture*, ed. Morris Dickstein (Durham: Duke University Press, 1998).
15. Poirier, *A World Elsewhere*, 6–7.
16. Ibid., 35.
17. Stanley Cavell, "What's the Use of Calling Emerson a Pragmatist?" in Dickstein, in *The Revival of Pragmatism*, 77.
18. Richard Poirier, *The Renewal of Literature: Emersonian Reflections* (New York: Random House, 1987), 16.
19. Cavell, "Calling Emerson a Pragmatist," 78.
20. Poirier, *The Renewal of Literature*, 13.
21. Richard Poirier, *The Performing Self: Compositions and Decompositions in the Languages of Contemporary Life* (New York: Oxford University Press, 1971), 83.
22. Ibid., xiii.
23. Poirier, *The Renewal of Literature*, 14.
24. Ibid., 45.
25. Poirier, *The Performing Self*, 82.
26. John Dewey, "The Moral Struggle or the Realizing of Ideals," in *Outlines of a Critical Theory of Ethics*, EW 3:372.
27. Poirier, *The Renewal of Literature*, 148, 195, 183.
28. Dewey, *Human Nature and Conduct*, 263; MW 14:180.
29. Ibid.
30. Poirier, *A World Elsewhere*, 35.
31. Poirier, *The Renewal of Literature*, 16.
32. Poirier, *A World Elsewhere*, 88.
33. Poirier, *The Performing Self*, 111.
34. It is interesting to note how Poirier thinks we experience a transition: "It is like catching a glimpse of a thing before it is possible to recognize it or name it, the moment just before it can be classified by language and thus become composed or reposed in a human corpus or text" (*The Renewal of Literature*, 47). A transition thus is a passage *to* language, something happening *before* language. Dewey's glimpses are more than a transition to another, composed state; when we catch a glimpse we are not simply waiting for the arrival of names and classifications.
35. Poirier, *The Performing Self*, 67.

36. Ibid., xiii.
37. Poirier "Why Do Pragmatists Want to Be Like Poets?" 359.
38. Poirier, *The Renewal of Literature*, 202.
39. Dewey, *Human Nature and Conduct*, 263; MW 14:180.
40. Richard M. Gale, "John Dewey's Naturalization of William James," in *The Divided Self of William James* (New York: Cambridge University Press, 1999), 335, 336.
41. Edmund Husserl, "Philosophy as Rigorous Science," in *Phenomenology and the Crisis of Philosophy*, trans. Quentin Lauer (New York: Harper Torchbooks, 1965), 79.
42. Edmund Husserl, *Studies in the Phenomenology of Constitution*, trans. Richard Rojcewicz and Andre Schuwer, book 2 of *Ideas Pertaining to a Pure Phenomenology and to a Phenomenological Philosophy* (Boston: Kluwer Academic Publishers, 1989), 294.
43. Ibid., 184.
44. John Dewey, "Antinaturalism in Extremis," in *Naturalism and the Human Spirit*, ed. Yervant H. Krikorian (New York: Columbia University Press, 1944), 2.
45. Husserl, *Phenomenology of Constitution*, 118.
46. Richard Cobb-Stevens, "Husserl's Understanding of Body and Spirit" (manuscript), 5.
47. The idea of "materializing" spirit and transcendence is to be found in Karl Jaspers. His brilliant account of transcendence, though certainly not congruent with Dewey's in all respects, is nonetheless provocatively similar in some important and interesting ways. See *Philosophy*, vol. 3, trans. E. B. Ashton (Chicago: University of Chicago Press, 1971).
48. Dewey, *Human Nature and Conduct*, 54; MW 14:40.
49. *The Correspondence of William James*, vols. 1–4, ed. Ignas Skrupskelis and Elizabeth Berkeley (Charlottesville: University Press of Virginia, 1992), 4:114.
50. Dewey, *Art as Experience*, 104; LW 10:109.
51. Quentin Lauer, introduction to Edmund Husserl, "Philosophy as Rigorous Science," in *Crisis of Philosophy*, 13.
52. Gale, *The Divided Self of William James*, 332.
53. Ray Carney, "When Mind Is a Verb: Thomas Eakins and the Work of Doing," in Dickstein, *The Revival of Pragmatism*, 379, 382.
54. Ibid., 384.
55. The other is from Emerson (*Nature*): "All to form the Hand of the mind;—to instruct us that 'good thoughts are no better than good dreams, unless they be executed!'"
56. Carney, "When Mind Is a Verb," 386.
57. Ibid., 385.
58. Dewey, *Human Nature and Conduct*, 263; MW 14:180. Note that the critical edition corrects the Modern Library edition "times" to "time."
59. Dewey, "The Moral Struggle," EW 3:373.
60. James Wood, *The Broken Estate: Essays on Literature and Belief* (New York: Modern Library, 1999), 168. This phrase occurs in an illuminating but not entirely balanced analysis of George Steiner, "George Steiner's Unreal Presence."
61. Irwin C. Lieb, *The Four Faces of Man: A Philosophical Study of Practice, Reason, Art, and Religion* (Philadelphia: University of Pennsylvania Press, 1971), 30.
62. Dewey, *Human Nature and Conduct*, 264; MW 14:181.
63. Carney, "When Mind Is a Verb," 380.
64. Richard Selzer, *Letters to a Young Doctor* (New York: Simon and Schuster, 1982), 50.

65. Carney, "When Mind Is a Verb," 401.
66. Dewey, *Human Nature and Conduct*, 263–64; MW 14:181.

Chapter Four
1. Martin Heidegger, "Letter on Humanism," in *Martin Heidegger: Basic Writings*, ed. David Farrell Krell (New York: Harper, 1977), 195.
2. Ibid., 231.
3. Henry David Aiken, *Predicament of the University* (Bloomington: Indiana University Press, 1971), 144.
4. Joseph Bensman and Robert Lilienfeld, *Craft and Consciousness: Occupational Technique and the Development of World Images* (New York: Wiley, 1973), 349.
5. Ibid., 1.
6. Paul Ricoeur, *Freedom and Nature: The Voluntary and the Involuntary*, trans. Erazim V. Kohák (Evanston, Ill.: Northwestern University Press, 1966), 289.
7. George A. Kelly, *A Theory of Personality: The Psychology of Personal Constructs* (New York: W. W. Norton, 1955), 68–72.
8. John N. Findlay, *Values and Intentions: A Study in Value-Theory and Philosophy of Mind* (New York: Humanities Press, 1961), 77–78.
9. Richard Rorty, *Consequences of Pragmatism* (Minneapolis: University of Minnesota Press, 1982), xxxix.
10. Ibid., xl.
11. Maurice Merleau-Ponty, *Signs*, trans. Richard C. McCleary (Evanston, Ill.: Northwestern University Press, 1964), 241.
12. John N. Findlay, "The Constitution of Human Values," in *Human Values*, Royal Institute of Philosophy Lectures, volume 11, 1976/77, ed. Godfrey Vesey (Atlantic Highlands, N.J.: Humanities Press, 1978), 206. An interesting feature of Findlay's approach to moral consciousness is his phenomenological argument that universalization is in fact an inherent tendency or trait of consciousness in general and not only moral consciousness. A fuller treatment of this argument is contained in his *Values and Intentions*, particularly section 2, "The Basic Modes of Consciousness," 45–92.
13. See chapter 3, "How Names Are Given," in Robert Sokolowski's book, *Presence and Absence: A Philosophical Investigation of Language and Being* (Bloomington: Indiana University Press, 1978), for an excellent account of "how naming is constituted by the play of presence and absence" (xvii).
14. John Dewey, *Experience and Nature*, second edition. (La Salle, Ill.: Open Court, 1929), 40.
15. Hannah Arendt, "Thinking and Moral Considerations," *Social Research* 38, no. 3 (autumn 1971): 421–22.
16. Hannah Arendt, *The Life of the Mind: Thinking* (New York: Harcourt, 1977), 15.
17. Arendt, "Thinking and Moral Considerations," 425.
18. Hans Küng, *Does God Exist? An Answer for Today*, trans. Edward Quinn (New York: Doubleday, 1980), 122.
19. Alasdair MacIntyre, "What Morality Is Not," in *Against the Self-Images of the Age: Essays on Ideology and Philosophy* (New York: Schocken, 1971), 99.
20. Ibid., 107.
21. Ibid.
22. Arthur Brittan, *The Privatised World* (Boston: Routledge, 1977), 140.
23. Ibid., 151.
24. See my review of Calvin O. Schrag's *Radical Reflection and the Origin of the*

Human Sciences, for a discussion of the primacy of lived experience; "Life-World as Origin," *Man and World* 15 (1982) 323–35.

25. Ernest Becker, *The Structure of Evil: An, Essay on the Unification of the Science of Man* (New York: George Braziller, 1968), 299.
26. Arendt, "Thinking and Moral Considerations," 418.
27. Ibid., 434.
28. Ibid., 441.
29. Arendt, *The Life of the Mind*, 185.
30. Ibid., 187.
31. An important discussion of the implications of pluralism in connection with religious commitment and affirmation is to be found in Peter L. Berger's book *The Heretical Imperative: Contemporary Possibilities of Religious Affirmation* (New York: Doubleday, 1979). Pluralization is a fact of institutional and social life, says Berger, with the result that taken-for-granted doctrines and world views come to be seen as far more fragile and uncertain. Modernity multiplies choices and Berger notes that the word "heresy" comes from the Greek verb *hairein*, which means "to choose." Pluralization, then, makes heresy an imperative and makes attractive a certain "mellowness" so far as absolutes are concerned.
32. Arendt, "Thinking and Moral Considerations," 442.
33. William Hare, *Open-mindedness and Education* (Montreal: McGill-Queen's University Press, 1979), 9.
34. Ibid., 9–10.
35. William James, "The Sentiment of Rationality," in *The Writings of William James: A Comprehensive Edition*, ed. John J. McDermott (New York: Modern Library, 1967), 322.
36. Ibid.
37. James, "Pragmatism and Humanism," in McDermott, *Writings of William James*, 449.
38. James, "Sentiment," 323.

Chapter Five

1. Michael Oakeshott, "Rational Conduct," in *Rationalism in Politics and Other Essays* (Indianapolis: Liberty Press, 1962), 129.
2. Ibid., 129.
3. Ibid., 117.
4. Oakeshott, "On Being Conservative," in *Rationalism in Politics*, 409.
5. Oakeshott, "Rational Conduct," 102–3.
6. The similarity to Dewey's criticism of the "already made" is striking.
7. Oakeshott, "Rational Conduct," 103.
8. Ibid., 104.
9. Robert J. Sokolowski, *Moral Action: A Phenomenological Study* (Bloomington: Indiana University Press, 1985), 59.
10. Ibid., 53.
11. Ibid., 110–11.
12. Michael Oakeshott, *On Human Conduct* (New York: Oxford University Press, 1975), 43.
13. Ibid.
14. Ibid., 44.
15. Ibid., 45.

16. Oakeshott, "Rational Conduct," 122.
17. Ibid., 129.
18. Ibid., 125.
19. Oakeshott, *On Human Conduct*, 88.
20. Peter Winch, "The Nature of Meaningful Behavior," in *The Idea of a Social Science* (New York: Humanities Press, 1958), 58.
21. Michael Oakeshott, "*Rationalism in Politics*: A Reply to Professor Raphael," *Political Studies* 13, no. 1 (February 1965): 92.
22. Winch, "The Nature of Meaningful Behavior," 63.
23. For an interesting discussion of Dewey's theory of deliberation, see Henry S. Richardson, "Reflective Sovereignty," chapter 8 in *Practical Reasoning about Final Ends* (New York: Cambridge University Press, 1994).
24. Oakeshott, "Rational Conduct," 118.
25. Ludwig Wittgenstein, *On Certainty*, trans. Denis Paul and G. E. M. Anscombe (New York: Harper Torchbooks, 1969), 15e.
26. John Dewey, "Interpretation of the Savage Mind," in *Philosophy and Civilization* (New York: Capricorn Books, 1931), 187; MW 2:51.
27. A strange irony, indeed, that Lars Engle, in a chapter titled "Dramatic Pragmatism in *Hamlet*," says: "Both performers and pragmatists focus on what works, on what can be made visible, and on the way human purposes pan out or display their values as they encounter diverse circumstances" (in *Shakespearean Pragmatism: Market of His Time* [Chicago: University of Chicago Press, 1993], 54–55).
28. John Dewey, "The Postulate of Immediate Empiricism," in *The Influence of Darwin on Philosophy* (Bloomington: Indiana University Press, 1910), 228–29; MW 3:159–60.
29. Ibid., 234; MW 3:163.
30. John Dewey, *Theory of the Moral Life* (1932; New York: Irvington Publishers, 1960), 134–36; LW 7:274–75 (emphasis added).
31. Jennifer Welchman, *Dewey's Ethical Thought* (Ithaca: Cornell University Press, 1995), 171.
32. Oakeshott, *On Human Conduct*, 40.
33. Ibid., 44.
34. Ibid., 70.
35. Ibid., 80.
36. Dewey, *Human Nature and Conduct*, 192–93; MW 14:134.
37. Ibid., 223; MW 14:154.
38. Ibid., 237; MW 14:163.
39. Sokolowski, *Moral Action*, 66–67.
40. Ibid., 70.
41. Ibid., 151–52.
42. Ibid., 152.
43. Ibid., 153.
44. Ibid.
45. Ibid., 153–54.
46. Oakeshott, "Rational Conduct," 122.
47. Oakeshott, *On Human Conduct*, 91.
48. Sokolowski, *Moral Action*, 154.
49. "From Absolutism to Experimentalism," in *John Dewey: On Experience, Nature and Freedom*, ed. Richard J. Bernstein (New York: Liberal Arts Press, 1960), 13; LW 5:155.

50. Oakeshott, "Rational Conduct," 111.
51. Dewey, *Human Nature and Conduct*, 67; MW 14:49.
52. Oakeshott, "Political Education," in *Rationalism in Politics*, 61.
53. Dewey, *Human Nature and Conduct*, 262; MW 14:179–80.
54. Ibid., 263; MW 14:180.
55. Oakeshott, "On Being Conservative," in *Rationalism in Politics*, 408. See Paul Franco, *The Political Philosophy of Michael Oakeshott* (New Haven: Yale University Press, 1990). Concluding his analysis of "Rational Conduct," Franco says: "The deeply contextual view of knowledge which was presented in *Experience and Its Modes* is precisely what is denied or overlooked in the rationalist view of human activity as the pursuit of independently premeditated ideals or purposes. Finally, and closely related to the last point, 'Rational Conduct' offers a positive account of human activity, and in particular of practical activity. This positive account follows, as we have seen, *Experience and its Modes* in its emphasis on context, coherence, the immanence of thought, and the interdependence of subject and object" (128–29).
56. John Dewey, *Art as Experience* (New York: Capricorn Books, 1934), 195; LW 10:199.
57. Dewey, *Theory of the Moral Life*, 149; LW 7:287.
58. Oakeshott, *On Human Conduct*, 80.
59. Oakeshott, "The Voice of Poetry in the Conversation of Mankind," in *Rationalism in Politics*.
60. Wallace Stevens, "Metaphors of a Magnifico," *The Palm at the End of the Mind: Selected Poems and a Play*, ed. Holly Stevens (New York: Vintage Books, 1972), 36.

Chapter Six
1. William Arrowsmith, "The Shame of the Graduate Schools—Revisited," *Proceedings of the Thirty-Sixth Annual Meeting of the Midwestern Association of Graduate Schools*, Radisson-Chicago Hotel, Chicago, Illinois, 30–31 March, 1 April, 1980, 50.
2. Richard Rorty, "The Contingency of Selfhood," in *Contingency, Irony, and Solidarity* (New York: Cambridge University Press, 1989).
3. Plato, "Protagoras," *The Dialogues of Plato*, trans. B. Jowett (New York: Random House, 1920), 86.
4. Susan W. Dilts, ed., *Peterson's Guide to Four-Year Colleges 1990* (Princeton: Peterson's Guides, 1989), 23.
5. Helen Lefkowitz Horowitz, *Campus Life: Undergraduate Cultures from the End of the Eighteenth Century to the Present* (New York: Alfred A. Knopf, 1987), 3–4.
6. Frithjof Bergmann, *On Being Free* (Notre Dame, Ind.: University of Notre Dame Press, 1977), 85.
7. William James, "The Stream of Thought," in *The Principles of Psychology*, (New York: Dover Publications, 1890), 255.
8. Bergmann, *On Being Free*, 84–85.
9. J. Glenn Gray, *The Promise of Wisdom: An Introduction to Philosophy of Education* (New York: J. B. Lippincott, 1968), 35–36.
10. John Dewey, *Experience and Nature*, second edition (1929); LW 1:47.
11. Ibid., 57.
12. Friedrich Nietzsche, "Schopenhauer as Educator," in *Unmodern Observations (Unzeitgemasse Betrachtungen)*, ed. William Arrowsmith (New Haven: Yale University Press, 1990), 165–66.
13. Karl Jaspers, *Philosophy of Existence*, trans. Richard F. Grabau (Philadelphia: University of Pennsylvania Press, 1971), 70.

14. Gray, *Promise of Wisdom*, 159.
15. E. M. Cioran, *A Short History of Decay*, trans. Richard Howard (New York: Viking Press, 1975), 95.
16. Alfred North Whitehead, *Adventures of Ideas* (New York: Macmillan, 1933), 278.
17. William Arrowsmith, "Turbulence in the Humanities," *Arion: A Journal of Humanities and the Classics* 2 (spring and fall 1992/1993).
18. John Dewey, "A College Course: What Should I Expect from It?" *EW* 3:54.

Chapter Seven

I am grateful to Calvin O. Schrag for his critical comments on this paper.
1. Hubert L. Dreyfus, "Holism and Hermeneutics," in *Hermeneutics and Praxis*, ed. Robert Hollinger (Notre Dame, Ind.: University of Notre Dame Press, 1985), 234–35.
2. Ibid., 235.
3. Ibid., 232.
4. Ibid., 233. That Dreyfus no longer holds the view that Heidegger was the first to fully appreciate the noncognitive may be inferred from his approving quotations from Dewey's *Human Nature and Conduct* (published in 1922) to be found in his recent book, *Being-in-the-World: A Commentary on Heidegger's* Being and Time, *Division I* (Cambridge MIT Press, 1991). See 67, 70, 347–48. Further, this superb book makes clear that Dreyfus's preference for the language of "practices" (and "skills") to challenge what he calls the "priority of mental content" (85) is not meant to limit or exhaust the ways in which the world is preontologically or pretheoretically available to us. Nonetheless, it is equally clear that Dreyfus does not believe he is losing anything by leaving habit unexamined and allowing practices and skills to do the work of revising our understanding of how the subject is related to the object. I, on the contrary, believe that a great deal about the "directedness of the mind" (51) cannot be understood without a phenomenology of habitual meaning of the sort provided by Dewey (and Merleau-Ponty).
5. John Dewey, Introduction to *Essays in Experimental Logic* (Chicago: University of Chicago Press, 1916), 4. For a fuller account of Dewey's theory of preobjective, habitual meaning, see my book *The Phenomenological Sense of John Dewey: Habit and Meaning* (Atlantic Highlands, N.J.: Humanities Press, 1977).
6. John Dewey, *Experience and Nature*, second edition (La Salle, Ill.: Open Court, 1929), p. 20.
7. Hans-Georg Gadamer, "The Problem of Historical Consciousness," in *Interpretive Social Science: A Reader*, ed. Paul Rabinow and William M. Sullivan (Berkeley: University of California Press, 1979), 154.
8. John Dewey, *Human Nature and Conduct: An Introduction to Social Psychology* (New York: Modern Library, 1922), 40–41.
9. John Dewey, "Interpretation of the Savage Mind," in *Philosophy and Civilization* (New York: Capricorn Books, 1931), 173–87. For an even earlier account of habit, see Dewey's *Lectures on Psychological and Political Ethics, 1898*, ed. Donald F. Koch (New York: Hafner Press, 1976), particularly chapter 2, "Interests and Habits in the Organic Circuit."
10. John Dewey, *Art as Experience* (New York: Capricorn Books 1934), 104.
11. *The Morning Notes of Adelbert Ames, Jr.*, ed. Hadley Cantril (New Brunswick: Rutgers University Press, 1960), 221.
12. Ibid.
13. John Dewey, *Experience and Nature* (La Salle, Ill.: Open Court 1925), 18–19.

14. J. Glenn Gray, *The Promise of Wisdom: An Introduction to Philosophy of Education* (New York: J. B. Lippincott, 1968), 84.
15. Dewey, *Experience and Nature* second edition, 20.
16. Ibid., 21.
17. Ibid., 23.
18. Dewey, "Epistemological Realism: The Alleged Ubiquity of the Knowledge Relation," in *Essays in Experimental Logic*, 276.
19. Dewey, *Experience and Nature*, second edition, 24.
20. Dewey, *Experience and Nature*, 4.
21. Dewey, *Experience and Nature*, second edition, 19.
22. Dewey, *Experience and Nature*, 13.
23. Ibid., 16.
24. John Dewey, "Body and Mind," in *Philosophy and Civilization* (New York: Capricorn Books, 1931), 308.
25. Dewey, *Experience and Nature*, second edition, 22.
26. Ibid., 30.
27. Dewey, *Experience and Nature*, 7.
28. Ibid., 7–8.
29. Dewey, *Experience and Nature*, second edition, 244.
30. Ibid., 245.
31. Ibid., 22.
32. Ibid., 247.
33. Ibid., 248–49.
34. Ibid., 249–50.
35. Dewey, *Essays in Experimental Logic*, 6.
36. Ibid., 4.
37. Dewey, *Experience and Nature*, 19.
38. Ibid., 21.
39. Ibid., 7.
40. Ibid.
41. Hans-Georg Gadamer, "The Universality of the Hermeneutical Problem," in *Philosophical Hermeneutics*, trans. and ed. David E. Linge (Berkeley: University of California Press, 1976), 9.
42. Hans-Georg Gadamer, *Truth and Method* (New York: Crossroad Publishing, 1976), xiii.
43. Dewey, *Essays in Experimental Logic*, 4.
44. Gadamer, *Truth and Method*, 263.
45. Dewey, *Experience and Nature*, second edition, 21.
46. Gadamer, *Truth and Method*, 247, 259, 265, 266.
47. Ibid., 314.
48. Ibid., 311.
49. Ibid., 310.
50. Ibid., 314.
51. Ibid., 320.
52. Gadamer, "The Problem of Historical Consciousness," 159–60.
53. Ibid., 108–9.
54. Gadamer, *Truth and Method*, 237.
55. For one of the most detailed and careful analyses of Gadamer's theory of *Vorurteile*, see Lawrence Kennedy Schmidt, *The Epistemology of Hans-Georg Gadamer: An Analysis of the Legitimization of "Vorurteile"* (New York: Peter Lang, 1985). Georgia

Warnke's discussion of Gadamer's central themes, though not offering such a close reading as Schmidt's, is also helpful: *Gadamer: Hermeneutics, Tradition, and Reason* (Stanford: Stanford University Press, 1987).

56. Gadamer, "The Problem of Historical Consciousness," 154.
57. Gadamer, *Truth and Method*, 315.
58. Ibid., 317.
59. Ibid., 319.
60. Ibid., 324.
61. Ibid., 320.
62. Ibid., 265.
63. Ibid., 263.
64. Ibid., 268.
65. Ibid., 266.
66. Ibid., 325.
67. Ibid., 325, 328.
68. Ibid., 337–38.
69. Ibid., 259.
70. Ibid., 261–62.
71. Gadamer, "The Problem of Historical Consciousness," 154.
72. Gadamer, "The Universality of the Hermeneutical Problem," 9.
73. Gadamer, "The Problem of Historical Consciousness," 151–52.
74. Gadamer, *Truth and Method*, 328.
75. Ibid., 261–62.
76. Gadamer, "The Problem of Historical Consciousness," 154.
77. *Selected Letters of Robert Frost*, ed. Lawrence Thompson (New York: Holt, Rinehart and Winston, 1964), 302–3.
78. Gadamer, "The Problem of Historical Consciousness," 154.
79. Ibid.
80. Dewey, *Experience and Nature*, 18.
81. Ibid., 6.
82. Ibid., 15.
83. Dewey, *Experience and Nature*, second edition, 20.
84. *Letters of James Agee to Father Flye* (New York: George Braziller, 1962), 101.
85. Gadamer, *Truth and Method*, 332.
86. Ibid., 247.
87. Ibid., 262.
88. Gadamer, "The Problem of Historical Consciousness," 152.
89. Ibid., 149.
90. Dewey, *Experience and Nature*, second edition, 21.
91. Dewey, *Experience and Nature*, 18–19.
92. *The Letters of Emily Dickinson*, ed. Thomas H. Johnson (Cambridge: Harvard University Press, 1958), 440.
93. Gadamer, "The Problem of Historica Consciousness," 149.
94. *The Letters of Emily Dickinson*, 490.
95. John Dewey, "The Postulate of Immediate Empiricism," in *The Influence of Darwin on Philosophy* (Bloomington: Indiana University Press, 1910), 229.
96. Gadamer, *Truth and Method*, xix.
97. Ibid., 317, 445.
98. Richard J. Bernstein, "From Hermeneutics to Praxis," in *Hermeneutics and*

Modern Philosophy, ed. Brice R. Wachterhauser (Albany: State University of New York Press, 1983), 98.
99. Ibid., 99.
100. Ibid., 100.
101. Gadamer, *Truth and Method*, xiii.
102. Dewey, *Experience and Nature*, 9.
103. Ibid., 11–12.
104. Ibid., 18–19.
105. Dewey, *Experience and Nature*, second edition 20.
106. Gadamer, *Truth and Method*, 433.
107. Ibid., 250.
108. Dewey, "The Experimental Theory of Knowledge," in *The Influence of Darwin on Philosophy*, 85.
109. Gadamer, "The Problem of Historical Consciousness," 154.

Chapter Eight
1. George Steiner, *Real Presences* (Chicago: University of Chicago Press, 1989), 4.
2. John E. Smith, *The Spirit of American Philosophy*, revised edition (Albany: State University of New York Press, 1983), 157. It is worth noting another instance of the "before us" criticism of naturalism and, eventually, Dewey. Langdon Gilkey says of Reinhold Niebuhr that "it is as if he wished to push the roof off an immanentist culture in which whatever *is* is confined to what comes before us in ordinary experience.". Dewey's pragmatism does not, I believe, contribute to a naturalist culture within which, in Gilkey's words, "whatever represents, or can represent, the ideal in life must be resident in, expressed through, and also confined to actual cultural life" (*On Niebuhr: A Theological Study* [Chicago: University of Chicago Press, 2001], 16).
3. Ibid., 156, 157–58.
4. John Dewey, *A Common Faith* (New Haven: Yale University Press, 1934), 3; LW 9:4.
5. Ibid., 6; LW 9:6.
6. John Dewey, "The Revival of the Soul," LW 17:13.
7. Ibid., 14.
8. John Dewey, *Outlines of a Critical Theory of Ethics*, EW 3:372.
9. Peter L. Berger, *The Heretical Imperative: Contemporary Possibilities of Religious Affirmation* (New York: Anchor Books, 1979), 62–63.
10. Ibid., 64.
11. For a fine treatment of regulative ideals, see Dorothy Emmet, *The Role of the Unrealisable: A Study in Regulative Ideals* (New York: St. Martin's Press, 1994).
12. Robert C. Neville, *God the Creator: On the Transcendence and Presence of God* (Albany: State University of New York Press, 1992), 237.
13. George Santayana, "Dewey's Naturalistic Metaphysics," in *Dewey and His Critics*, ed. S. Morgenbesser (New York: Journal of Philosophy, 1977), 349; the article originally appeared in *Journal of Philosophy* 22, no. 25 (3 December 1925).
14. .George Santayana, *Interpretations of Poetry and Religion*, critical edition, ed. William G. Holzberger and Herman J. Saatkamp, Jr. (Cambridge.: MIT Press, 1989), 3; Dewey, *Common Faith*, 17; LW 9:13.
15. Dewey, *Common Faith*, 19; LW 9:14.
16. Ibid., 18–19; LW 9:14.
17. William M. Shea's discussion of the "whole" in Dewey suggests a number of

interesting paths for further analysis. See pages 131–41 in *The Naturalists and the Supernatural: Studies in Horizon and an American Philosophy of Religion* (Macon, Ga.: Mercer University Press, 1984). Shea's fundamental point regarding Dewey and transcendence is that "the transcendent does emerge in Dewey's language on the qualitative wholeness and unity of human experience." This is not a limp or weak transcendence for Shea; it simply is the best Dewey could do given his "inability to deal with an ontologically meaningful language for the transcendent" (136). Thus, on one hand, "there is no truly transcendent ideal in Dewey's Naturalism," and on the other, "Dewey's 'experience of the whole' has hit religious experience on the head" (136, 139). This cannot be right: if Dewey does justice, in some measure, to religious experience, it is precisely because he does justice, in some large measure, to the transcendent ideal.

18. I specifically have in mind three chapters in *Experience and Nature*: chapter 1, "Experience and Philosophic Method" (particularly the 1925 edition), chapter 2, "Existence as Precarious and Stable," and chapter 8, "Existence, Ideas, and Consciousness." David L. Hall is helpful with respect to the matter of wholes and unities in Dewey's turn toward the transcendent, or what he prefers to term the "mystical." See "From Loneliness to Solitude: The Pragmatist's Path to Salvation," in *Pragmatism, Neo-Pragmatism, and Religion: Conversations with Richard Rorty*, ed. Charley D. Hardwick and Donald A. Crosby (New York: Peter Lang, 1997).

19. .Dewey, "The Good of Activity," in *Human Nature and Conduct* (New York: Modern Library, 1922), 288–89; MW 14:199.

20. Dewey, *Common Faith*, 19; LW 9:14.

21. Ibid.

22. Steven C. Rockefeller, *John Dewey: Religious Faith and Democratic Humanism* (New York: Columbia University Press, 1991), 379.

23. Dewey, *Common Faith*, 19–20; LW 9:14–15.

24. Rockefeller, *Democratic Humanism*, 396. His "guides to action" conception of the ideal in Dewey leads Rockefeller to a predictable, but fundamentally misleading, view of faith in Dewey's philosophy of religious experience: "The comprehensive idea in Dewey's philosophy of religious experience is not the idea of faith but the idea of the religious quality of experience generated by all the factors contributing to a deep enduring adjustment" (512).

25. Dewey, *Common Faith*, 19–20; LW 9:15.

26. Ibid., 20; LW 9:15.

27. John Dewey, *Art as Experience* (New York: Capricorn Books, 1934), 29; LW 10:35.

28. Dewey, *Common Faith*, 43; LW 9:30.

29. John Dewey, *The Quest for Certainty: A Study of the Relation of Knowledge and Action* (New York: Capricorn Books, 1929), 72–73; LW 4:59.

30. Ibid., 69; LW 4:56.

31. Dewey, *Common Faith*, 20–21;LW 4:15.

32. Dewey, "The Moral Struggle or the Realizing of Ideals," in *Outlines of a Critical Theory of Ethics*, EW 3: 373.

33. Dewey, *Common Faith*, 21; LW 4:15.

34. Ibid.

35. Dewey, *The Quest for Certainty*, 138; LW 4:111.

36. John N. Findlay, "Intentional Inexistence," in *Ascent to the Absolute: Metaphysical Papers and Lectures* (New York: Humanities Press, 1970).

37. Dewey, *The Quest for Certainty*, 301; LW 4:240.

38. Dewey, *Common Faith*, 21; LW 9:15.

39. Dewey, *The Quest for Certainty*, 300–301; *LW* 4:240.
40. Dewey, *Common Faith*, 21; *LW* 9:15–16.
41. Dewey, *The Quest for Certainty*, 299; *LW* 4:239.
42. Ibid., 299–300; *LW* 4:239.

43. It is, I believe, unaccountable why Findlay's work has been neglected since his death in 1987. There is no exaggeration in John Silber's remark that Findlay is unique in western philosophy, a uniqueness "thrown into sharper relief by the very existence of so comprehensive a philosopher in a century dominated philosophically by efforts to restrict arbitrarily the scope and the depth of philosophical investigation" (preface to *Studies in the Philosophy of J. N. Findlay*, ed. Robert S. Cohen, Richard M. Martin, and Merold Westphal [Albany: State University of New York Press, 1985], vii–ix). The essays contained in this collection shed critical and appreciative light on Findlay's work. Also to be noted is the careful, patient study by Michele Marchetto, *Impersonal Ethics: John Niemeyer Findlay's Value-Theory* (Aldershot: Ashgate Publishing, 1996).

44. Findlay, "Intentional Inexistence," 228. In seeking to look deeper into Dewey, it might appear odd to seek illumination from an absolutist, a mystical absolutist, at that. I think it makes good sense, for three reasons. First, Findlay's range of expertise encourages us to notice some incidental and consequential resonances in Dewey of philosophers as diverse as Meinong, Hegel, Plato, Kant, Husserl, and Wittgenstein. Second, Findlay's own rather unique philosophy, particularly his views on consciousness and intentionality, has some remarkable affinities to Dewey's philosophy of experience. These affinities became clear to Findlay in the last years of his life. When I first met him in 1972, he was, when in a generous mood, indifferent to pragmatism, although he did have some admiration for James. Toward the end of his life, he had come to have a quite different view of Dewey, calling him "one of the great philosophers of experience of the twentieth century" (personal communication). This is an example, I believe, of the comprehensive vision noted by Silber, that is, Findlay's desire to see further and deeper. A close study of *Values and Intentions* yields considerable rewards for the study of James and Dewey. The final reason for not being too reluctant to think Dewey and absolute in the same thought is that at least one other philosopher has done so. I refer to John R. Shook, *Dewey's Empirical Theory of Knowledge and Reality* (Nashville: Vanderbilt University Press, 2000). See chapter 4, "The Absolute of Active Experience." Shook, I think, has absolutized the active, effortful dimension of Dewey and tends to give inadequate attention to the transcendence inside of action, effort, and practice.

45. Findlay, "Intentional Inexistence," 229.

46. In that essay Dewey says: "Things are what they are experienced *as* being; or that to give a just account of anything is to tell what *that* thing is experienced to be. By these words I want to indicate the absolute, final, irreducible, and inexpugnable concrete *quale* which everything experienced not so much *has* as *is*. To grasp this aspect of empiricism is to see what the empiricist means by objectivity, by the element of control" (John Dewey, "The Postulate of Immediate Empiricism," in *The Influence of Darwin on Philosophy and Other Essays in Contemporary Thought* [Bloomington: Indiana University Press, 1910], 234; *MW* 3:162–63).

47. Findlay, "Intentional Inexistence," 230.

48. For just a few examples, see *Democracy and Education: An Introduction to the Philosophy of Education* (New York: Free Press, 1916), chapter 18 "Educational Values," where Dewey discusses the nature of appreciation, what he calls having a "realizing sense" of something. See also *Experience and Nature* (LaSalle, Ill.: Open Court, 1929), chapter 8, "Existence, Ideas, and Consciousness," in which Dewey says: "Except as a reader, a hearer repeats something of these organic movements, and thus 'gets' their

qualities, he does not get the *sense* of what is said; he does not really assent, even though he give cold approbation" (244; *LW* 1:227). And, finally, in *Art as Experience*, Dewey says: "We cannot grasp any idea, any organ of mediation, we cannot possess it in its full force, until we have felt and sensed it, as much so as if it were an odor or a color" (119; *LW* 10:125). For an interesting and compelling discussion of "sense" in Dewey, see Timothy V. Kaufman-Osborn, *Politics/Sense/Experience: A Pragmatic Inquiry into the Promise of Democracy* (Ithaca: Cornell University Press, 1991).

49. Findlay, "Intentional Inexistence," 230.
50. Ibid., 233.
51. Ibid., 234.
52. Ibid., 235.
53. Ibid., 236.
54. John Dewey, *Experience and Education* (New York: Collier Books, 1938), 43–44; *LW* 13:25.
55. Findlay, "Intentional Inexistence," 236.
56. Findlay, "Intentional Inexistence," 237.
57. Ibid.
58. Ibid., 238.
59. Dewey, *Common Faith*, 21; *LW* 9:16.
60. John N. Findlay, "The Realm of Notions and Meanings," in *The Transcendence of the Cave* (New York: Humanities Press, 1967), 38–39.
61. Findlay, "Intentional Inexistence," 238, 239, 241.
62. Ibid., 241.
63. Ibid., 241–42.
64. Dewey, *The Quest for Certainty*, 304, 301; *LW* 4: 243, 240.
65. Dewey, *Art as Experience*, 276; *LW* 10:280.
66. John Dewey, "Changed Conceptions of the Ideal and the Real," in *Reconstruction in Philosophy*, enlarged edition (Boston: Beacon Press, 1948), 118 and 122; *MW* 12:147 and 149.
67. Ibid., 122; *MW* 12:149–50.
68. Ibid., 114–15; *MW* 12:145–46.
69. Findlay, "Intentional Inexistence," 236; Dewey, *The Quest for Certainty*, 306; *LW* 4:244.
70. Dewey, *Common Faith*, 21; *LW* 9:15.
71. Ibid., 23; *LW* 9:17.
72. For an account of conflict in Dewey, see William R. Caspary, *Dewey on Democracy* (Ithaca: Cornell University Press, 2000). Unlike some recent readings of Dewey, this work proposes at least an interesting approach to Dewey. It should be apparent, though, why I regard "conflict" or "conflict resolution" as phenomenologically abbreviated categories which dilute the nature of moral and spiritual struggle.
73. Dewey, *Common Faith*, 20, 23; *LW* 9:15, 17.
74. Ibid. (emphasis added).
75. The concepts of "atmosphere" and "atmospheric" serve a very important function in Dewey which extends beyond the realm of religion. "The flying moment is sustained by an atmosphere that does not fly, even when it most vibrates" (*LW* 1:370). This is a metaphysical presupposition for Dewey, one which works its way into virtually all areas of his philosophy. It is not always easy to discern, however, precisely what Dewey intends by "atmosphere." I believe it is one of his principal ways of calling upon the invisible and intangible as pathways to transcendence. A good indication of this movement toward the intangible is found in his "Tribute to S. J. Woolf." He notes that

Woolf is recognized for his ability to capture "salient traits" of persons who talk to him. Dewey continues: "Readers know also of his power to convey the intangibles, the atmosphere in which men live and do their work" (*LW* 17:526). The intangible is never further away in Dewey than atmosphere, never more hidden or revealed than transcendent context.

Chapter Nine
   1. Helen Vendler, "Wallace Stevens: The False and True Sublime," in *Part of Nature, Part of Us* (Cambridge: Harvard University Press, 1980), 1.
   2. Wallace Stevens, "The American Sublime," in *The Palm at the End of the Mind* (New York: Vintage Books, 1972), 114.
   3. The meaning of "context" in Dewey is far from clear, despite the ease and frequency with which it is taken to be an essential feature of his philosophy. To say that Dewey advances a "contextual approach" to a problem, issue, or idea is to say very little. Early in "Context and Thought," when he is discussing why "neglect of context" is such a "disaster," context is virtually equivalent to "limiting," that is, to "limiting conditions." Without limits, without specifiables, absolutes or contextless universals are inevitable. However, when Dewey turns "to consideration of the content and scope of the context that philosophizing should take into the reckoning," it is "background" (and "selective interest"), not "limiting conditions," to which he attends. The temporal background constituted by intellectual traditions is specifiable, to some degree, but the specifications are themselves limited and limiting. Of these traditions, Dewey says that "they are the circumambient atmosphere which thought must breathe; no one ever had an idea except as he inhaled some of this atmosphere" ("Context and Thought," in *John Dewey: On Experience, Nature, and Freedom*, ed. Richard J. Bernstein [New York: Liberal Arts Press, 1960], 100). Context is not a denial of the transcendent in any area of Dewey's philosophy. It is a reminder of the atmosphere which leads out from particulars to something no less universal than "some sense of the structure of any and all experience" (ibid., 110; *LW* 6:21). Dewey's use of such terms as "expanding spheres of context" and "the next wide circle or deepened stratum of context" bring to mind Emerson in "Circles."
   4. The literature on Stevens is *very* large. I note just a few of the works concerning Stevens relevant to this chapter. Joseph Carroll, *Wallace Stevens' Supreme Fiction: A New Romanticism* (Baton Rouge: Louisiana State University Press, 1987); Thomas C. Grey, *The Wallace Stevens Case: Law and the Practice of Poetry* (Cambridge: Harvard University Press, 1991); Frank Lentricchia, *The Gaiety of Language: An Essay on the Radical Poetics of W. B. Yeats and Wallace Stevens* (Berkeley: University of California Press, 1968); Frank Kermode, "Dwelling Poetically in Connecticut," in *Wallace Stevens: A Celebration*, ed. Frank Doggett and Robert Buttel (Princeton: Princeton University Press, 1980); Denis Donoghue, "Stevens's Gibberish," in *Reading America: Essays on American Literature* (New York: Alfred A. Knopf, 1987); J. S. Leonard and C. E. Wharton, *The Fluent Mundo: Wallace Stevens and the Structure of Reality* (Athens: University of Georgia Press, 1988); Robert Pack, *Wallace Stevens: An Approach to His Poetry and Thought* (New York: Gordian Press, 1968); Michael T. Beehler, "Kant and Stevens: The Dynamics of the Sublime and the Dynamics of Poetry," in *The American Sublime*, ed. Mary Arensberg (Albany: State University of New York Press, 1986); *The Act of the Mind: Essays on the Poetry of Wallace Stevens*, ed. Roy Harvey Pearce and J. Hillis Miller (Baltimore: Johns Hopkins University Press, 1965); Joseph N. Riddel, "Stevens on Imagination—the Point of Departure," in *The Quest for Imagination: Essays in Twentieth-Century Aesthetic Criticism*, ed. O. B. Hardison, Jr. (Cleveland: Press of Case

Western Reserve University, 1971); David M. LaGuardia, *Advance on Chaos: The Sanctifying Imagination of Wallace Stevens* (Hanover, N.H.: University Press of New England, 1983); Glauco Cambon, "Wallace Stevens: 'Notes toward a Supreme Fiction,'" *The Inclusive Flame: Studies in Modern American Poetry* (Bloomington: Indiana University Press, 1963).

5. Dewey, "Emerson—Philosopher of Democracy," MW 3:189–90.

6. Thomas M. Alexander, *John Dewey's Theory of Art, Experience, and Nature: The Horizons of Feeling* (Albany: State University of New York Press, 1987); Russell B. Goodman, *American Philosophy and the Romantic Tradition* (New York: Cambridge University Press, 1990); Steven C. Rockefeller, *John Dewey: Religious Faith and Democratic Humanism* (New York: Columbia University Press, 1991).

7. Wallace Stevens, "The Sail of Ulysses," in *Opus Posthumous*, revised edition, ed. Milton J. Bates (New York: Alfred A. Knopf, 1989), 129–30.

8. John Dewey, *Psychology*, EW 2:168.

9. I am deeply indebted in this chapter, as I was in chapter 8, to John N. Findlay's "Intentional Inexistence," for insights into the nature of intentionality which are critical to questions concerning imagination. See *Ascent to the Absolute: Metaphysical Papers and Lectures* (New York: Humanities Press, 1970).

10. Dewey, *Psychology*, EW 2:168.

11. Ibid., 170, 171.

12. Ibid., 171–72.

13. Ibid., 173.

14. Ibid., 270.

15. Ibid., 173.

16. Ibid., 172–73.

17. Ibid., 173.

18. Ibid., 174.

19. Wallace Stevens, "The Noble Rider and the Sound of Words," in *The Necessary Angel: Essays on Reality and the Imagination* (New York: Vintage Books, 1951), 6.

20. Ibid., 7.

21. Wallace Stevens, "Holiday in Reality," in *The Collected Poems of Wallace Stevens* (New York: Alfred A. Knopf, 1965), 313.

22. Dewey, *Psychology*, EW 2:172.

23. Stevens, "Chocorua to Its Neighbor," in *The Palm at the End of the Mind*, 244.

24. Dewey, *Psychology*, EW 2:174.

25. Stevens, "Imagination as Value," in *The Necessary Angel*, 150–51.

26. John Dewey, "The Live Creature," in *Art as Experience* (New York: Capricorn Books, 1934), 3; LW 10:9.

27. Ibid., 13; LW 10:19.

28. Ibid., 16; LW 10:22.

29. Ibid., 17; LW 10:23.

30. Dewey, "The Live Creature and 'Etherial Things,'" in *Art as Experience*, 20; LW 10:26.

31. Ibid., 20, 21; LW 10:26, 27.

32. Ibid., 22; LW 10:28.

33. Ibid., 25; LW 10:31.

34. Ibid., 29; LW 10:35–36. It should be remembered that in *The Public and Its Problems*, vision and the seen are—phenomenologically, socially, and politically—less fundamental than hearing. Dewey says: "The connections of the ear with vital and out-

going thought and emotion are immensely closer and more varied than those of the eye. Vision is a spectator; hearing is a participant." (*The Public and Its Problems* [Chicago: Swallow Press, 1927], 218–19; *LW* 2:371).

35. Dewey, "The Live Creature and 'Etherial Things,'" 29; *LW* 10:36.
36. Ibid., 32; *LW* 10:38.
37. Ibid., 33; *LW* 10:39, 40.
38. Keats to John Hamilton Reynolds, 19 February 1818, in *John Keats: Selected Poems and Letters*, ed. Douglas Bush (Boston: Houghton Mifflin, 1959), 265.
39. Dewey, "The Challenge to Philosophy," in *Art as Experience*, 274, 281; *LW* 10:278, 286.
40. Dewey, "The Human Contribution," in *Art as Experience*, 268; *LW* 10:272–73.
41. Ibid.; *LW* 10:272.
42. For this reason, I think that Russell B. Goodman is not entirely correct when he says that "Dewey remains a realist in *Art as Experience*, committed to the existence of the physical world" (*American Philosophy and the Romantic Tradition*, 120). With Stevens, we might say that the "difficult inch" of the physical world is "soon unconfined" through the commitment-softening intentionalities of imagination.
43. Dewey, "The Human Contribution," 270; *LW* 10:274.
44. Dewey, "The Challenge to Philosophy," 272, 275, 276; *LW* 10:276, 279, 280.
45. Ibid., 276; *LW* 10:280.
46. Ibid., 277; *LW* 10:281.
47. Richard Poirier, *A World Elsewhere: The Place of Style in American Literature* (New York: Oxford University Press, 1966).
48. Dewey, "The Challenge to Philosophy," 277; *LW* 10:281.
49. Dewey, "The Act of Expression," in *Art as Experience*, 72; *LW* 10:79.
50. Keats to Richard Woodhouse, October 27, 1818, in *Selected Poems and Letters*, 279–80.
51. "Nature," in *Ralph Waldo Emerson: Selected Prose and Poetry*, ed. Reginald L. Cook (New York: Holt, Rinehart and Winston, 1950), 6.
52. Stevens, "The Noble Rider and the Sound of Words," in *The Necessary Angel*, 24.
53. Dewey, *Art as Experience*, 297; *LW* 10:301.
54. Stevens to Bernard Heringman, *Letters of Wallace Stevens*, ed. Holly Stevens (New York: Alfred A. Knopf, 1966), 710.
55. Dewey, *Art as Experience*, 281; *LW* 10:286.
56. Stevens, *The Necessary Angel*, 23.
57. Roger Shattuck, "The Innocent Eye and the Armed Vision," in *The Innocent Eye: On Modern Literature and the Arts* (New York: Farrar, Straus, Giroux, 1984), 353.
58. Geoffrey H. Hartman "Criticism, Indeterminacy, Irony," in *Criticism in the Wilderness: The Study of Literature Today* (New Haven: Yale University Press, 1980), 269–70.
59. Ibid., 270.
60. Stevens, letter of 8 March 1943, *Letters*, 441.
61. Shattuck, "The Innocent Eye," 347. Habit complicates Shattuck's position. Were we not habitual beings, living beyond our means would not be necessary; neither, though, is it clear how it would be possible. Shattuck's confidence that the loop road will, and ought, return you "to your original path," depends upon what sort of "means" he believes habit makes possible.
62. Wallace Stevens, *Notes toward a Supreme Fiction* (Cummington, Mass.: Cummington Press, 1942), 15.

· INDEX ·

absence: and continuum of meaning, 154; habit as middle term between presence and, 70, 143; as positive, 86–87; vigilance and, 87, 88–89, 96
absolutes, 90–91, 97, 197
actual, the: aesthetic experience subordinating existence to meaning, 219; continuous readaptation of, 41–42; end-in-view versus actual end of desire, 42–43; God as union of ideal and, 175; the ideal and, 40, 45, 46–48; imagination as excess of meaning over, 206; more than meets the eye in, 178; as opening to possibility of ideal meanings, 179; Plato on the intelligible versus, 38; projected ideal versus actually enjoyed good, 28, 31–36, 39–40, 58, 63–64; seen in light of imagination, 192; as subordinated to possibilities of imagination, 181–82
adaptation, 41–42
aesthetic experience: as consummatory, 12, 17; existence subordinated to meaning in, 219; horizons of meaning opened by, 12–13; imagination in, 200; as imaginative, 217; Levin on Dewey's account of, 56–59; "make-believe" theory of, 196, 217–19, 230n.70; ordinary experience as lacking aesthetic quality, 209; as pure experience, 214–15, 218; religious faith compared with, 184–85; reverie in, 217–18; the self as disappearing in, 220–21; working back into ordinary experience, 218–19. *See also* sublime, the
Agee, James, 166–68
Agnew Clinic, The (Eakins), 72–77
Aiken, Henry David, 79, 136

Alexander, Thomas M., 5–6, 202
"American Sublime, The" (Stevens), 201
Ames, Adelbert, Jr., 143
Ammons, A. R., 138
"Antinaturalism in Extremis" (Dewey), 66
appreciation of the ideal: "appreciation" in Dewey's works, 51; art and religion as source of, 49, 52, 64; in Dewey's theory of deliberation, 112; faith and aspiration steadied by, 77; and inner vision's control of the outer, 59; surrendering to, 58
Arendt, Hannah: on destructive effect of thinking, 94–95; on meaning on model of truth, 139, 174; on reason and quest for meaning, 89, 139, 141; reason and thinking distinguished by, 89–90; on thinking and the invisible, 26
Aristotle, 105, 134
Arrowsmith, William, 122, 134, 136, 137–38
art: as consummatory, 12; loop analogy for, 223–24; make-believe theory of, 196, 217–19, 230n.70; and nature, 211, 212; nature and spirit intersecting in, 67; and normal experience, 209–10; pure idealism and pure realism in, 206; purpose in, 219–20; reverie in, 217–18; as source of appreciations and intimations of the ideal, 49, 52, 64; understanding and wonder in, 216. *See also* aesthetic experience; literature
Art as Experience (Dewey): on art and normal experience, 209–10; on environment as condition of life, 210, 214; habit as central to, 2; on having an experience, 12; on imagination, 214–21; on make-believe theory of art, 217–19,

Art as Experience (continued)
230n.70; on mind as a verb, 72; on negative capability, 205, 213–14, 215, 219, 220, 223, 224, 225; on phenomenology of sensing, 190, 248n.48; primacy of meaning thesis in, 2; rehabilitation of sense in, 211–13; on sense of being founded on a rock, 57; on sensuous experience absorbing the ideal, 30; on the sublime, 202; on surrendering ideal to objective material, 57–59

aspiration: and faith, 186; glorifying at expense of thought, 45; intimations of ideals steadying, 77; morality as life of, 36; possible ideal good stirring, 66; practical limitations on, 39; realization of ideals requiring, 50

Barzun, Jacques, 136
Beaufret, Jean, 78
Becker, Ernest, 94
Being-in-the-World: A Commentary on Heidegger's Being and Time, *Division I* (Dreyfus), 242n.4
Bensman, Joseph, 80–81, 93
Berger, Peter L., 20–21, 123, 178, 239n.31
Bergmann, Frithjof, 125, 128, 131, 134
Bernstein, Richard, 170–71, 173
Bourdieu, Pierre, 233n.22
Bourne, Randolph S., 11
Brentano, Franz, 189, 193
Brightman, Edgar S., 4
Brittan, Arthur, 92–93

Carney, Ray, 72–77
Caspary, William R., 248n.72
categorials, judgmental, 116–17
Cavell, Stanley: on Dewey's account of experience, 11–15; Dewey's and Wittgenstein's pictures of thinking compared by, 28–29, 34; on Emerson and pragmatism, 15, 60, 61, 62
character, 115, 116
"Chocorua to Its Neighbor" (Stevens), 208, 250n.23
choice: in Dewey's theory of deliberation, 114; of a major, 124–33; in Oakeshott's theory of deliberation, 103–5, 113–14
Cioran, E. M., 134
classics, the, 135
Cobb-Stevens, Richard, 69–70
"College Course, A: What Should I Expect from It?" (Dewey), 137
Collins, James, 9–10, 228n.26
commitment, humanism and, 83–86
Common Faith, A (Dewey), 175–89, 198–99
conduct, rationality of, 99–121

consciousness: experience as not reducible to, 147–48; historical versus knowing, 153; the ideal as present to, 48–51; mind distinguished from, 150–51; the subconscious, 149–50; understanding as not restricted to, 153
"Context and Thought" (Dewey), 249n.3
control, capacity to, 58–59
convictions, 90–91
Cornforth, Maurice, 5
Coughlan, Neal, 3, 230n.64
Craft and Consciousness (Bensman and Lilienfeld), 80–81
creative imagination, 205, 208

declaring a major, 124–33
deliberation: Dewey's theory of, 109–21; habits of mind in, 99; Oakeshott's theory of, 101–9
Democracy and Education (Dewey), 137, 144
DeMott, Benjamin, 62
desire: versus duty, 33–35; end-in-view versus actual end of, 42–43; the good versus the desirable, 118; habits as forming, 43–44; the ideal regulating, 186; ideals as objects of, 44–48; intelligence converting into plans, 44, 45; moral practice as grounded in, 37–39; as obstruction-dependent, 42–45; in Sokolowski's account of virtue, 116
Dewey, John: on absence, 86–87; "Antinaturalism in Extremis," 66; "atmosphere" in work of, 248n.75; "A College Course," 137; *A Common Faith*, 175–89, 198–99; on context, 100, 119–20, 249n.3; "Context and Thought," 249n.3; on deliberation, 109–21; *Democracy and Education*, 137, 144; on education as growth, 130, 133, 137; *Experience and Education*, 11, 192; "Experience, Nature, and Art," 230n.70; on faith and the unseen, 175–99; "From Absolutism to Experimentalism," 9–10; from-to perspective on, 9–11; and Gadamer on meaning, 139–74; on the good as struggle, 28–53; idealism of, 3–6, 10–11, 137; instrumentalist and naturalist interpretations of, 1; "Interpretation of the Savage Mind," 109, 110, 143; "Knowledge as Idealization," 26; moral idealism of, 28; on the "more," 24–25; *Outlines of a Critical Theory of Ethics*, 28–39, 177, 186, 231n; as philosopher of the ordinary, 202; Plato compared with, 38; "Poetry and Philosophy," 6; "The Postulate of Immediate Empiricism," 2, 110–11, 189, 247n.46; primacy of

meaning in, 2, 17, 21; *The Public and Its Problems,* 250n.34; *The Quest for Certainty,* 185, 187, 188; on rationality of conduct, 99–121; *Reconstruction in Philosophy,* 230n.70; "The Revival of the Soul," 177; spiritual character of experience in, 122–23; and Wallace Stevens, 200–225; *Studies in Logical Theory,* 5; *Theory of the Moral Life,* 111–12; the transcendent dropping out of discussions of, 54–77; "Tribute to S. J. Woolf," 248n.75; and the undeclared self, 122; on understanding practice and action from inside, 26–27; unification seen as goal of, 202–3. See also *Art as Experience; Experience and Nature; Human Nature and Conduct; Psychology*
Dewey's Empirical Theory of Knowledge (Shook), 10–11
Dickinson, Emily, 168–69
dramatic rehearsal, 112–13
Dreyfus, Hubert L., 140–41, 160, 170, 242n.4
duty: versus desire, 33–35; and the good, 36–37; Kant on highest good and, 232n.20

Eakins, Thomas, 72–77
education: as adventure for Gray, 129, 131–32, 133; as dealing in tangibles and invisibles, 122–38; as growth for Dewey, 130, 133, 137; specialism and humanistic, 79–83
Eldridge, Michael, 15–17
Emerson, Ralph Waldo: "Beyond and Away" disavowed by, 202; Cavell on pragmatism and, 15, 60, 61, 62; Dewey on aesthetic experience of, 185, 212; "Experience," 12; on good thoughts, 237n.55; on past greatness, 135; poetics of transition in, 56, 57, 61; Poirier on pragmatism and, 62; on the self as disappearing in aesthetic experience, 220, 221; skepticism of, 60–61, 64
empathy, 88
ends-in-view: versus actual end of desire, 42–43; hypothetical functioning of, 43; ideals contrasted with, 47, 48, 53, 183; and the infinite, 50–51; instrumentalism on ideals as, 16
Engle, Lars, 240n.27
experience: art and normal, 209–10; as broader than what is known, 141, 142, 166, 172, 174; deep structure of, 148; dividing, 34; Gadamer's theory of, 156–60, 170, 171–72; getting beyond itself, 11; habit as basis of Dewey's theory of, 144; habit constituting, 81;

habit's transcendental contribution to, 17; imagination as highest contribution to, 214; imagination as reaching beyond, 182–83; knowledge as simplification of, 146; as not reducible to consciousness, 147–48; openness to, 158, 159–60; phenomenology's return to, 92; qualitative, 12–13; reconciling ideals with, 6–8; religious, 178–79; science for understanding, 11–12; spiritual character of, 123; transcendence and ordinary, 19–22. See also aesthetic experience; lived experience
"Experience" (Emerson), 12
Experience and Education (Dewey), 11, 192
Experience and Its Modes (Oakeshott), 241n.55
Experience and Nature (Dewey): on art and nature, 212; and authority of an ideal, 185; field theory of meaning in, 50; as grounding human activity in the consummatory, 3; on habit, 2, 142, 144; on phenomenology of sensing, 247n.48; on the precarious and the stable, 130; on problem of real and ideal, 26; on recalcitrant particular and the sublime, 225
"Experience, Nature, and Art" (Dewey), 230n.70

faith, 175–99; aesthetic experience compared with, 184–85; as anticipatory, 183, 199; the ideal as object of, 179; the ideal as work of, 46, 47; intimations of the ideal as steadying, 77; and knowledge, 183–84, 188, 199; morality as life of, 36; in the moral order, 74; in religious experience, 178; staking oneself on, 53; and the unseen, 179, 183, 198–99; and work, 45, 46
fancy (fantasy), 204–5
field theory of meaning, 49–50
Findlay, John N.: affinities with Dewey of, 247n.44; on drawing distinctions, 82; as influence on this study, 8; on intentional existence, 187, 189–99, 250n.9; uniqueness of work of, 247n.43; on universally pursuable values, 85, 238n.12
finitude, 75, 84
Franco, Paul, 241n.55
"From Absolutism to Experimentalism" (Dewey), 9–10
from-to perspective, 9–10
Frost, Robert, 164–66

Gadamer, Hans-Georg: Bernstein's criticism of, 170–71; Dreyfus's criticism of, 140–41, 160, 170; on experience,

Gadamer, Hans-Georg (*continued*)
  156–60, 170, 171–72; as influence on this study, 8; "The Problem of Historical Consciousness," 163; on questioning, 160; on reading a letter, 162–69; on temporal distance, 159; theory of *Vorurteil*, 154–62; *Truth and Method*, 155, 165; truth as measure of understanding for, 139; "The Universality of the Hermeneutical Problem," 154–55
Gale, Richard M., 66–72
Gilkey, Langdon, 245n.2
God, 175
good, the: and the better, 16–17; the desirable versus, 118; duty and, 36–37; giving tangible expression to, 32–33; harmonizing the self as, 180; projected ideal versus presently enjoyed, 28, 31–36, 39–40, 58, 63–64; in Sokolowski's account of virtue, 116; as struggle, 28–53; as transcendent, 19, 29–30, 32; unification of spirit and habit in good life, 4
Goodman, Russell B., 6, 202, 251n.42
Gouinlock, James, 18
grace, pragmatic, 52
Gray, J. Glenn, 2, 129, 131, 133–34, 145
greatness, 135–36
Grene, Marjorie, 232n.13
Griswold, Charles W., 233n.25
Gross Clinic, The (Eakins), 72–77

habit: and aspiration, 36; background and horizons provided by, 148, 150, 154; conservative and creative functions of, 30; constancy as based on, 36; as creating and constituting our experience, 81; current custom and, 14; and desire, 43–44; in Dewey's theory of deliberation, 109–10, 117, 118, 119; in Dewey's theory of experience, 144; the flexible habit, 81, 91; habitual meaning, 2, 3, 30, 55, 67, 70, 99, 139, 146, 148, 150, 152–54, 192; as history naturalized, 143; Husserl on, 3, 67, 69–70, 71; intentionality of, 3, 192; James on, 70; Levin on, 54, 55; meaning set loose by, 17; as middle term, 70; and Oakeshott's theory of deliberation, 106; postmodernism suppressing, 109–10; preservation of the past through, 173; as revealing, 174; and the sublime, 23; surrendering, 32, 33–34, 35; thinking versus good habits, 118; as transcendent, 2, 3; transcendental contribution to experience of, 17; in understanding, 148–50, 153–54, 173; unifying spirit and, 4, 27; and *Vorurteil*, 139–

74; worth as conveyed to the senses through, 30. *See also* habits of mind
habits of mind: consciousness forming naturally into, 80; and continuum of meaning, 154; critical, 71; in deliberation, 99; dramatic, 109, 111; as foundation of intentional life, 150; humanism as habit of vigilance, 87, 88; phenomenological, 92; range of convenience of, 81–82; specialization and, 81, 83; as vehicles of vision, 81; vigilance calling into question, 78, 91, 96, 97
habitus, 69, 233n.22
Hall, David L., 246n.18
Hampshire, Stuart, 19–20
Hare, William, 96
Hartman, Geoffrey H., 224
Hegel, Georg Wilhelm Friedrich, 118, 158
Heidegger, Martin, 78, 111, 139, 140, 145
heresy, 239n.31
Heringman, Bernard, 222
hermeneutic circle, 151, 161
hermeneutics, 8–9, 140, 169, 172, 173
Hoernle, R. F. Alfred, 4–5
"Holiday in Reality" (Stevens), 207
Homer, 134
hope, 46, 47
Horowitz, Helen Lefkowitz, 124–25
Hudson, W. H., 185, 212
humanism: and commitment and value, 83–86; concrete, 85, 92–93; and contingency, 83–84; conventional interpretations of, 78; creedal view of, 86, 87, 94; humanistic values, 84–85, 88–89, 92; specialism and humanistic education, 79–83; universal, 85, 93; and vigilance, 78–98
humanities, the, 131, 134
Human Nature and Conduct (Dewey): on habit, 2, 55, 142–43, 144; integration of opposites in, 58; on "little island" of the foreseen in the "infinite sea," 49, 59; on morality as struggle, 28, 39–53; on plasticity of the young, 14; on sense of an enveloping whole, 57; on unification of spirit and habit, 4, 27; on what to do next, 181
Hunter, James Davison, 233n.22
Husserl, Edmund: and Dewey's theory of deliberation, 111; on habit, 3, 67, 69–70, 71; on naturalism, 68–69, 71; and Oakeshott's flow of sympathy, 106, 108; and Oakeshott's idiom of activity, 105; on science of the lifeworld, 13; and specialism, 80
hypotheses, 38–39, 115, 233n.27

idealism: as coming first, 40; Dewey and, 3–6, 10–11, 137; Dewey's moral idealism, 28; as easily brought to naught, 44; sentimental, 45; as wanted rather than existing, 25

ideals: action as fulfilling, 40–41; and the actual, 40, 45, 46–48; as already in existence, 187–99; authority of, 185, 186–87, 188, 193; as campaigns, 31; in consciousness, 48–51; desire regulated by, 186; as ends-in-view, 16–17, 183; experimental sciences changing conception of, 197; as faith's object, 179; God as union of actual and ideal, 175; idealizing imagination, 206–7, 208; ideal meanings, 2, 4, 7, 16, 18, 25, 30, 46, 58, 73, 179, 187, 192–93, 196, 205–6, 212; as immanent and transcendent, 197; infinity of connections as ideal, 48, 51, 64, 74; instrumentalist and naturalist interpretations of, 1; as at intersection of tangible and intangible, 1; Kant's regulative, 17; Levin on, 55; in Levin's account of Dewey's aesthetics, 56–59; light/dark and visible/invisible in Dewey's analysis of, 50; in nature, 48; nature as agreeable to idealization, 212; as objects of desire, 44–48; as outrunning the seen and touched, 46–48, 52, 58; as possibilities, 48, 183; projected ideal versus actually enjoyed good, 28, 31–36, 39–40, 58, 63–64; reconciling experience with, 6–8; seen as fixed and absolute, 7; as significances to be appreciated, 51–52; a stable world as without, 131; translating into practice, 73–77; the whole self as ideal, 180; working ideals, 46–47. *See also* appreciation of the ideal

imagination: the actual seen in light of, 192; the actual situation as subordinated to possibilities of, 181–82; aesthetic experience as imaginative, 217; creative, 205, 208; and Dewey's naturalism, 8; in Dewey's *Psychology*, 30, 203, 204–9, 225; in Dewey's theory of deliberation, 112; Dewey's uncertainty regarding, 201, 215; environmental context of, 210–11; as excess of meaning over actuality, 206; as highest contribution to experience, 214; idealizing, 206–7, 208; inner and outer reconciled in, 215–16; insubordinate, 209, 211, 213, 218, 220, 223; natural, 209, 213; and natural environment, 213; in Oakeshott's theory of deliberation, 104, 120; particularity of object of, 204; perception and memory distinguished from, 204, 205; pragmatism giving practical bent to, 200; as reaching beyond experience, 182–83; and the real, 207, 221–25; in religious experience, 178; the self harmonized through, 179–82; three stages of, 204–5; universalizing, 206, 207, 208

"Imagination and Value" (Stevens), 209

immediatism, 110

infinity: of connections as ideal, 48, 51, 64, 74; "little islands" of the foreseen in the "infinite sea," 49, 59

instrumentalism: and idealism in Dewey, 5, 7, 9; on ideals as ends-in-view, 16; on ideals as tools, 1

intellectualism, 145, 167–68

intelligence: as converting desire into plans, 44, 45; as illuminating, 50

intentionality: desire's intentional object, 34; in Dewey's theory of meaning, 22, 70; Findlay on intentional existence, 187, 189–99, 250n.9; habit as intentional, 3, 192; habits of mind as foundation of intentional life, 150

interests, 126–27, 220

"Interpretation of the Savage Mind" (Dewey), 109, 110, 143

Interpretations of Poetry and Religion (Santayana), 179

intuitions, 149

James, Henry, 60

James, William: on the "bottom of being," 19, 27, 98, 127; on free water of consciousness, 126; Gale on Dewey's essays on, 66–72; on habit, 70; on the human contribution, 209; Husserl influenced by, 3; and the imagination, 182; and Oakeshott's theory of deliberation, 106; on otherness infecting our commitments, 97; *Psychology*, 7; on psychology as natural science, 7; realism in idealism of, 6; on single-word answers, 97; and skepticism, 13, 60; transition as central to, 61

Jaspers, Karl, 87–88, 130, 132, 135, 182, 237n.47

Jay, Paul, 235n.12

judgmental categorials, 116–17

Kampf, Louis, 62

Kant, Immanuel: on habit, 30, 33; on the highest good, 35, 232n.20; and Oakeshott's theory of deliberation, 105; regulative ideals of, 17; on the sublime, 24, 200; on thought as averse to accepting its results, 90

Kaufmann, Walter, 136
Keats, John, 211, 213, 214, 220–21, 224
Kelly, George, 81
knowledge: Arendt distinguishing between knowing and thinking, 89; being and knowing as not equivalent, 110, 144–47, 168; experimental knowing, 31; faith and, 183–84, 188, 199; self-knowledge, 123, 126–27, 129, 165; as simplification of experience, 146; tacit knowledge, 105; and truth, 165–66; understanding as broader than, 141, 142, 166, 172, 174
"Knowledge as Idealization" (Dewey), 26
Kohák, Erazim, 235n.6

Lauer, Quentin, 71
Lawrence, D. H., 23, 59, 62, 169, 205
Leavis, F. R., 136
letters, Gadamer on reading, 162–69
Levin, Jonathan, 54–59
Lieb, Irwin C., 76
Lilienfeld, Robert, 80–81, 93
limitations, human, 75
literacy, 136–37
literature: the classics, 135; and life, 62–63; loop analogy for, 223–24; Poirier on pragmatism and, 59–66. *See also* poetry
lived experience: being-there-for-me dimension of, 191; Dewey on substituting intellectual outcome for, 143; and Dewey's theory of deliberation, 110; habit and lived meaning, 71; and Oakeshott's theory of deliberation, 106

MacIntyre, Alasdair, 91–92
major, declaring a, 124–33
meaning: aesthetic experience subordinating existence to, 219; art as consummating possibilities of, 12; art as expressing ideal meaning of nature, 212; continuum of, 154; creative imagination penetrating hidden, 205, 208; environment as condition of, 210; field theory of, 49–50; Gadamer on inappropriate foremeanings, 157–58; habit and lived meaning, 71; habit as setting loose, 17; habitual, 2–3, 30, 55, 67, 70, 99, 139, 146, 148, 150, 152–54, 192; horizons of, 13, 25; ideal, 2, 4, 7, 16, 18, 25, 27, 30, 46, 58, 73, 179, 187, 192–93, 196, 205–6, 212; imagination as excess of meaning over actuality, 206; imaginative, 205, 213; intentional arrows of, 22; and intentionality for Dewey, 70; in Levin's account of Dewey, 56; in literature, 61, 62–63; man presupposed by, 84; meshed in, 24; and mind, 150, 151; on the model of truth, 139–74; in Oakeshott's theory of deliberation, 103–4, 113; as outrunning the tangible, 25–26; pragmatic, 74, 76; as prelude to truth for Gadamer, 160; of present act as vast, 51, 64, 66, 74, 120; primacy of meaning thesis, 2, 17, 21; reason as quest for, 89, 139, 141, 173; of religious faith, 185; "road of meaning," 27; and sense, 211–12; truth distinguished from, 89, 139, 168; unity of understood, 161
Melville, Herman, 60
Menand, Louis, 11
Merleau-Ponty, Maurice, 2, 68, 83, 84, 105
Metaphysical Club, The (Menand), 11
Miller, John William, 17
mimesis, 63
mind: consciousness distinguished from, 150–51; open-mindedness, 95–97; as a verb, 72. *See also* habits of mind; thinking
morality: aspiration and faith in, 36; desire as ground of, 37–39; Dewey's moral idealism, 28; faith in the moral order, 74; as striving, 31; universalizability in, 91–92, 238n.12. *See also* duty; good, the
Murdoch, Iris, 17–18, 19, 32–33

Natanson, Maurice, 21, 22, 229n.55
naturalism: in *Art as Experience*, 211, 216; and being meshed in meaning, 24; Gale on Dewey's, 66–72; Husserl on, 68–69, 71; and idealism in Dewey, 5, 7, 9; on ideals as tools, 1; and the "more," 24–25; and religious experience, 178
Naturalism and the Human Spirit (Krikorian), 66
nature: as agreeable to idealization, 212; art and, 211, 212; the ideal and, 48; and spirit intersecting in religion and art, 67. *See also* naturalism; supernatural, the
Neville, Robert C., 179
Nichols, James H., Jr., 232n.22
Niebuhr, Reinhold, 245n.2
Nietzsche, Friedrich, 123, 130, 131–32, 134, 136
"Noble Rider and the Sound of Words, The" (Stevens), 207, 221–22

Oakeshott, Michael: on context reinforcing immanence, 100; on deliberation, 101–9; on education, 136; *Experience and Its Modes*, 241n.55; on flow of sym-

pathy, 100, 106, 107, 108, 112, 113; on idiom of activity, 105–6, 110; as influence on this study, 8; "Rational Conduct," 101; on rationality of conduct, 99–121; on tradition of behavior, 119, 120; "The Voice of Poetry in the Conversation of Mankind," 120
objectivity, 191, 215, 219
"Ode to Arnold Schoenberg: On a Performance of His Concerto for Violin" (Tomlinson), 24
open-mindedness, 95–97
Otto, Max, 7, 31, 45
Outlines of a Critical Theory of Ethics (Dewey), 28–39, 177, 186, 231n

Palmer, Richard E., 8
Pappas, Gregory F., 234n.48
patience, 61
Peterson's Guide to Four-Year Colleges 1990, 124, 133
phenomenology: appeal to lived experience of, 93; of religious experience, 178–79; return to experience of, 92; of sensing, 190
"Philosophy as a Rigorous Science" (Husserl), 68
phronesis, 105, 173
Plato, 38, 118, 134
pluralism, 79, 95, 97, 239n.31
Poetics of Transition, The: Emerson, Pragmatism, and American Literary Modernism (Levin), 54–59
poetry: approaching transcendence through, 22–24; and interaction with the environment, 212; and normal experience, 210; Santayana comparing religion and, 179; as significances to be appreciated, 52
"Poetry and Philosophy" (Dewey), 6
Poirier, Richard, 59–66, 219, 236n.34
Polanyi, Michael, 105
postmodernism, habit suppressed by, 109–10
"Postulate of Immediate Empiricism, The" (Dewey), 2, 110–11, 189, 247n.46
practical, the: and caring about finitude, 75; Dewey's definition of, 37; Dewey's pragmatism seen as practical, 172–73; pragmatism giving practical bent to the imagination, 200
practice: as guarding its integrity, 76; requirements of, 39; translating ideals into, 73–77; understanding from the inside, 26–27
pragmatism: and the actually experienced, 39–40; Carney on Eakins and, 72–77; Emerson and, 15, 60, 61, 62; the foreground as dominating, 179;

Levin on immanence in, 54–55; Poirier on literature and, 59–66; pragmatic grace, 52; pragmatic meaning, 74, 76; and skepticism, 13–14; and the sublime, 200–201; and transcendence, 1, 11, 15, 36; on transcendence as a temptation, 75
prejudice. See *Vorurteil*
presence: habit as middle term between absence and, 70, 143; humanistic values and, 88–89; to the mind, 192; vigilance as middle term between absence and, 87
primacy of meaning thesis, 2, 17, 21
principles: in Dewey's theory of deliberation, 115; in Oakeshott's theory of deliberation, 102, 105–8, 117, 118–19
"Problem of Historical Consciousness, The" (Gadamer), 163
Psychology (Dewey): idealism in, 3, 5; on imagination, 30, 203, 204–9, 225
Psychology (James), 7
Public and Its Problems, The (Dewey), 250n.34
purpose: in art, 219–20; in Oakeshott's account of rational conduct, 101. See also ends-in-view

qualitative, the: horizons of meaning opened by, 12–13; qualitative immediacy, 18, 111, 184, 190, 191
Quest for Certainty, The (Dewey), 185, 187, 188
questioning, 160
Quine, W. V. O., 140, 160

Randall, John Herman, Jr., 38
Raphael, D. D., 107
"Rational Conduct" (Oakeshott), 101
reading: Dewey on, 151–52; a letter for Gadamer, 162–69
reason: Arendt distinguishing intellect from, 89; in choosing a major, 125, 128, 131; and interaction with the environment, 213; and intuitions, 149; invisibility of, 99; quest for meaning inspiring, 89, 139, 141, 173; the rationality of conduct, 99–121; *Vorurteil*'s preservation of past as achievement of, 173
Reconstruction in Philosophy (Dewey), 230n.70
reflection: Dewey on intellectualism, 145; in Dewey's theory of deliberation, 111–12; habitual background of, 150; imagination as extending beyond, 183; in Oakeshott's theory of deliberation, 103, 105, 107–8; religious experience

reflection *(continued)*
    as beyond, 184; the whole self as unapprehensible in, 180, 183
relativism, 83
religion: aesthetic experience compared with, 184–85; God as union of ideal and actual, 175; imagination in, 200; nature and spirit intersecting in, 67; phenomenology of experience of, 178–79; pluralism and, 239n.31; Santayana comparing poetry and, 179; as source of appreciations and intimations of the ideal, 49, 52–53, 64; and the unseen, 176; in wider social and natural context, 198
Renewal of Literature, The (Poirier), 65
reverie, 217–18, 220
"Revival of the Soul, The" (Dewey), 177
Ricoeur, Paul, 81, 91
Rieff, Philip, 136
Rockefeller, Steven C., 48, 182, 183, 202, 246n.24
Romantics, 6
Rorty, Richard, 82–83, 122, 123
Rosenthal, Sandra B., 234n.48
Roth, Robert J., 233n.27

"Sail of Ulysses, The" (Stevens), 203–4
Santayana, George, 179–80, 181, 182
Schneider, Herbert W., 3
Schwartz, Delmore, 39
science: conceptions of real and ideal changed by, 197; in Dewey's naturalism, 67; as inadequate for accounting for all experience, 11–12; and the qualitative, 13
self, the: as always at the wheel, 39; as disappearing in aesthetic experience, 220–21; divided selves, 34; the imagination harmonizing, 180–82; interests as identification of material world with, 220; Nietzsche's definition of, 123, 134; as not fully specifiable, 122; perfecting ourselves, 38; staking of, 32, 34, 37, 53, 58, 74, 177, 235n.6; as in transition for Levin, 55; the undeclared self, 122–38; the whole self as ideal, 180; words taking us outside our selves, 63
self-cultivation, 30–31
self-discipline, 133–34
self-discovery, 131
self-knowledge, 123, 126–27, 129, 165
self-realization, 120, 135
self-transcendence, 35, 37
Selzer, Richard, 77
sense: Dewey's rehabilitation of, 211–13; of an enveloping whole, 57; in experimental knowing, 31; the ideal absorbed by, 30; phenomenology of sensing, 190. *See also* aesthetic experience
Shakespeare, William, 213
Shattuck, Roger, 223–24, 225, 251n.61
Shea, William S., 245n.17
Shook, John R., 10–11, 247n.44
Silber, John R., 232n.20, 247n.43
skepticism, 13, 14, 60–61, 64, 158
Smith, John E., 176, 177, 179, 199
Socrates, 123–24, 132
Sokolowski, Robert, 102, 115–17, 118
specialization, 79–83
Spencer, Herbert, 86
standards, educational, 137
Steiner, George, 50, 51–52, 175, 235n.55
Stevens, Wallace, 200–225; "The American Sublime," 201; "Chocorua to Its Neighbor," 208, 250n.23; "Holiday in Reality," 207; on imagination and the real, 207, 221–22, 223, 224; "Imagination and Value," 209; on imagination as agreeable to the imagination, 209, 211; on imagination creating images independent of the originals, 211, 217; as influence on this study, 8; Levin on, 59; the "more" in poetry of, 201–2; "The Noble Rider and the Sound of Words," 207, 221–22; as poet of the ordinary, 202; "reality-imagination complex" of, 202, 203; "The Sail of Ulysses," 203–4; and skepticism, 60; on the sublime, 200, 201; "That will not declare itself / Yet is certain as meaning," 121
stress, vigilance introducing, 94
struggle, for the good, 28–53
Studies in Logical Theory (Dewey), 5
Stuhr, John J., 228n.18, 229n.55
subconscious, the, 149–50
sublime, the: and ordinary experience, 218–19, 223; pragmatism and, 200–201; recalcitrant particular as standpoint for beholding, 225; as seeing what was hidden in the particular, 209; Stevens's concern with, 200, 201; Weiskel on, 22–24
supernatural, the: and authority of an ideal, 185; Dewey and that of the Romantics, 6; and Dewey's phenomenology of religious experience, 178; imagination attributed to, 182; versus the supersensible, 175, 184
supersensible: versus the supernatural, 175, 184. *See also* unseen, the
superstition, 87
surgery, 74, 76–77

surrender: of the artist to objective materials, 57; in struggle for the good, 28, 31–32, 33–34, 35, 58, 63; to the unseen, 177

tacit knowledge, 105
Taylor, Harold, 136
temporal distance, 159
Thayer, H. S., 5
Theory of the Moral Life (Dewey), 111–12
thinking: Arendt on the invisible and, 26; as dangerous to all creeds, 95; Dewey and Wittgenstein on, 28–29; versus good habits, 118; progressive correction of, 193–94; vigilance compared with, 89–90, 94–95. *See also* reason; reflection
Tocqueville, Alexis de, 1, 200
Tomlinson, Charles, 22, 24
transcendent, the: as background and stimulus for Dewey's work, 27; as dropping out of discussions of Dewey, 54–77; the good as transcendent, 19, 29–30, 32; habit as transcendent, 2, 3; hypotheses as transcendent, 38–39, 233n.27; as nature opening to spirit, 67; and ordinary experience, 19–22; poetry for approaching, 22–24; in pragmatism, 1, 11, 15, 36; self-transcendence, 35, 37; starting point with, 18; supersensible transcendence, 175; as a temptation, 75; the transcendental contrasted with, 227n.1; transcending human limitations, 75; wager on, 175, 176, 179, 181. *See also* ideals
Transforming Experience: John Dewey's Cultural Instrumentalism (Eldridge), 15–17
transition, 56–57, 59, 65, 236n.34
"Tribute to S. J. Woolf" (Dewey), 248n.75
truth: imagination exceeding, 205; and knowledge, 165–66; in letters, 162–65, 170; meaning distinguished from, 89, 139, 168; meaning on the model of, 139–74; as measure of understanding for Gadamer, 139; time in assessment of, 159; unity and, 161; and *Vorurteil* for Gadamer, 154–62, 166, 169–70
Truth and Method (Gadamer), 155, 165

understanding: art as beginning in, 216; as broader than knowledge for Dewey, 141, 142, 166, 172, 174; for Gadamer, 139, 141–42, 158, 161–62, 166, 171, 172; habit in, 148–50, 153–54, 173; a letter for Gadamer, 162–69

"Universality of the Hermeneutical Problem, The" (Gadamer), 154–55
universalizability, 91–92, 238n.12
unseen, the, 175–99; Dewey's openness to, 176–77; experience of, 178; faith and, 179, 183, 198–99; in religious experience, 178; staking the self on, 177; in wider social and natural context, 198–99

value: humanism and, 83–86. *See also* good, the
Vendler, Helen, 200, 201
vigilance, 86–98; abitrariness reduced by, 91; and absolutes, 90–91; and belief, 88; as dangerous to all creeds, 95; for doing justice to the phenomena, 85, 92, 93–94, 97; as expanded awareness, 87–88; and feeling, 88; habits of mind called into question by, 78, 91, 96, 97; humanism and, 78–98; as middle term between presence and absence, 87; open-mindedness contrasted with, 95–97; as quiet and gentle, 94; stress introduced by, 94; thinking compared with, 89–90, 94–95
"Voice of Poetry in the Conversation of Mankind, The" (Oakeshott), 120
Vorurteil (prejudice): confrontations to, 158; as continuity-making structures of experience, 157; Dreyfus on Gadamer's use of, 140; Gadamer's theory of, 154–62; habit contrasted with, 172–74; and letter reading, 166, 167, 169; as obscuring, 174; preservation of past as achievement of reason with, 173; temporal distance from, 159; and tradition, 171; and truth, 139, 141, 155–62, 166, 169–70

Weiskel, Thomas, 22–24
Welchman, Jennifer, 112–13
Whitehead, Alfred North, 135, 235n.6
"Why Do Pragmatists Want to Be Like Poets?" (Poirier), 59
Winch, Peter, 106–8
Wittgenstein, Ludwig: Cavell comparing Dewey's picture of thinking with that of, 28–29; and Oakeshott's theory of deliberation, 108, 109
Wölfflin, Heinrich, 9
wonder, 216–17
Wood, James, 75, 235n.55
Woolf, S. J., 248n.75
Wordsworth, William, 230n.70

www.ingramcontent.com/pod-product-compliance
Lightning Source LLC
Chambersburg PA
CBHW031548300426
44111CB00006BA/213